TOO LONG
IN THE
BUSINESS

TIM TOPPS

Matador
9 Priory Business Park,
Wistow Road, Kibworth Beauchamp,
Leicestershire. LE8 0RX
Tel: (+44) 116 279 2299
Fax: (+44) 116 279 2277
Email: books@troubador.co.uk
Web: www.troubador.co.uk/matador

ISBN 978 1784620 080

British Library Cataloguing in Publication Data.
A catalogue record for this book is available from the British Library.

Typeset by Troubador Publishing Ltd, Leicester, UK
Printed and bound in the UK by TJ International, Padstow, Cornwall

Matador is an imprint of Troubador Publishing Ltd

NOTE: This is a work of fiction, and a gross misrepresentation of the seven splendid colleagues I had the good fortune to work with in real life; fine, charming, blameless folk and good businessmen to boot: none of them swore offensively, nor licked his knife, at least not in public. I have depicted not them, but the awful people they might have been. Ron, for example, was in real life the staunchest person I've ever known. If any of us had faults, it may well have been myself. What is more, I still can't believe my father was an assassin... He was staunch, too. But as regards the CIA – and their activities among our University students in the Fifties and Sixties until the 'Ramparts' exposure – and probably long after – well, what do *you* think?

To all small-business owners, getting through life's financial jungle by swinging from straw to straw.

And to Sarah, Olivia, the girl in the Peter Jones window, the one in the E-type, Elsa from the Oxford office, plus a few more (who know who they are); not to mention the late Freda McMurdo... **

... and in memory of Bobbie, who put up with a lot.

** (I said not to mention her)

vii

PROLOGUE

A curious thing to admit, right at the start, but if you were at a British university in the 1950s, 60s or 70s, I know where you went to the lavatory. Don't tell anyone, but I dream about it all the time.

I am walking along endless Hall corridors, looking on scrawled cards for the residents' names, looking also – and urgently – for an unoccupied loo. Always there is either a queue outside it, or if it is surprisingly vacant, I find, when I sit down, that all four walls are made of glass, or that people are strolling through and talking to each other a little too loudly about insurance, or I am doing it crouched in a laundrette, which is worse… Worst of all, where has the bogstrap gone? Usually, that's enough to wake me up. It sure did, this time.

Downstairs in the darkness, the hall clock chimed apologetically, the fourth note a bit flat as always. It was half past something.

I was due downtown this morning for probably the most important meeting of my life. Also here in Cambridge, back at that happy start to the Sixties before, under The Stones and their ilk, it all went so wrong, this was Poppy Day, the annual Rag Day, so my clients would be everywhere and the traffic would be sluggish; I'd better get up.

Little wonder that my nights so often found me roaming in my twitchy dreams countrywide around those Halls of Residence. My work with students had taken me everywhere from Aberdeen to Exeter, repeatedly, over the past fifteen years, and when you've an appointment every thirty minutes right through a long day you really do need to know where the facilities are. No problem here in Cambridge itself (the basement in Trinity's Whewell's Court; King's Hostel behind the Arts Theatre; that weird place at the far end of Downing) nor in Oxford for that matter as I'd lived there for four years and favoured that cell down all those stairs at the Radcliffe Camera, or if time allowed and the bladder permitted, the less frequented and better-heated loos at Rhodes House (the Americans like to be cosy); but when I was touring my clients at other Universities, all those Wilmslow Road Halls in Manchester used to worry me a bit, (except St Gabriel's where I knew the Warden). And as for Loughborough, to reach some bogs in places like Hazelrigg you needed to be an athlete – as of course they were, most of them, on their 'Athletics Scholarships'.

Mind you, I am writing about the early days, as I had already been in this business a long time: advising students about things they didn't want, but ought to have, made it seem even longer sometimes. But this was now 1964, second week of November. My highly unpleasant but momentous and prematurely-named Board Meeting loomed ahead, yet in all other ways this was an enjoyable occasion. I had experienced many Rag Days at other Universities, which usually brought with them a feel of slight embarrassment: a bit contrived, a bit intrusive, with the general public in Edgbaston or Clifton, or the folk along Woodhouse Lane, Leeds, or even around Aldwych (with both King's and the LSE hamming it up) as somewhat reluctant outsiders, paying up with a thin smile and wishing it was tomorrow. But for some reason, Cambridge was always different. The town willingly joined in, in those days as I still remember them: where else, anywhere at all, would the Banks in a Market Place consent to be raided by masked young men and girls, everyone around looking on with a smile? A good theme for an unmade Ealing comedy?

Nothing else was going to be comic, though, today. How was I going to keep control of the company I'd been building up across the UK ever since 1950? Countrywide, every undergraduate knew of us and our endless insurance circulars; thousands were our clients, covered for their flutes and trumpets, cycles, books – and above all, their lives. But now the seven men I'd carefully chosen to be my associates were beginning to come together against me – well, certainly some of them – just when I'd managed to detach us from the hidden disasters of my late Senior Partner and the others in the shadows…

The only real consolation I had today was that those seven were in two groups, and I would have to try to play one against the other. That would be one in the eye for them... If only it worked...

And, as it strangely turned out, one in the eye for Moscow too.

★ ★ ★

I rolled over and spreadeagled across the big bed like some ecstatic Saint Andrew, corner to corner without impediment. Someone – was it Thurber? – once wrote a piece 'You can't sleep with women' and he was so right. There had been many marital years of that well-known but so little mentioned syndrome: clinging to the cliff-edge at my ordained half of the bed after long, tense business days, my free arm dangling to the carpet and the accumulated tiredness dripping out of my fingers... Years tinged by a reluctance to cause offence by even hinting a wish to sleep alone.

It is only as we grow older that we start to appreciate that blessed self-indulgence of aloneness. While young and unattached, we become obsessed by the desire to be merged with someone else: the animal need to share, on which of course Life depends. Then we have, unavoidably, those actual 'sharing' years with a half-bed... Only after that fraught stage, which can end jaggedly in tears or providentially in a mutual understanding, can we hope to achieve the nirvana of being alone when we want to be: a truth neatly put recently, was it by the writer Zoe Heller: 'Solitude is wasted on the lonely'.

★ ★ ★

Heading for the car an hour or so later, I was reminded by the wheezing hall clock how careful I would have to be today, how easy it is to make a fatal mistake. There was a rather pushy girl who fancied her vocal skills in a Durham pub once, who marched up to sing 'My Grandfather's Clock' and confused her joy and pride very rewardingly for the rest of us:

"It was bought on the morn of the day that he was born

And was always his pride and his joy;
But it stopped short, never to go again,
When the old man – er – "

My Jaguar was a recent indulgence, but I was taking care round corners because this was the old Mark One with the narrow wheelbase which, they muttered, had let some good drivers down somewhat. To be honest, I still missed my beloved old Sunbeam Talbots, HCE 577 and then KER 602, both blue-and-grey, that used to glide me across country on my regular Oxford to Cambridge bunny-run in an aerodynamic cocoon, so that on that slope just outside Newport Pagnell (the hilly hiccup between the Chilterns and the Northampton Uplands, where the weather always seems to have changed as you go through) your ears would pop. I had the student President of Cranfield with me once on that stretch, and he offered to buy her on the spot. Mind you, I had bought her from the top Rootes man at Herbert Robinson's and he had fitted some esoteric Alpine accessories, whatever that meant, so she had been a bit special.

I turned down past Girton College towards the centre of town. A police car doppled past, so I assumed Poppy Day had started. That side entrance to Girton, framed by its pines, always clicked my memory back to a girl's face: I never knew her name. Over the years I have visited so many students in their rooms that I normally had trouble remembering what they looked like from one brief meeting to the next, so that on any campus or in the nearby streets, I tended to wear a fixed smile to avoid hurting the feelings of some passing client or prospect. No doubt I have been thought either daft or queer as a coot. But that one face lingers…

(Yes, of course, over all those years I have had a few passing affairs with some of the girls, in those free-and-easy days of the 1950s when so many of us were fully laid-back and 'liberated', without having to wait for a 1960s permit from that screwed-up late-developer librarian… Up in Hull, wasn't he though? Well, then…).

This complete stranger is the one I recall. It was getting dark, and after a non-productive sales pitch with somebody on the first floor, I was going down the main Girton staircase, and came upon this unknown vision who was going up; nobody else was around. It was close to the end of Term, and coming up to Christmas and that must have had a lot to do with it; but we smiled.

Then, full of the party spirit, I suppose, I said: "You are so beautiful, we'll never meet again, but Merry Christmas", and I kissed her, and she me, very thoroughly, and then we both went on our way, and we didn't even look back... (OK, OK, I did, so that's how I know: why do you have to point that out?) I wonder who she was. I always see that face so clearly. There's a cafe that features in one of my night-time dream campuses, (I think it seems to be on Nicholson Street in Edinburgh, or else on that turning just off Tottenham Court Road towards Senate House and ULU) where one of the fantasy waitresses reminds me of her – so I can't escape her even then. Not that I want to. Do you know Picasso's 'Sylvette'? That sort of girl, you can imagine what she must have looked like in real life, uncorrupted by a mad painter.

★ ★ ★

As I got to the end of the Huntingdon Road, at the top of Castle Hill, there was a zebra crossing.

No, really, a zebra was crossing. It was on its hind legs and it held a striped bucket for coins. A little further on, I could see a lion and a unicorn prancing about in combat. Motorists were all being held to ransom. Well prepared for all this, I paid the zebra my shilling, it issued me with a 'passport' and said: "Keep away from the lion", so I steered clear and went on down the hill to safety. In my rear mirror the lion and unicorn were giving a pretend hard time to somebody, probably from out of town, who didn't want a passport. At Magdalene I was stopped by an officious 'policeman' who examined my passport and told me, inevitably, that it was out of order, so I had to pay a sixpenny fine. However do foreigners cope with this?

On the bridge, a client of mine from Corpus was about to douse himself in something inflammable, burst into flames, and leap into the Cam, where presumably he hoped, first, that a punt was waiting, and secondly, that it wouldn't end like that lovely disaster for Baron

Von Stupp in the splendid film "The Great Race"… He waved to me, and I drove on, wondering how I should word the claim form. A short way on, the traffic stopped opposite Przibozki the barber shop, much patronised by this end of town and surreptitious supplier of something for the weekend; and next door, that well-favoured pub where, in the Gents, I once saw my favourite graffito of all time. It may have been there for years because surely nobody with any wit at all would have wanted to delete it. It ran across the wall just above the porcelain, saying in a long, tragic droop down to the floor:

Whoever he was I hope he felt he'd relieved himself.

That sad diminuendo
has always supported
me in times of
stress and hardship.

It is so good to
know that other
people are
as fraught as
oneself.

So much better
if they are
even worse off.

On this particular day
the memory did me
a power of good
as I drove on, past
the Round Church
and right into my
old familiar
St John St.

BALLS TO THE MODERATOR OF THE GENERAL ASSEMBLY OF THE FREE CHURCH OF SCOTLAND

Here were my old second-floor offices of the mid-fifties, in their lopsided rooms above the cabbage-infested hallway of Bernard Adams's 'Continental Comestibles' emporium. Those fruity premises of mine, (later occupied by 'University Aunts' and thus a most rewarding hunting-ground for students on the lookout for newly-arrived au pair girls, home-sick but adventurous and once including Brigitte Bardot's sister whom, tragically, I missed out on), had been advertised in 1954 in the accident-prone Cambridge Daily News at a rental of "£500 per anum". When I showed this to Bob Huff my estate agent friend, he said: "Well, it's better than paying through the nose." He may well have been right.

Next came that iconic Indian restaurant the 'Taj'. In recent years, we have been subjected to idiotic newspaper articles which claim that the country was devoid of ethnic restaurants until smart-arses like the Larkinians woke up in the late Sixties and tried to claim 'modern life' as their own, egged on by a horde of ungifted cooks who have talked their way into TV chefdom because they have the gift of the gab and can be seen thrillingly swearing for the cameras while their long ragged hair and dandruff falls into the soup. If you take the trouble to check with the Kelly's Directories of the Fifties, you will soon see we were not short of Chinese and Indian eateries in the big cities (and in Oxbridge too) though you might have had to drive to Dockland for anything authentic.

Turning left towards the rag-active Market Square, I remembered those two old familiars one would see hereabouts, but long gone: the dreadful shabby raincoat of E M Forster, outstaying his long welcome somewhere in King's; and hovering on the corner by the bookshop, under his wide-brimmed hat, the sinister figure of Monsignor Gilbey, that antidote to the benign Father Brown, who apparently hated women so much, he tried never to accept small change with the Queen's head on it: it must have got tougher all through the 50s – but we used to wonder if he had refused his Victorian pocket-money as a child.

Outside the cinema a lone student had set up his charity patch for the day: sitting on a stool, he was fishing through a grate into the drain; beside his collecting-box, in a net, lay two kippers. I envied his sense of detachment, wishing that I could start all over again, perhaps as a quiet researcher at one of these colleges, emerging just once a year to fish in the drains or hurl myself blazing into the river... I had never really been cut out for business, even for one that prospered – let alone the mess I was in now. For all I knew, it suddenly struck me, I might indeed be starting again after this morning. Four Area Managers and three HQ Directors. I had handpicked them, every bloody one. Now, as I turned past Christ's and towards our new base in the somewhat pretentious Prudential Building they were no doubt up there drinking my coffee, eating my biscuits and pretending to be nice to one another.

I slid into the long slope of the Pruhaus car park. The eponymous firm had the first floor, another big international was at the top; and most of our middle floor was a huddle of small businesses which probably, as Chandler's laconic Philip Marlowe would have said, had "crawled there to die": several grey one-man accountancies left high and dry when this or that tax dodge had been exposed and swept away from them. Alongside them, were we, selling our insurance wares to students and, as you will just have observed, grammatically irreproachable.

Our offices, I have to say, were rather pleasant once you got in the door, but carefully modest, in order not to alarm our impecunious student callers ("but think of their future potential"). The furnishings and decor owed much to Robert Sayle's emporium across the road.

More to the point, we were well equipped with a range of bottles for the benefit of the never-ending stream of Insurance Company Inspectors, weary and needing sustenance, but paradoxically a splendid source not only of commercial scandal which was very boring, but the very best utterly unprintable jokes that were going the rounds. (I'll tell you, but only if all the machines are switched off). These Company Reps were obliged by their Head Offices to call regularly on Brokers like us. Except that hardly any Brokers were at all like us and I think they enjoyed those eccentric visits.

I had started as a maverick, and I still was. What would I be tomorrow, with revolution in the air?

How to play my cards? "Divide and rule", Palmerston used to say – but it was all right for him – he had gunboats: mine had all sunk. But to put you fully into the picture, I must take you back 18 years to a very different boat, where it all started, when I left school.

CHAPTER 1

November 1946, Canada. She was ageing and had become scruffy; she swayed slightly; could have done with fresh make-up; but she was still well able to give brief comfort to a long procession of weary soldiers coming home from the War. As my boat-train pulled up alongside her in Halifax docks, Nova Scotia, at this anticlimactic end to my long trans-Canada CPR journey, I wondered if perhaps the SS Illyria was not a genuine Cunarder after all. I had never heard of her and frankly she was a bit undersized. Had she been captured from retreating Italians like so much other hardware, and renamed? Or was she part of that dubious Lend-Lease deal we had done a few years ago with Roosevelt, for which subsequently we had to seem so grateful throughout the Empire-crippling half-century of repayments – and if so, would she break her back on the next high wave?

As it turned out, I was being unfair. Certainly, we passengers were all slotted into indiscriminately shared cabins in this ex-troopship, built at Barrow in the 1920s, and the facilities below deck were still meanly wartime; but she would battle and plunge her way through solid walls of autumnal seas as resolutely as the finest of her Line, wheezing with her one gritty funnel all the way to the beckoning Liver Bird – if one has to get poetic about it.

To my bewilderment – though it was certainly flattering – when I approached the Customs shed I was taken aside and escorted straight up the gangplank by a Mountie who, in his red coat and big hat, was a pure cartoon impression of his homeland: he was built like the Rockies with a face like a moose. My first thought – the first thought of most late-teenagers in those circumstances, I guess – was that I had been arrested, and I began to think back to the train, and whether I had purloined the towels or the teaspoons from the CPR; but it emerged much later that because my passage home had been booked through my father's British Government office in Winnipeg, where I had been visiting for a few weeks, my papers had been marked in some way to indicate that I was 'Consular and Diplomatic' and so must have special help and gentle handling. Since I was only 18 and just three months out of school in England, where all my youthful instincts had been veering towards anti-establishment rebellion, this unexpected anointment came as a shock. But like some pompous and recently incoming Socialist Minister, I learnt at once to accept all available privileges smoothly (though of course reluctantly) and I saw no point in rocking the boat as soon as I'd boarded it.

Anyway, my berth was nothing much to write home about. The cabin was cramped but at least it was 'outside' with two portholes which I judged to be safely above sea level given good weather. I was to share with two others: a large drunken Army captain and a remote and introverted professor-type who somehow exuded the aura of having around him a permanent haze of mental dust; he never spoke but was constantly making nervous notes in the margins of tattered textbooks. I thought he might be returning from work in the States on the first atom bombs and was now busy with unspeakable improvements for the next. The Army captain was eloquent enough every night, but largely incoherent. His talk was aimed at neither of us, but to the world in general, its sad state, and his own guaranteed answers to everyone's problems. He never volunteered any information about himself, which was not unusual at that time, but I noticed he – or someone – had removed all the Unit badges from his frayed uniform and greatcoat. I assumed that he was either on deeply secret service or being shipped home to his Regimental HQ in some sort of disgrace that didn't quite merit handcuffs. Several nights he was sick, in calm weather. Why is it one always hears about drunken, raucous subalterns and captains, while most fictional majors or colonels are merely subdued and withdrawn? Is there some staff course at Sandhurst on 'How to hold your liquor', only available to the senior ranks? With my National Service looming in a few weeks, I might find out soon enough.

This inebriation spread, very acceptably, far beyond our Army passengers. The Illyria's engines may have run on coal or oil – I never knew which – but the internal operations of the ship seemed to be fuelled largely by alcohol. My dubious 'diplomatic' status had placed me, impressively, at the Purser's table, where the juice flowed freely at the expense of the Line. (I have since learnt that the Purser's table is the traditional placing for first-class passengers who are not quite as important as they think they are, so somewhere on board was a realist with a perceptively raised eyebrow). There were four other passengers at his table, three of them rather old and Departmental-looking with a range of thick unidentifiable accents, who harrumphed and mainly spoke economics among themselves after the initial exchange of formalities; and an intriguing younger man with whom I quickly palled up. This was Matt.

Mid-twenties probably, perhaps a little more... Dark and slim, quick-witted, and every girl's cinema-going idea of a young English Naval Officer, charming with a ready smile (so, obviously not Stanley Baker, but one of the others in that wardroom), though I never saw him in a uniform. In fact, despite appearances, he described himself as being "attached to the Colonial Police" and he was evidently in the same nurtured category as myself because every evening, when we phoney 'specials' were invited to drinks each sundown, successively with the Ship's Doctor (gin and tonic), my friend the less sophisticated Purser (gin and orange), the Chief Engineer (Scotch, what else?), and ultimately the Captain himself (pink gin, or vodka as a surprising alternative – he'd been on the Arctic convoys), Matt was always there.

Second day out, as we were working our way in thick fog past an invisible Newfoundland and presumably ploughing through dense layers of codfish, Matt and I got into conversation while strolling around the decks. It started as we leant against the rail and found ourselves watching an intensely beautiful girl saunter by. My poor unpractised eye followed her past the lifeboats and into the misty distance…

"Hm," said Matt. "Great scenery. Nothing much else worth watching in this weather, so let's keep that in focus for a while."

I fell into step beside him (you can always tell who's been in the Forces or the OTC) and this is how we got acquainted: each morning, around coffee-time, and at first quite unplanned, we would meet up on the same deck and wait for that pleasing moment when the girl – or sometimes another we deemed a suitable qualifier – flowed past; then we repeated our stroll, quite undetected but alas, equally unrewarded at least in my case. What Matt got up to in the later evenings I never knew.

Indeed, in telling me about himself he was nearly as bad, in the beginning, as my cabin companions, and he only opened up a little as he knew more about me. This didn't strike me as at all unusual: the War was not long over, little more than a year, and one was quite used to people of military age being reticent or entirely silent about their occupations, their comings and goings. For six years we had lived alongside posters by Fougasse or David Langdon, in every bus and tube train, warning that "Careless Talk Costs Lives", and "Even the Walls Have Ears". At school, last year's departed sixth-formers would visit when they came shakily home on leave, and one knew not to ask questions, often noting an unfamiliar haunted look in the eye, so much at odds with the remembered face of young triumph on the rugby field just twelve months ago.

On the other hand, I myself was still almost a sixth-former and – so far – had no secrets worth hiding. A one-way conversation with Matt, this interesting and intelligent fellow only a few years older, but with masses of experience, was perfectly acceptable. As we followed those swinging hips on that first day, Matt turned to me.

"Apart from chasing skirts around a troopship, what else brings you here?"

Throughout the war I had been at boarding-school in England, while my parents were stuck in East Africa in the Overseas Civil

Service. I hadn't seen them for seven years, and one couldn't even telephone. In term-time I was fifty miles north of London, and during the holidays ten miles south in a vulnerable suburb, with a premium view of first, the Battle of Britain, and then the London Blitz. (Age 12, when not collecting shrapnel souvenirs or putting out incendiaries with our stirrup-pump, I had written an excited diary which described the events happening over my head, and it was published in the 'Kenya Sunday Post' – does anyone know where the original diary is, in its faux-leather cover?).

Now, in the calmer but less exciting days of precarious peacetime, though I was due for the National Service call-up, my father – by now posted from Africa to Canada – had applied for a couple of months' grace, so that I could go across and spend a little time getting to know them all over again. Strangely, when they came to meet me at the station in Winnipeg, though I am six-foot, I was looking high up above them, as I had done when I was nine, from long-remembered habit. The same phenomenon was reported by two of my boarding-school contemporaries: Peter Parker, of British Rail memory; and John Fowles, the novelist, who was in my form (and only into print 15 years later than me, though I concede that he then went some way towards making up the gap).

"So now you're being shipped back as a special parcel." Matt was evidently as curious as I was, to know why, at my teen age, I had been the recipient of all this staff attention; but now he had the answer. "Any passage booked by the government must get priority," he explained, "though transatlantic tourists are starting to be welcomed if they're heavy with dollars. I reckon they let you visit your folks because if not, their Government Department would have to allow both of them back to the UK on compassionate leave: two top-class tickets and an empty chair in Winnipeg. High cost."

It was logical but deflating. I was the cheap option. It was time I turned to a different subject. By day three I felt I knew him well enough.

"How about you then, Matt? How come you're special?"

5

It seemed silly then, but like a clip from a B-movie, he really did look cautiously up and down the deck; then pulled from his pocket a small silver badge of a greyhound.

"I do various things, whatever they want me to. Just now I'm what's known as a King's Messenger, filling in for one of their fulltime people: they normally use retired senior officers… Send them all over the shop, carrying documents or packages and seeing them safely through other people's checkpoints and so on… "

"I thought I heard you say you were in the Colonial Police?"

He nodded. "That too, but we're all chopping and changing nowadays. I'm on detachment, we're moved around."

This I knew. My father had disappeared for several months from Kenya in late 1940 and alarmed my mother by re-appearing as an Air Force Officer with a ribbon on his uniform and sand in his hair.

Matt went on, as we hung over the stern rails watching the long yellow wake: "These people get me into all sorts of trouble and I have to describe myself whatever way I think best. Look at this," and he produced a newspaper cutting. It was a photo of the Big Three at a late wartime conference: Churchill, Stalin, Truman. Big smiles and tobacco smoke… Behind them was a row of grim-looking bodyguards – if they had been in dark glasses one would have thought Chicago rather than Yalta – and one of them was Matt.

I was impressed by this and by his willingness to open up to me. But I supposed that if his duties changed so often and so completely, there couldn't be very much depth to them really, so perhaps little of real importance that he needed to hide? But at the same time I was just a bit cautious: I found myself, as we walked off for a coffee, trying to picture him in the dark glasses… It honestly wasn't difficult.

"I'll tell you one thing," he went on later, twiddling his spoon, "I'll be damn glad to get back to our own side of the Atlantic. Bernard Shaw was right… "

He tailed off as if I was supposed to know what that witty but daft old man had been right about, but I had read so many of his

Prefaces, I couldn't guess. So Matt continued: "He said, more or less, that there is a fifty-year hiatus between the more intelligent American and, on the higher ground, all of us in Europe."

"A bit harsh?"

"There is just a built-in lack of outside-US comprehension. Do you know why our Arctic convoys had such a hard time for so long in the first years of the War? Why the Germans always seemed to know where we were? Believe it or not, the American ship-owners were still insuring their cargoes in Hamburg! I ask you!" He sat back and lit a cigarette. "I'll be glad to get to normal duties, whatever they are. So far as I know, it will be with the police, but they'll advise me when we dock. A good old quiet life in the Colonies, I hope: you know," and I knew he was teasing me, "Fuzzy-wuzzies, Whirling Dervishes, quick curved knives in dark alleys. The Great Game, if you can believe Kipling." A deep drag on the cigarette. "But really, Tim, it's all a bit more subtle than that, these days. For instance – "

But I never knew what that example would be, as he suddenly clammed up. He had acted like this before when anybody came too close while he was talking, and it had become a habit. A couple of Military Police came past in deep conversation and shouting against the wind. And then, to my annoyance, our conversation was to be finally killed by a pair of over-enthusiastic but gormless Canadian kids, brother and sister from Ottawa, straight from school and embarking upon a commendably early Grand Tour of the western Old World, if they knew where to find it. We had chatted with them a few times, as with many other passengers, but honestly we found their starry enthusiasm for everything at all historical – "Gee, the Old World!" – just a bit over-powering. Rod and Julie meant no harm, and were – one hoped – suitably grateful for the fantastic holiday being given by their industrialist father as a reward for getting their College entrance; but Matt and I secretly winced at the thought of the gigantic rides for which they were about to be taken, by every crooked hotelier, taxi-driver and starving souvenir-shop in accessible Europe.

"Gee, are you really going to Arx-fud?". That was Rod.

"Well yes, actually, I was lucky to get a place there, for when I'm finished in the Army?"

"The Army? Holy cow, I hope you don't have to shoot anybody." Yes, you've got it – Julie.

"Not very likely now, thank God," I told them. "I'm not a professional like – " and here I had a warning nudge from Matt. " – like all you Canadians. D'you know, Matt," I twisted the conversation, "there's a single street in Winnipeg that's produced three VCs!"

They, and Matt, asked what I planned to do after Oxford, which was something I had been debating in depth parentally a few days before, as we stood on the station platform beneath a spectacular electric-green Aurora that curtained its way right across the northern sky. My father naturally hoped I would follow him into some branch of the Diplomatic Service: I had done quite well in my scholarship and entrance exams in French and German. But I also rather leaned towards being my own boss, if I could only hit upon the right formula, a product to sell and a market that needed it. A multitude of post-war windows were opening, it must surely be a time of opportunity?

★ ★ ★

So many of my friends were heading off to university, either straight from school or after two years of National Service. I had especially been considering the possibilities of selling something to students. There must be a huge potential: for several years we had seen a build-up of would-be undergraduates behind the massive dam caused by the war. Many of them would be married, which was hitherto unheard-of. Where would they all live? What would all the wives do? Would the wives be students too? Who would look after the children? Since all this education was going to be provided free by a grateful Government, so cash would be no great problem, what would they be spending their money on? So far as I knew, nobody had yet done their sums on this and it intrigued me.

Chatting like this, I told the young Ottawans my intended College and invited them, just that little bit reluctantly, to visit me in my rooms if and when Oxford was on their itinerary (but I suspect I omitted to point out that this would be a good three years hence). I had nothing against them really, but they were just so immature. They wandered off after asking my advice on where to go on the Mediterranean, as if it were some small island. Oh dear, I thought...

I then put my earlier question again to Matt. "Do you know where your people are going to base you?"

He shrugged. "I'll send you a postcard," as we went in to avoid a squall and a slanting sea. And indeed he did: I have them still. Early 1947 from Aden ('The Storage Tanks'); October that year, Nairobi ("You may remember Torr's Hotel?") and I certainly did, and those marvellous chocolate cakes at teatime with Mum when I was seven; Late 1949 ("Just leaving Fiji"). Then they stopped, but I noticed that the last postcard, leaving Fiji, actually had a French stamp and was postmarked Marseilles, just at the time when there were disastrous strike threats by the Communists, against whom some Sicilian groups were recruited by the West. Naturally, this rang no bells at all with me at the time. I certainly worried about Matt though, now and then as the years passed, and was sadly led to the conclusion that those who wear cloaks invite daggers. He had very likely ended up, I told myself, just as he had joked one evening: "floating in small circles down the Irrawaddy" or, as we had sung across the stern rail on a windy morning, like the unfortunate Ivan Skavinski Skavar, who fought Abdulla Bulbul Amir in the old music hall song, and in the coda "A splash in the Black Sea one dark stormy night caused ripples to spread wide and far; it was made by a sack, fitting close to the back," of the aforesaid gentleman. (Has anyone noticed how the song's sympathies are all with the Muslim, not the Russian? Abdulla gets a fondly inscribed tomb, Ivan just the splash and the sack fitting close to the back!). I must swot up on the Ottoman Empire...

Wait a minute though: Ivan, let's remember, is the one for whom the Muscovite maiden mourns so touchingly "by the light of the pale Polar star", so maybe it was a draw after all.

I was going to miss Matt though, he had the makings of a good friend in those days; perhaps I saw him subconsciously as the brother I might have had. But for the next couple of days I didn't see him. More than halfway across and making for the north of Ireland before dropping down to Liverpool, we had run into some really nasty weather. My bunk being next to a porthole which I optimistically (fighting off the smell of socks and vomit from my renegade Captain) kept slightly open, I was positively soaked by a mixture of salty spray and driving rain, all in a couple of minutes. The resultant chill or whatever, sent me staggering to the ship's doctor, who mixed me a grim-looking opaque brew which made me feel perfectly well again almost at once. Bismuth and chlorodyne – and I've sworn by it ever since.

When I did next meet up with Matt we were only a day before docking – he, too, had been out of circulation: "Pressure of business," he said surprisingly. I commented jokingly (was bismuth alcoholic, or the other stuff?) that this was rather incongruous on board ship in mid-ocean: had he perhaps been searching for Ethel Le Neve, or keeping a lookout for all those fuzzy-wuzzies hiding behind all those icebergs? It didn't go down well. He rather stiffly replied that some people were always 'on call', and I would understand that if I ever got into the Foreign Service; or even, he added, made any success as an entrepreneur. He was evidently under some sort of pressure so I shut up.

Later that day he was himself again. He had been in touch with his people by cable, and they were messing about with his postings so that he no longer had any idea what lay ahead of him before he could rejoin the Police. Meanwhile, what had I been doing?

Oh, not much. Coffee with the young Ottawans. No lunch with the Purser until my stomach was fully mended… A twenty-four hour steamy session behind closed doors with our lusted-after girl with the wiggle on the boat-deck… ("Ho-ho" we both went). Then, back to reality, tea and sandwiches in the ship's library, with the kids again.

"What did you talk about?" It struck me as interesting that Matt should betray just a hint of irritation because I had been, if not enjoying, at least passing the time with, people and conversations which omitted him.

I reflected on his peripatetic job: no doubt chasing around the world, putting down no roots, however exciting it might sometimes be, was a lonely affair and must leave him short of friends and relationships. I said we had been looking at maps of the safer and warmer parts of south and western Europe and sketching a possible tour for them.

I had also expounded, as I often did in those days, about the book I had long planned to write, imaginatively illustrating the Old World through the history linked to, of all things, its bridges: Avignon and the Anti-Pope... The unfortunate Harold winning at Stamford Bridge but therefore too depleted and deflated at Hastings... Arles and Nimes and the Romans... Rubicon and Caesar... The Tiber and Horatius... The Venice 'Bridge of Sighs'. The 'Ponte Vecchio' and the lovesick Dante... The upstream battle-bridge of the Ponte Flaminio where Constantine was converted, and in turn with the help of his British mother, converted the entire Roman Empire, to Christianity.

It turned out the Ottawan pair had a smattering of Art History and a book on it; but it appeared there was an interest in 'easy classics' music too, and we had drifted on to Lehar – still alive in Vienna – and that led them to want to have a glimpse of the Blue Danube.

"God!" cried Matt "Haven't they heard about the Iron Curtain?" Churchill had made his speech in the States very recently. I supposed not, and assumed that they were simply wanting to visit the shrines of Mozart, Beethoven, Schubert and that crowd. We decided to advise them to stay close to the Mediterranean ("but don't drink the water") and buy a book on the Baroque to study in their hotels, leaving it at that.

"Did they have any thoughts for you about things students may want to buy?"

★ ★ ★

We had not even touched on my thoughts for post-Oxford, and anyway, from my observation of them, I was pretty sure these kids had a level of maturity so far short of the general undergraduate standard at home in the UK, that Canada and the States would be a hopelessly dissimilar market. They just didn't know anything: Bernard Shaw was on to something, the hairy old walnut.

Matt and I strolled round the deck for the last time, early that evening, as we steamed south skirting the Scottish coast. I remember it was windless with a glorious battleship sky…

"Battleship?" he queried, looking up puzzled. "Battleship means grey."

No, I said, rather proud of myself, "Clearly you don't collect cigarette cards". There had recently been a series – Players, I think – featuring paintings of some of the chief vessels in the Fleet. It was obvious that the artist, though very accomplished, was bored to tears using that dreary bluish-grey time after time, and had reacted rebelliously by going to town enthusiastically with his skies and clouds in what was supposed to be the background. Every one of those cards is fervent in exciting sunsets, and believe me, they reward collection for those backgrounds alone, never mind the Fleet.

But Matt had, rather touchingly, taken it upon himself to try to offer some career help to the naive and younger me. He had been reflecting on my student selling idea.

"I think you're on to a very good proposition, Tim, I really do. Because, as you say, there will be hundreds of thousands of these students, all open to new ideas and all pretty serious-minded because of their service and often their family commitments. It is a vast pool of young people, wide open for you to dive in… " His voice trailed off. "Before the war," he went on, "one had the impression they were all over-rich pampered Daddys' Boys – "

"Well," I objected, "I don't know about that. Most of our Prime Ministers have come from – "

"Daddys' boys." He said it firmly and I heard the full-stop. It was clear that Matt ever so slightly resented the fact that he hadn't been to university. I wondered to what extent his current occupation (not even a 'profession', really) was acting in compensation for that. But that was unworthy of me.

"Keep pressing on." He patted my shoulder. "While you're in the Forces, do all the research you possibly can. Especially if you go for a commission – and you should because you've been in the OTC for years at school – you've passed basic training by miles – you'll be right in there alongside your future market, won't you?"

That gorgeous young woman sashayed by for one last time and we watched her nostalgically. She turned and smiled. We smiled back – well, wouldn't you?

"Don't let me keep you," I told him as we came within sight of the lights of Liverpool: the pilot would be coming aboard soon, to take us in early tomorrow.

"Maybe later," said Matt, and I still don't know the truth behind all that. "But just for now, Tim," he urged me, taking my arm, "Talk, talk to everybody, to find out their needs, their incomes, and what they are thinking. That most of all: what they are thinking. But don't tell them why." His voice dropped. "Never, ever, tell people why." Then, a bit clearer as he went on:

"The world is going to be full of smart young tricksters. Slick operators, not all of them just after the quick buck, but a lot of wild-eyed idealists too. Watch out for the politics."

"Are students really – really – interested in boring politics?" I stupidly asked. He nearly threw me over the side with his desperate look.

"Europe is split in half. Your English students are going to be in the new Front Line, and they won't even know it. But they will be targeted. Wait and see," he ended.

I have to tell you: I waited, and I saw.

★ ★ ★

13

Quite late that last night, as we lay at anchor outside Liverpool I suppose, he came to find me, just reaching for my pyjamas, and suggested a chat in the lounge, which was by then almost deserted. Sitting there while he went to get us a couple of scotches, I saw the renegade Captain from my cabin in close conversation with two stuffed-shirts who seemed intent on clapping him in irons, or whatever the phrase is. They had come out from the harbour in a launch, and no doubt they had all the authority they needed to cart him off under arrest for whatever-it-was he had done; but I looked at them, fresh-faced and straight out of college; and then I looked at him; not a medal-ribbon on show, but I knew from his talk that he had been across North Africa with Monty, then up the agony of Italy, and finally in a foul diseased prison outside Rome where half his companions had been dragged outside and shot for no clear reason. On rescue, of course he had cracked in some way. He was being taken back to account for whatever it was. All this, one had to accept. What I could not accept was the faceless, unblinking, hopelessly uncomprehending attitude of those two smug young well-cushioned bureaucrats for whom this was just another minor 'operation'. A nice rare steak on the way home, Justin?

Matt came back with not just two large scotches, as expected, but the bottle. You must picture us steadily working our way through it as the conversation developed. Many self-righteous people just can't understand how incredibly easy it is, to get through a bottle of scotch. One or two Holmes-like problems, and it goes nowhere; but perhaps, nevertheless, less toxic than his three-pipe formula?

"Tim," he said "I might be able to help a bit with your university ideas, because I'm always going to be in touch with people in the Colonies." What the hell, I thought. "British Councils, for instance, and local Colleges wanting to send young people to the UK", he went on: "I am always in contact with the top local people who are spreading the gospel about the education we can offer. So do keep in touch – "

But then, at once he corrected himself.

"Or rather," he stumbled slightly, "better I think, for me to do the liaison because I'm all over the globe and only I will know when I'll be close to the UK… "

So he didn't want me to know even where he was, let alone what he would be doing.

He was getting more and more confidential, lowering his voice and edging closer. Then – was it the whisky? – he put an arm round me, a clumsy demonstration, usually of false bonhomie, which amazed me.

I have to admit I have always hated that. I was nonplussed by it, and rather rudely resisted it. So American… Was he American?

But in my innocence I was underestimating him. Under the cover of the encircling arm, he half-whispered to me urgently and with complete clarity: "Listen Tim, I'll keep in touch as long as I can. We are very interested in the student connection. I've just heard, I have to go to Holland on a direct student arrangement set up by some Americans. I don't think we ought to have met and talked about student affairs, so I am going to delete it – "

I then realised that other people had come into the lounge, well past midnight though it was. So I became all confidential too.

I said, whispering in return: "How in Hell can you 'delete' or however you describe it, something that has actually happened? We have talked. That's it."

Matt removed his arm, and I remember thinking that I seemed to be on the brink of getting sucked in to the Great Game, despite myself. I had to avoid this. All I wanted after Oxford was the quiet life.

We drained our glasses. Unsurprisingly, we had finished that bottle. As we walked back along the deck he said casually: "We dock in the morning, but the Americans are picking me up by launch before dawn."

Oh come off it, I thought. 'Before dawn.' Why not by bloody helicopter? But he was serious – I decided not to pull his leg, and was glad at once.

"Tim, I have to ask you a favour."

"Of course."

"Two favours actually."

"All the better." Here was a delightfully mysterious friend, who might have been my elder brother, who had guarded Churchill, who carried the Greyhound badge, and was off in the tracks of Kipling, asking for my confidence and assistance as we dramatically parted. Would Buchan have refused? Would Dornford Yates, even, he whose heroes passed their time driving around the Balkans in a Bentley, hanging miscreant peasants from trees without anybody's permission.

"Never say you've met me. Don't attempt to get in touch or write to me, ever."

I nodded, swelling with secret pride.

"Next: don't say you were on this ship."

"What? Me?" He was my friend but was he getting paranoid?

"If anyone asks you, say a different ship. Say it was – " he waved his hand as he thought. "Say it was the 'Scythia', that'll do. But," and he took my hand in both of his before leaving me at my cabin door, "keep on with your student ideas. Secretly. And," this was with a pat on the back, "good luck in the Army, old lad."

When I joined the disembarking assembly the next morning, Matt had indeed already gone. I went south by train with the two gabbling and simplistic Canadians, and I got off and changed trains at Crewe just to escape, and praying they had lost my address.

CHAPTER II

The first back-to-work day after New Year is never a thrilling time, but 1947 had a particularly gloomy start for those of us in National Service call-up Group 101 who had been met at Canterbury station, steaming in the cold, by a genial corporal – red face under red beret – from the Parachute Regiment. That in itself was thoroughly alarming; already nervous in the extreme, we envisaged ourselves being hurled in and out of aircraft for six weeks; but to our relief he was now grounded after an energetic war, and attached to The Buffs, who were to give us our Basic Training, 'The Treatment', at a barracks just up the hill from Canterbury Cathedral.

It would culminate in meetings with the rather self-regarding PSO (Personnel Selection Officer) who lurked in a hidden office somewhere in the tangle of the Headquarters Block, but into whose hands we would be irrevocably committing ourselves in a few weeks' time, as soon as we could call ourselves soldiers.

To read about other people's Army service is always boring, so to write about it calls for brevity. I must remember and act upon the thoughtful philosophy of our diminutive Glaswegian platoon sergeant when, that first afternoon, he wheeled us into the lecture-room. He told us: "Pull your fucking fingers out and fucking pay attention to me and the bleeding Medical Officer and shut up for fuck's sake." We fucking did, as I recall.

To sit through a graphic lecture, with vivid pictures, on Venereal Disease before we had even unpacked, bizarrely set the scene for the next six weeks. I surreptitiously looked around at the thirty of us: a strange mix, but that was to be expected. About half were straight from public or grammar schools, a little gauche in this greater Outside World; the others had been roped in from the murkier areas of South-East London and had probably already been working in factories or around the markets for at least a couple of years. The division between the two sectors was immediate, as one would expect: we all homed in for comfort on the people in whom we thought we detected a possible bond, or at least a shared fear.

Each sector had its strengths. In the freezing barrack-room, with fifteen beds down each side and two smoking coke-stoves in the middle, my group settled at one end and the apparent street-urchins at the other. We eyed each other: my lot in open, and them in concealed, alarm. But it slowly dawned at our end that in one respect at least we must have the advantage: most of us had spent years – a full nine in some cases – in dormitory life, and were well acclimatised, (and incidentally had thus gained much experience of how to live with and cope with a lot of very mixed personalities! Those unthinking and too hasty critics of boarding-schools show their lack of understanding when they fail to take this into account, and blindly judge schools only on the silly league tables: my nine years growing up night and day with forty others taught me pretty well how to handle most types of people, a few of them a bit dodgy, and in my last year, to be largely in charge of them: answer that, you petty trouble-makers!). The crowd at the other end, however, were probably away from their own bedrooms and their family firesides for the first time ever. So, who was at the most disadvantage, we wondered, comforting ourselves a little.

The VD lecture turned out to be the catalyst, which nobody could have foreseen. At lights-out, after hearing the gruesome warnings of the bleeding Medical Officer (who appealed to the higher aesthetics of our group by speaking less than romantically about the discomforts of Schubert, Donizetti and Delius and nearly all the Romantic Poets) and watching some hideous films, we had settled into our beds when the conversation at the far end began to turn to their absorbing sexual experiences.

In the darkness at our end we listened in awe. Not bewilderment because, of course, we knew what it was all about and such chat was not at all new to us; but amazement, I suppose, that one could be so experienced and blasé as to talk openly about one's intimacies in a bleak barrack-room to all and sundry whom they had just met. Clearly our virginal crowd had little, more likely nothing to declare: but why, we were thinking, declare at all like this? We were being deliberately talked into an embarrassing 'loser' position, that was evident, and there was nothing we could do about it unless we could find some common ground, which seemed pretty unlikely. We would be a hut divided. At the other end they bragged on and on...

I remember thinking: if this basic division between Us and Them pervades the next six weeks, life won't be easy. I'm sure the rest at my end were silently thinking the same...

But memorably, the crisis was averted. There was an almost un-noticeable little Cockney bloke, stationed – appropriately – towards the centre and opposite the leaking stoves, who had said nothing so far, but his bridge-building genius saved the day by uniting us all. We had been listening in our hushed silence to endless loud reminiscences about all-night sessions, a torrent of multiple orgasms, group activities in various unlikely permutations, and then the subject turned to premature ejaculations, and other unhappy male disabilities came up (so to speak), and he piped up:

"Did you hear about the chap who couldn't 'come'?"

"No?" A very medico-sexually-absorbed chorus from the far end, greatly intrigued.

"They had to go and fetch him."

We all erupted. The hidden tension was broken at once: they must have heard the laughter in Dover. Soon after, we were asleep and when our Parachute corporal came round to raise us at six in the morning, we were all friends and helping each other with our kit. Simple as that.

★ ★ ★

The utter bawdiness of life in the ranks must be experienced to be believed. With its timeless adjectives, the 'bad language' is nothing more than an easy solution to the constant need by NCOs to get results as fast and abruptly as necessary, in a way recognised at once by all. One very soon forgives this. A strict Salvationist friend of mine, post-National Service, did so readily; as he put it: "In a vital emergency, it is simply quick communication – there isn't time for 'I say, you chaps', nor to search for more variety of words".

After our all-platoon bonding on the second day, I made my own small contribution to mutual togetherness by concocting a short verse to throw more helpful light on what we had been told at the VD lecture. I can't say that after all these years I am even slightly proud of it, but it went down quite well at the time:

"You can tell a man with clap, as against a man with pox;
He's a less unhappy chap but he dribbles down his socks."

Yes, I know, but they were trying days.

Smutty verse is at the very heart of Army life. We all knew, from schooldays, the rude classics such as (sung to Road to the Isles):

Oh my little sister Lily is a whore in Piccadilly
And my mother is another in the Strand,
And my father sells his arsehole at the Elephant and Castle
We're the finest fucking family in the land.

It was useful to have among us a selection of experts from various sixth-forms. One night we enjoyed an erudite metallurgical discussion about the Old Man of Madras, from which it emerged that even in the stormiest weather he would have been sparkless.

Only in the Army have I met someone – later a QC – who could and often did recite the whole of 'Eskimo Nell', let alone that Scottish epic 'The Ball of Kirriemuir' ("you couldna hear the music… "). Then there was the romance of the cowboy, "out there in Texas where the bullshit lies thick," who rather messily meets up with Charlotte the harlot the cowpuncher's whore. And it was my American medical friend Bill, called up by mistake, who brought us the worries of a certain young lady:

In the midst of her sexual contortions,
Despite contraceptive precautions,
Little Ermintrude
Let a sperm intrude –
Do you know a good man for abortions?

Many of the best of these come out of the medical schools. Perhaps there is a link, since both medicine and combat involve death, and one benefits by being able to laugh incongruously. It was the medics among us who sang 'Balls to Doctor Finkelstein' which was apparently based on fact – there had reportedly been a lecturer of that name, I think at Bart's, who was rumoured to have "kept us all waiting while he was… " er, attending to some private and personal function. Tra-la-la-la.

Some of the finest rude lyrics must have been invented to offset the boredom of a long march, perhaps after the gloomy cheerfulness of 'Goodbye Piccadilly' or – centuries earlier – to enliven tunes such as the Irish 'Lilliburlero', first published in the 1600s and then described as a quickstep, the word at that time simply referring to troops on the march. The tune soon "acquired satirical verses", my reference book tells me, and I bet there were some fruity ones, probably about Cromwell.

Closer to our own times, many inspired words have been attached to the rousing marches of people like John Philip Sousa and Kenneth Alford. Sousa died in 1932 and I wonder if he knew about the settings, with such well-known lines as:

"Bollocks," (two, three) "and the same to you"

or my own absolute favourite because of its utter craziness (and oh! the pain!):

"Have you ever caught your bollocks in a rat trap?"

where it is difficult to think of any other words, rude or not, that would so beautifully fit that joyful tune; I love the aching abruptness of the last two syllables (reminiscent of Gilbert's "Dull dark dock… Short sharp shock") following the cheerfully implied happiness of the music immediately before. I would love to know what inspired luminary thought it up – on the march, or in the barracks after a few beers? I am sure Sousa would have approved: after all, as well as those marches he wrote several operettas, but much more to the point, he had been in the Marines.

Those of us who didn't know all these naughty verses, had plenty of time to learn. Knowing the spiteful tricks of our climate we were suspicious when mid-January was unusually mild; and then icily vindicated when, at the end of our third week of training, it went – how can I put this? – cold. Very, very cold: we had snowdrifts twelve feet deep; amid great heaps of it, everything froze. The latrines were the first to go and you had to pee strategically to thaw out the moving parts: in some huts I'm told the NCO organised a pee rota, which must have been an idea remembered from somewhere nasty a few years earlier. I hate to think how the ATS girls managed... (Well, no, I don't actually *hate* to, to be frank, but, you know...)

The parade-ground had to be abandoned when, smoothed by a cutting wind into a sort of skating-rink, it made dozens of us in our hobnailed boots skid and topple in all directions at the "about... turn!". Instead, we continued learning our drill in the gym, in our socks and just pretending to hold rifles so that we wouldn't make dents in the PT Sergeant's hallowed woodblock floor. It wasn't quite the real thing and we began to wonder how, in the steps of Napoleon and then Hitler, we could ever win against Russia if the call came.

The Buffs officers in charge of us, seldom actually seen, were handling the situation fairly well, in particular making hot soup available several times a day. In the cookhouse, though, we saw lots of large rats running up and down along the overhead hot water pipes, tempted from their usual lairs under the floorboards. We didn't begrudge them their warm feet, but one or two of the extremists among us started muttering about events in Paris during the siege of the Franco-Prussian War... Then, the coke for the stoves ran out.

We were all put on fatigue duties, which under normal conditions would have been a punishment only for miscreants; but as we couldn't carry out any normal duties, there wasn't a miscreant in sight. So when a convoy of coke lorries slithered into the camp, we just shovelled it all day, and sat around it in the stoves all night and watched it burn itself away. One small consolation was to read, by the yellow barrack-room light, that people in Australia were in trouble too, being hospitalised by hailstones the size of billiard-balls. I forget why this pleased us so much – maybe something to do with cricket?

The snow was still in control of the place when we were brought abruptly to the end of our intended Basic Training, well ahead of the scheduled six weeks. The next intake could not be postponed, so we all went off, after a PSO's frosty deliberations about our various strengths and – more likely – weaknesses, to many far-flung Regimental or Corps Training destinations. One of my friends, who suffered (far less than he was claiming) from flat feet, was whimsically posted to a cavalry regiment, but they had recently been fully mechanised, so he ended up in tanks and armoured cars, one of which shortly ran over, and flattened still more, at least one foot. The little chap whose timely joke had so neatly eased all our relationships that first night, being in civilian life a qualified carpenter, went bemusedly to the Army Catering Corps, where he did very well, became a Regular, and was killed in Korea some years later: whether this was connected with his cooking I never knew. (But that was a war I am glad I missed, where capture led not just to physical torture and likely starvation, but to the far more subtle manipulations of the brain, as – come to think of it – you will see much later).

I had been sounding out a few of the platoon at 'our end' about any ideas they might have for selling something to students; and I was delighted when my medical friend, who had brought us the verse about 'Ermintrude', was posted with me to Tidworth. Bill was unique, having been somehow inducted into the British Army because of not one but two confusions: first, he was an advanced medical student which should have given him exemption until fully qualified, when he would have had an immediate commission; and moreover, his father was a top Harley Street surgeon whose influence ought to have ensured that deferment. But secondly, he was in fact a US citizen and passport holder, though living in London. I could see no reason for his presence with us amid, first, the frozen Downs outside Canterbury, and now the slanted sheet-ice of a Wiltshire hillside. Bill seemed to bear no grudges whatever, and was perfectly happy and philosophical, and as I got to know him I suspected that he had simply come along for the experience: I reckoned he was at heart a novelist rather than just a doctor. Nevertheless, shovelling coke had not been his forte. "My hands" he would cry, waving them about, "My surgeon's hands!"

Tidworth is a – what exactly is Tidworth? – I suppose some ordinary people do live there, civilians I mean, but by and large it is an Army Camp, like a number of other settlements nearby, on the unfashionable side of Salisbury Plain, that centre of pre-history. Even in the Iron Age and before, all the best people settled further South, the other side of the A303 or whatever they might have called it then, leaving our northern riparians to console themselves by idly cutting white horses in the chalky turf. Those horses are such a bore: there is only one really original and imaginative one, King Alfred's (and Chesterton's) at Uffington, a sort of Celtic *art nouveau* – celebrating a great victory, they say, yet clearly visible in those days only to the Gods. And anyway, why a horse?

Our earliest pre-Roman coins also carried a similar skeletal horse figure. I have always thought that in those days, to portray a horse on a hunk of silver must have implied that the value of the coin was equivalent to the price of a good horse. It seems logical, would have seemed so to a pretty primitive man trudging along the Ridgeway around 100 BC. But at that same time in more sophisticated countries such as the widely scattered Mediterranean Greek colonies, their local silver carried pictures of bees, dolphins, tortoises… Some of them were symbols of their State of origin, back in the Aegean (and of course there was the Owl of Athens); some are thought to denote the main export product of the region (corn, fish, mussels), which is also sensible. But I still want to know about our home-grown Celtic horses. Did we actually have home-grown horses in 100 BC?

I do tend to wander a bit these days – but so I did even back then, let's face it.

Tidworth has been an Army centre for generations, indeed my grandfather had been stationed there as a Ninth Lancers quartermaster-sergeant in the early 1900s soon after coming back from the Boer War. That same barracks now housed the Training HQ of my destined unit: The Royal Army Ordnance Corps.

When the PSO told me this, I had been delighted, I thought it meant I would be map-making and maps have always been something of an obsession. He put me right, up to a point, by saying No, it was all about guns and bombs and bullets. This, too, was marginally exciting. But on arrival we learnt that my part in the War Office's dusty version of Matt's Great Game was to be a junior assistant bureaucrat supervising a bunch of truculent labourers, all sunk in the Army's worldwide network of warehouses devoted to the supply of stores – of every kind of goods except food. Not for me the dizzy High Life and macho postings of those famous regiments named after a county or a king or queen, with the traditional nicknames my grandfather had told me about, those sleepless nights as we sat in the indoor Morrison shelter and listened to the doodlebugs' engine cutting out overhead. There were the 'Cherrypickers' (a rival cavalry regiment, and so he relished the story of this supposedly disgraceful epithet: caught in an orchard when they should have been facing the enemy, and made to wear cherry-coloured breeks forever after, or so he said, though the story got longer as did the air-raids). More gung-ho were the 'Death or Glory Boys' whose story I now forget, though I have in mind something about skulls and crossbones. There were more, dating back to the Modder River, I think in the Transvaal, where he had been shot, though not too badly. One of those nicknames, however, I only learnt later as it was omitted by Grandad in his strict Methodism; and even now I am warned never to mention it north of the border. I don't know which regiment, or what happened, or what they got up to, but somewhere up there are the 'Sheep-shaggers' and I'm not going to say it again…

So I was unexotically deemed appropriate for a backroom desk life, though possibly with a pip on my shoulder later in the year. Yankee Bill and I hit Tidworth's sub-Las-Vegan wonders on the same day, to start our indoctrination into the thrills of receiving, holding and issuing stores. There were about twenty of us in this intake from all around the UK. We were officially the '24th ORTS' and I never found out what that stood for, except that we had to learn the basic functions of that branch of the RAOC. (At the far opposite end of our Corps were the heroic men of Bomb Disposal – I suppose I should be grateful to that PSO in Canterbury for recognising me as totally unsuitable for such work – but how did he know?).

If we passed our ORTS course, we would go to a WOSB (War Office Selection Board) where a group of well-fed regular officers would set us more tests, chat over dinner and then in comfy armchairs, watch how we drank our soup and what sort of sherry we favoured (and, no doubt, how quickly it went down), whether we stood up when ladies came in the room (rarely, and only if it was an officer, mind you), and at the end of three days, decide who should be recommended for OCTU (Officer Cadet Training Unit).

Now, a permanent job at a WOSB! – *that* would have been my idea of serving my country…

However, the dreaded OCTU beckoned, where we would be drilled ruthlessly; insulted incessantly by uncouth NCOs who – I still suspect – had been handpicked for the work because of their irretrievable unpleasantness; and forced to conform to an insane regime where the utmost importance was attached to tiny matters of microscopic tidiness in the hut. Then, after eight weeks including a battle-course on Dartmoor with live ammunition, we would be illogically given the King's Commission and turned into officers and gentlemen. I thought back to the defrocked captain on the ship. H'm.

I'm not 'knocking' the process, not in the least, it's probably as good as any other way of selecting officers. And, in retrospect anyway, I wouldn't have missed it; though many experiences are of course good only in retrospect and the more retro the better. It is sometimes said that for us commissioned National Servicemen, with little more than a year to serve as an officer, the exercise was wasteful; but we must look at the world situation at that time and judge accordingly: we were all available to be re-called if necessary, and many found themselves in Korea, or Malaya, Aden, Suez in due course. For the War Office we were a good investment.

★ ★ ★

I said to Bill one day as we slid down the hill (still freezing in late March, and even Big Ben had been iced up the other night): "What d'you think students at university would be most interested in?"

"Sex."

"Yes, but they'll get that anyway. What would they want to buy?"

He nearly repeated, but thought better of it. "Music?"

"How come, music?"

"Well, they'll all have their separate courses and hobbies and interests, but whatever those are, they can play music in the background so it would have a general appeal... Popular."

"Do you mean a cheap range of popular classics, like the Boston Pops – "

"Holy cow!" He looked at me as though I'd just emerged from The Ark. "If that's their thing, they'll join a music club and borrow the records. I mean the latest hits – Sinatra and so on. Over in the States, the kids go to his shows and shout and scream and get hysterics and wet their knickers and fall over – that's what they'd want to buy and take home, to relive their kicks." (About twenty years later a young man would contact my Student Insurance office asking us to advertise in a new magazine he was starting, for students. One of so many; it'll never catch on; we declined with a sad smile. His name was Branson. Moral: sell people what they want, not what they need).

27

Bill had this interesting idea, though. Perhaps a closed-membership record club, advertised at all the Colleges in the JCR and the Halls? Maybe some system of Term-long hire instead of outright sale? (Idea for a clever advert: Term-long… Long-term??) Would the craze for a new 'hit' spread slowly out from London via the dance-halls, or splash everywhere spontaneously via the BBC? How about selling the used returned records to a firm in some other country which was slower on the uptake?

"I guess you'll have to research into that; but I tell you, in the States the NSA will be getting its act together, now the war's over, and they'll want to link up with student union leaders over here." I queried. "National Student Association," he explained. "I'll find out a bit more if you like."

"Would they know about trade if they're a bunch of students?"

"You're joking? It's going to be run by full-timers, professionals, now everyone's back. I'm told they're getting some pretty heavy financial backing. Politics are coming into it: anti-Commie and all that. Like your Churchill said last year."

This was beginning to sound like Matt.

"The Iron Curtain – how can that come into it – we're talking about fresh young innocent students, aren't we?"

Bill shook his head sadly. "Don't you people ever read the papers? Over in Russia they really focus on using students for propaganda – "

"Oh, well, Russia – " I was mentally switching off. "What they do with their students is their business."

He dug a heel into the ice and turned to me. "I'm not talking about their students, but ours."

I forget whether I actually laughed but must at least have smiled. "You Yanks are getting a bit too paranoid," I told him.

"Well, we'll see." This was over his shoulder as he skidded off to the NAAFI for a cup of our terrible English coffee. I went to the Camp Library and checked in Whitaker on total UK student numbers.

Later that week, the last few days before our visit to the WOSB, we dejectedly drifted into a lecture which threatened to be the most boring of the entire course: the complicated documentation that is involved when a Unit somewhere needs to order an item from the RAOC Depot back in England. It was a revelation.

The unlikely officer who presented this talk – the austere Captain Clements, I remember, who looked like Somerset Maugham's elder brother on a bad day – had developed over the years on the Plain a brilliant style, able to enliven and jokingly embroider the most mundane facts. Since we were not the first but the 24th ORTS, he would have been sharpening his act for ages. I have to put this on record, though you must imagine his sales-patter as I couldn't possibly compete.

At that time (and now, for all I know) a standard order-form, an 'Indent for Stores', was a half-foolscap (i.e. roughly A5 in today's printer-speak) set of carbon-backed forms, a layer of six joined copies in other words, all in different colours. The quartermaster out in Kuala Lumpur or Lagos would fill in the form ('press firmly') keep the bottom copy (white) and send the next-to-last (yellow) to his Unit's accounts office. The other four came back to the Central Ordnance Depot such as my eventual destination COD Donnington, and when we fulfilled the order, those bits of coloured paper dispersed sort of prismatically. One went with the item, one to our Accounts, one we filed, and so on. (You will guess that I never knew where that one went). Apparently this mechanism had been copied from the routines at Marks and Spencer. But here's the worrying thing:

Captain Clements presented all this as if it was some kind of adventure story or soap-opera. We felt ourselves drawn into it: what would happen to that green copy? Would it at last be re-united with the blue one?

★ ★ ★

It was, it was! At the end of all the recording, the statistic-gathering and the cross-referencing, nearly all those bits of paper were reconciled at Central Accounts, brought together from the ends of the earth. The way it was told, I honestly was quite excited at this happy denouement. I then at once felt an idiot and looked around sheepishly to check other reactions. It was a relief, later, to compare notes and find that most of us had had the same ridiculous experience. Were we, though, all being brainwashed and sucked into The System?

★ ★ ★

We had carefully drunk the soup and languidly chosen the dry sherry; we had knowingly chatted about the world's problems (for God's sake, where's yesterday's Times?). We had then devised ways, given a six-foot pole and a bucket, to lead our section across a ten-foot chasm and over a barbed-wire fence. In short, we (or most of us) had passed WOSB. Now we were returned to Tidworth to await our summons to OCTU at Aldershot, where the terrifying and nationally-known Sergeant-Major Brittain doubtless looked forward to our arrival.

But a temporary, paradisal interlude made life worthwhile. RAOC Tidworth had one overwhelming asset – it was completely out of control. Even when achieving a senior rank, a storekeeper is not a natural regimentarian. In due course I was going to bump into Majors who were published poets or thriller-writers; a Colonel who successfully sold his paintings; one or two who sang professionally – and these were the Regulars. It used to be said, (admittedly, only by us) that the RAOC were the real Intelligence Corps, while the latter outfit existed in the hope of gaining some intelligence, if possible, before demob). But our superiors were not essentially military. On the drill parades which we had to attend every Saturday as our token nod to the real Army, one officer couldn't even march properly: he swung his arm in line with the same leg, which the ORTS watched in disbelief and we found it really difficult to do, up and down our Nissen hut. And with this lack of organisation, everything descended upon Lance Corporal Osborne.

Those of us who came back to await OCTU were shunted sideways into a small squad under this pleasant and self-deprecating man, whose job was merely to keep us occupied in any reasonable way until the call came for individuals to be sent for, to proceed to Aldershot and the Brittainarium. Our Camp HQ staff were not to know that some idiot politician in remote Whitehall had decided to slow up on OCTUs for several months. In the beginning L/ Cpl. Osborne had eight supernumeraries to take care of, and was suitably relaxed about his job. He went on leave. When Bill and I arrived, which was when Osborne came back, there were *seventy-one* of us. What was more, we were now all potential officers, and a few were anxious to be regarded as such, let alone looking forward to getting the appropriate pay, in expectation of which most of us were in deep trouble at the bank. We were a bit rebellious.

I don't think there is anyone from those days that I remember with more admiration than Lance Corporal Osborne. He was presented with a problem and he solved it. On that first day when seventy-one of us were lined up, he stood and looked at us for quite a long time. Then he marched us up the hill into a clump of woodland and asked us how we would design a tree-high obstacle course. When we had offered our suggestions on the sheets of paper he had provided, he chose one and made us build it. A lorryload of planks and ropes and nuts and bolts came from the stores (I don't remember him filling in any rainbow-coloured forms, so he evidently had his sources). As soon as it was constructed and after we had then for a couple of weeks swung and blundered across it, he told us to dismantle the damn thing and rebuild it further into the wood, which we did. This was repeated a couple of times, until we got right into the central depths of the wood where we were fully out of sight of the camp, and life got easier: we sat around playing cards and Osborne, who was smoking quite heavily, disappeared for hours at a time, I think to the library, and perhaps to seek some new ideas out of Foulsham's Fun Book.

31

After that, with no more woods to build in, he once marched us to a big hilltop field that was full of rabbit warrens. He made us count the rabbits but it was evident that he was getting desperate. The following day, and regularly thereafter, two big TCVs (Troop Carrying Vehicles) awaited us every morning. We drove first to the remains of a Roman villa. "In a ditch nearby," he told us, "has been found a family of edible snails, originally imported by the Romans. In eighteen hundred years they have travelled only half a mile. So if you are waiting for a posting away from Tidworth, take heart: others are worse off than you lot." He took us to Old Sarum and told us about Rotten Boroughs ("If you think the Borough of Tidworth is rotten, look at this"); he took us to Winchester, and as we debussed by the statue, "This man was famous for burning some cakes; our friends back at the cookhouse still await their memorial but I'm working on it. Be back here at four."

★ ★ ★

I like to think that it was only to ease the pressure on poor L/Cpl. Osborne that Bill and I devised our own way of filling the days, while we waited for the War Office to pull itself together. It was he (and I insist on this for fear of being visited by the Military Police after all these years), he – Bill – who discovered a crucial loophole: whereas, if you were taken ill during the night, you had to report sick at eight in the morning and be marched down the hill to the CRS (Casualty Reception Station) and then be examined and grilled by the MO, if on the other hand you happened to be struck by some fearful disease between eight a.m. and half-past, it was left to you to stagger down on your own.

The CRS was on the far side of the main road from Andover to the outside world: to Bath, to Salisbury, to anywhere… That road, deep as it was within the post-war Army HQ network, was alive with lorries and the more friendly 'tillies' ('utility truck', a modest but rather accommodating two-seater with a van section at the back). Moreover, as well as helpful Army drivers, all the civilian motorists at that time, mostly commercial travellers, would happily give a lift to someone in uniform.

Shortly after eight in the morning Bill and I would suddenly feel terrible. Down we would limp, as far as the main road.

"Where do you want to go?" a driver we flagged down would say; we asked where he was headed, and cry joyfully: "That's just where we are aiming for, how lucky."

And true enough, that is where we went. This technique, purely to help Lance Corporal Osborne you understand, would get us all over Southern England: Cheddar, Lyme Regis, Glastonbury... Another time I took Bill to Oxford and introduced him to a school friend in The Queen's College where he was enthralled by the idea of one's staircase Scout who brought in a jug of hot water and a washbowl each morning ("Gee! How great, how mediaeval!). We avoided London, partly because Bill knew the city as well as I did, and partly also because the MPs would be prowling (Military Police, though maybe some Members of Parliament prowled too, who knows – whatever happened to Tom Driberg and the guardsmen?). But all in all we made pretty good use of our time. I often think that Bill must have taken back to the States a better idea than most, of early England: both Stonehenge and Avebury were very close at hand, we had already done Old Sarum and Winchester; now we worked on King Arthur as well, with Cadbury, even Dozemary Pool, though Tintagel would have to wait. And we were always, amazingly, back by lights-out.

Other members of our expanding squad found their own hazardous ways to cope. One of my intake was a rather flamboyant Londoner from somewhere like Swiss Cottage who hadn't enjoyed being cut down to an unacceptably small size by the NCOs, with whom he clearly didn't get on. Not a 'spiv' exactly, but his uncles probably were: a streetwise character who knew the ropes and how to pull them. He had managed, on arrival, to bribe a Company Office clerk, who was about to be demobbed, to delete his name from all the records except the payroll; and while still living his hedonistic life around the West End, he would drive down to

Tidworth once a week to join the pay parade. He came down in uniform but had left his equipment – belt, pouches, gaiters, and so on – with a friend.

One day, there was a fire in the office and all the routine records were lost; they had to be reconstructed from the data on the payroll which came in from elsewhere. Two nights later, his name appeared on the roster for guard duty. His friend alerted him in London. He sent a telegram: "Arriving six p.m. please blanco all kit". But he had forgotten that the local Post Office was run by the Army.

We saw him no more. I got his little-used gaiters.

★ ★ ★

Eventually somebody woke up at the War Office, and the main beneficiary was our Corporal, at last de-stressed but whom nobody at Tidworth HQ ever bothered to promote. I hope he found his reward in civilian life, somewhere in Human Resources. We all drifted off to OCTU.

Mons Barracks just outside Aldershot was the domain of that dreaded icon, Regimental Sergeant Major Brittain, the artificial scowl beneath the frowning peaked cap, later destined to play parodies of himself in Ealing films. A pleasant man in fact, but to us he was terror itself, as was his immense side-kick, Company Sergeant Major Parnaby. Across from the distant side of the bleak Mons parade ground, as we marched and counter-marched ("Higher with those arms, gentlemen, higher") you would hear Brittain's mock concern: "Mr Parnaby. Mr Parnaby. That little round man, is he going to catch up or do you want me to slow the squad down for him?" We were told that with the wind in the right direction, a shouted command from RSM Brittain at Mons could have a squad leap to attention miles away in Camberley, or perhaps even Sandhurst, where he really belonged.

One evening in our hut, we were sitting on the floor 'bulling our boots'. This idiocy involved rubbing endlessly at the leather to make it completely smooth so that the polish gave a better shine:

'bulling' was an acquired knack which many of us never really mastered, and most barrack-rooms included one or two specialists – obsessives, one would say today – who would bull your boots for you, over a few days, if kept supplied with cigarettes or the odd pint... At OCTU however, we felt obliged to do such things in person – a bit 'infra dig' to pay another cadet, don't you know? – and anyway most of the initial hard work had been done long ago, so by now it was mainly a matter of massaging-in the layers of polish, against the ever-present risk of a sudden inspection.

That was also why we were all sitting on the floor. By far the most absurd suffering invented for us cadets by the junior NCOs who ruled our daily lives, was the insistence that our beds must be absolutely perfect when made in the morning – not just neatly squared off, but geometrically so. Inevitably, the result over God knows how many years was for everyone to stuff strips of thick cardboard along the edges of their mattress, below the top blanket. At night-time these strips were taken out and hidden under the mattress so that we slept on the evidence of our cheating. At the end of your course, with any luck you would sell your cardboard to a new cadet coming in; or more likely, to one of the permanent staff NCOs at a discount, for selling on...

The real absurdity lay in the fact that this activity was so transparent: it was perfectly obvious that all the inspecting NCOs knew about the cardboard and always had done; as did the Duty Officers, however naive, who paid an occasional visit when nothing good was happening in the Mess: of course they would remember the farce from their own days. It was just an unspoken conspiracy between everybody involved, and accepted mutely as 'part of the routine'. But we dared not sit on our bed, let alone anyone else's.

On this evening Bill was squatting opposite me, reading the paper.

"Tim, I've got your answer. Dirty laundry."

I put down my boot and nervously examined myself.

"Your students... What they need... That Oxford pal of yours... "

I cast my mind back to our visit to The High. I didn't remember any dirty clothes lying around.

Bill waved his paper at me. "If things are so primitive, water supply and all that, I guess they all have to send stuff to a big laundry that serves the whole College, and I'll bet it doesn't come back for a week. But look."

The item in the paper was complete with a photograph of a shop that contained a battery of domestic-sized washing machines, and the write-up was hailing the arrival soon in England of our first 'laundrette', where the public could go and get all their washing done self-service, on the spot; and dried, too. So obvious, now. I think it was going to be somewhere in London's bedsitter-land, probably Paddington where so many 'pads' are, after all.

I could see the student appeal. "Ready for wearing the next day – they won't have to buy so many clothes." At the time clothing was still in short supply and, in effect, rationed.

"A room at the back, for doing your ironing," said somebody.

"Charge extra for that."

Bill suggested selling the students a three-year season-ticket, with a cut rate for each visit, which would give me a lump sum up-front to cover the premises, machines, plumbing, advertising…

The more I thought about the idea, its novelty and its attraction for young people away from home, the more I felt I may at last have homed in on a viable scheme. My imagination galloped away: a student laundrette in every university town, economically sited in a nearby side-street but still central, with music playing, near shops where students go… Close to a cafe… Or maybe with its own tea and coffee-making facilities… Perhaps sell the records that we were playing? Whyever not?

★ ★ ★

I continued doing all the tantalising laundrette sums as we worked our way towards our commissions and the passing-out parade. (And it would take me a full two years to discover whyever not). We were measured for our uniforms by a mob of the local tailors who had been doing this for a couple of hundred years. We were buttered up by all the local bank managers in turn, who (through what dubious arrangement with the Mess Secretary I don't like to speculate) were able to chat to us in small groups with large sherries, and then, they hoped, individually down at the Bank where the application forms were already on the table. We bought our Sam Browne belts, our swagger-sticks, our insurance in case we lost our baggage anywhere from Paddington to Polynesia; smooth young men tried to interest us in sports cars, skiing holidays, club memberships… We were then dumped on the sharp edge of Dartmoor for a week, where one of my friends got a bullet ricochet up his backside, another dropped his Bren gun into a bog and had to pay for it…

… And I was very nearly beheaded. I survived, lying there in a sooty cloud in the heather, only because the idiot in question mercifully made two mistakes instead of just one. He was in charge of the mortar. First, he fired it at our section instead of at the target we were attacking: the shell missed my head by about a foot, landing with a dull 'plop'. Second because, thank God, he had wrongly loaded a smoke bomb instead of high explosive. So far as I know, nothing was ever said. Today, no doubt there would have been salivating ambulance-chasing lawyers lining the road back to Okehampton.

The narrowness of my escape only really sank in down at the pub that night, when – also sinking in – there was quite a lot of 'scrumpy' or 'tanglefoot' cider in circulation. As we walked back to the Camp, we saw – a 'first' for all of us in the UK – an incredible display of the Aurora, a great shimmering blush across the sky but crimson instead of the electric green I remembered from Winnipeg. A member of my section suggested it was God celebrating my survival but the rest threw him into some nettles.

★ ★ ★

Back at Mons, we bulled our boots for the last time, polished our buttons, generously stacked our strips of cardboard in the corner ready for the next intake, and went on parade. Then lunch with our families and friends and, here and there, a tailor and bank manager fervent to the last. After that, it was goodbye time. We had come together at Mons from every conceivable Corps or Regiment, so we dispersed widely and there had been no great sense of togetherness as at RAOC Tidworth, which is where Bill and I returned briefly.

Bill, I remember, gave me some useful advice as we shook hands and parted; it was straight out of Hollywood.

"Do what Tom Destry said, before Marlene got shot. Be like a postage stamp: just stick to one thing till you get there. Adios."

Some of us – maybe all of them, I never knew – had signed the Official Secrets Act. So as things stand, unless I get dispensation, there's not much I can tell you about the next eighteen months, but it was largely pretty enjoyable and in good laidback company.

Maybe some other time. (Note 1, back of the book).

And then I came up to Oxford.

CHAPTER III

Immersed in my own quasi-military world, and especially after getting my commission, I had no awareness whatever of some significant murky developments on the international student scene. Many of the snippets of fact that follow were in any case unknown at the time, to all but a few insiders; indeed I am told that a large number of files on student affairs (MI6 for instance) remain nursing their secrets in their dusty archives. Nor will our UK National Union of Students be of much help: as their ex-President (late 1960s) Jack Straw is fond of saying in his more grown-up capacity: "Some secrets must remain secret." And the NUS seems notably touchy about allowing me access to its own archive held at Warwick University, though that may just be because – understandably – they don't like me much... You'll see why.

★ ★ ★

In view of my later involvement, in the twenty-odd years following National Service, it seems sensible at this point to list some of those events of which I was so blissfully ignorant. Though chronological order can sometimes be a little confusing, anything else would be worse. I will be as brief as clarity allows.

1945 (late) Moscow, well ahead of the West in its understanding of the power of propaganda, and the ease of 'spinning' it to the young, wishes to hold a 'World Youth Congress' and stage it in London: they have cleverly talked Eleanor Roosevelt into giving it her blessing. Our Prime Minister Attlee, a socialist evidently looking over his shoulder, allows the event, as he puts it: "to give the Communists the benefit of the doubt". Thousands attend, from many countries, among them a phalanx of muscular Russian ex-army 'students' nearing middle-age. The Congress launches the 'World Federation of Democratic Youth', clearly promoting Communism and with a definition of 'democratic' that is unfamiliar to Western ears.

1946 Early. A second Congress has been fixed for Prague. The UK's man on the spot suggests we should try to find somebody in our NUS to send non-Communist delegates and make their presence felt. In the US there is at this time no authoritative body equivalent to our NUS, but the NSA will soon be formed, so a couple of dozen students from the States go anyway.

1946 Middle. Churchill's 'Iron Curtain' speech at Fulton in the US. Atom bomb test at Bikini Atoll. British cartoonists have field days.

1946 Autumn. 17,000 students from 71 countries attend Prague Congress, where "crowds stood and cheered Stalin" whilst crowds also didn't. (The UK students were given the money to go, by a far-sighted Foreign Office man called Montagu-Pollock). Sponsored as always by Moscow, the 'International Union of Students' (IUS) is formed, membership being open to all the national Unions. Obviously Communist from the start, but there is no other international alternative, Russia having stolen a march. The Dutch refuse to join, which may be significant in the light of future developments, much later in this book; the Irish, Canadian and Scandinavian Unions very likely to withdraw. (The first Vice-President of IUS later became the Head of the KGB, no less, but even then retained his position for a year! This top-job promotion *must* imply that he had been a professional spy for years).

1946 Winter. Elections in France: Communists the largest party.

Churchill speech: "Relations with USSR have deteriorated steadily and more than a third of Europe is under Russian control." British students show their deep concern for world crises by protesting in London – for the return of the Eros statue to Piccadilly Circus.

1947 January. A Branch Director of MI5 (an ex-NUS President) says: "we want student unions infiltrated, especially peace-loving Lefties." BBC reporters who went to Bishop Rock lighthouse on Christmas Day to do a five-minute interview, are still there on January 6. (Quote: "This bad weather comes from Russia.")

1947 Summer. US students form their National Student Association and set up a student travel service. Austria votes to leave the IUS as it's a 'political instrument'. NSA extraordinarily votes to *join* the IUS! great alarm in the US… US National Security Act creates the CIA. Its staff at the end of 1947 totals 302 personnel, its budget is $4,700,000. (See two years later, end of 1949, below).

1948 January. Awake at last, a remote department of the UK Foreign Office organises an International Youth Congress at London University. This department becomes 'Information Research Dept.' (IRD – our first undercover unit for political shenanigans, i.e. parallel to the new little CIA). The Congress led to the 'World Assembly of Youth', in obvious competition with Moscow's organisations. After initial meetings elsewhere, it makes its HQ in Paris. *(After 1952 it was funded by the CIA).* Denmark leaves IUS.

1948 Summer. UK Government imposes very strict travel currency limits. In the US, the National Security Council, in its now notorious Directive 10/2, approves covert action by the CIA. (Later it will ordain that illegal acts by CIA personnel are to be reported only to the CIA itself, and not to the Law, thus *putting the CIA above the law*). The 'American Committee of United Europe' (ACUE) is founded, to fund CIA's surreptitious financial aid to 'The European Movement', and thence via countless channels to a horde of non –

or anti-Communist causes: magazines, radio stations, trade unions... And students.

1948 September. A two-day Conference, set up by the Foreign Office, and held at Worcester College Oxford, secretly decides: "... atomic war with Russia is almost a certainty... The only method of preventing the USSR threat from ever materialising is by utterly defeating Russian Communism." UK university departments are seething almost everywhere with Left-leaning dons.

1949 Late. A meeting of Western Student Unions forms the 'International Student Travel Confederation'. It is unclear who instigated and funded this: I have been denied access to the relevant files. But read on, later in the book... By the end of the year, (compare with Summer 1947 above) the CIA has not 302 but 5,954 staff and annual budget of $ 82,000,000. They have set up or adapted dozens of 'funds' which supply scores of worthy causes in Western Europe and elsewhere, through 'charitable' outlets created for the purpose, such as:

Congress for Cultural Freedom, Council of European National Youth Committees, European Youth Campaign, Foundation for Youth and Student Affairs, Independence Foundation, International Institute for Youth Affairs, International Research Services, National Education Association, World Assembly of Youth, World University Service, Young Christian Democrats, and more...

1950 Spring. NUS wisely leaves IUS. Grants approved for UK students to visit US under a joint scheme funded by the 'International Research Fund' and 'Student Travel Service' (who?).

1950 Summer. Meeting in Stockholm of Western SUs to form an acceptable alternative to the IUS. The intention is said to be an avoidance of politics: (e.g. "most of the time we talked about student travel"...). They establish 'The International Student Conference' ISC). From the US, the NSA attend; one of their delegates later joins the CIA, and the CIA's covert masterminds Tom Braden and later Cord Meyer, then assist in establishing the ISC's co-ordinating Secretariat (COSEC) based at Leiden in Holland. (They have both written about their activities, somewhat cautiously). The CIA presence in Holland is mysterious: the British MI6 had recently been expelled from Holland as a hangover from the unexplained destruction in London of wartime Resistance files; the CIA appear to have taken over, in strength, but that too is confused. Some writers say it was a very small CIA presence and list only a handful of names; one or two others list nearly a hundred... In June, at an International Labour Conference held in Geneva, the Czech, Hungarian and Polish delegates walk out because Nationalist China (i.e. non-Communist) is attending... Back here, the Oxford Union votes its regret at US domination of the democratic world.

1950 Autumn. Attlee condemns the proposed 'Peace Congress' at Sheffield, referring to bogus selection of delegates. Some of the foreign groups are refused entry to UK. Small attendance: after one session the Congress decamps to Warsaw... The ever-consistent Oxford Union now elects an American as Secretary... At year-end some Scottish students with nothing more important to think about, steal the Stone of Scone from Westminster Abbey.

1951 Feb. UK Army Reservists (ex-National Service) called up for the Korean War... May: Burgess and Maclean turn up in Moscow... Summer: Huge 'Communist Youth Rally' in East Berlin, estimated to have cost Moscow fifty million dollars. Two million delegates. TWO MILLION!!

US is prompted by this to form the European Youth Campaign... In US, the NSA plans an 'international information centre' to combat the "loaded" IUS news bulletins to students.

1952 Early. ACUE (see June 1948 above) now starts, with the apparent blessing of the US Senate, to funnel millions (and millions) of dollars secretly to the EYC and those other outlets, supporting youth organisations to such an extent that commentators now speak of 15 national committees, sixteen million members, two million brochures, nearly 3,000 study sessions and shows. It has since emerged that four of ACUE's Directors were top CIA men... In March, Fred Jarvis, President of the UK's NUS, warns the NSA that the IUS are trying to discredit them over "outside sources of funding". Now whoever could that be? And did Jarvis know?

1952 August. COSEC opens its Leiden office to administer the ISC (see above, 1950 Summer). On the very same day, FYSA opens its New York offices (see list in 1949) and appears to have funded ISC and COSEC from then on, until all this (or more likely, just some) was exposed in the 'Ramparts' scandal of 1967, which I will come to later (end of book: Matters Arising – 2), though it's worth Googling: "NYT-Ramparts-CIA".

Also in those days, some of the more serious preoccupations of British students included:

    * Manchester University students form a Custard Appreciation Society.

    * Bradford students launch an Apathy Society; at the inaugural meeting, nobody turns up.

★ ★ ★

So that was student international politics at the time, so I am told. I was oblivious to all of it, but it may help to fill in the background to this work of fiction. On the other hand, it doesn't make much difference to the story, so you needn't really read it, but it's a bit late to tell you that.

CHAPTER IV

"So, how was your crossing on the old 'Illyria', then?"
That was a fine start. This was the first thing my Senior Tutor said when I visited his paper-strewn rooms, after checking in at the Lodge of my Oxford College, that 1949 Michaelmas Term.

I had almost forgotten the old floating barrel of secrets, what with all the involvements of my past two years; but I suddenly remembered how Matt had asked me to avoid mentioning the ship. I mumbled something, and he went on with the patriarchal welcoming chat he had been doling out to nervous freshmen for thirty years... I looked round the room: paper-strewn I had thought; but paper-lined as well, since every inch was taken up by extremely tired-looking books; and one might even add paper-infested as the whole place was full of the mustiness you normally only get in the stockroom of a very old library.

He was chatting away. I have since been told that after 1945 he had schooled himself to adopt an entirely new patter for those of us who had done our military service; indeed, only a couple of years before me, he would have been talking to men returning from some very grown-up experiences, which must have taken him back to his own days on the Western Front and his DSO at Gallipoli. It must have been quite a shock, not just to the dons but to all university staff, in the immediate post-war days, to find their charges so adult and so unsuited to the pre-war rules and regulations. It is on record that the 'Bulldogs' (the University's 'heavy mob' of college servants employed to enforce discipline when necessary, under the command of a Don who was the Proctor) had rebuked in 1946, for drinking on the pavement outside a pub, a student who turned to be a Colonel with an MC.

There is a very much older, delightful story of the undergraduate who was stopped in the street one night by the Proctor because he was arm-in-arm with the most notorious lady of the town. In the accepted routine, the student was asked: "Sir, will you kindly introduce me to your companion?"

"By all means." Equally straight-faced, "Please meet my sister."

The Proctor exploded. "Are you not aware that this woman is the most renowned harlot in Oxford?"

"Yes, Mummy and I are very worried about it. Goodnight."

★ ★ ★

"Let's see," the Senior Tutor continued, "it's Languages, isn't it?"

"Well, that was the scholarship subject, but I've been having second thoughts as I said in my letters, and it's been agreed I should do PPE instead."

"Ah," he sighed, "economics, the gloomy science – what a pity." The Senior Tutor was an Ancient History man as one might have guessed. He went on: "Did you know that the Minister for Economics in Singapore is called Dr. Dam Rong?" His shoulders heaved silently, and when I left ten minutes later it was in the pretty firm knowledge that I was in good hands.

Dick at the Lodge had directed me towards my rooms and also given me some mail that had awaited my arrival. There was that last postcard from Matt; one from Bill, now Stateside and settling into student life on the West coast; he said they already had laundrettes, but they also had hot and cold running water; on the other hand they had no building earlier than 1934. Could I buy the Radcliffe Camera and ship it over?

In the second quad, under the arch with the statue, I met my Scout, Arthur, who would be servicing my staircase and its six occupants, bringing in the inevitable jug of hot water at seven every morning, and laying my coal fire when necessary: I could have done with him in Canterbury. He was also destined to greet my huddled form an hour later, most days, with a shocked: "Mr Topps, Sir, it's almost *eight*!" as he came into the bedroom with a cup of tea: he must have practised that tone of voice for years. "Oh Mr Topps, your jug's gone all cold again".

I next introduced myself to my neighbour across the landing, Richard, also just arrived. Reading English, he was destined for great things in the theatre as a producer and sometimes actor; but in those first College days Richard and I devoted many late nights to planning the quick fortune certain to burgeon from our eldoradan chain of student-oriented self-service laundrettes, whose success the Americans had apparently demonstrated. In front of one or the other of Arthur's blazing fires, we worked out that with adequate direct-marketing and sales promotion, plus those inspired three-year season tickets, we could open a second place in six months, then two more at the end of the year, and so on... Before we were thirty we would be opening one a week and then we'd sell up and retire to somewhere warm and libertine in the Colonies...

Not only were there fewer and fewer Colonies, and those less and less libertine, but I – of the two of us, the economist – took a full fortnight to realise we had overlooked income tax and rates. We went back to our essays and Richard joined the Dramatic Society.

★ ★ ★

It was largely the shortage of Colonies and Dominions that persuaded me away from thoughts of the Overseas Civil Service which had shunted my parents around the world; and any temptations to stay on in the Army as a regular officer had already been rapidly dispelled when I had seen some of the ex-Indian Army subalterns now rejoining their original British units, and realised that they would all be senior to me by the time I signed on.

Not only that but they all seemed so depressed, so serious. My fond memories were of my own unorthodox and frankly rather unmilitary group, irredeemably 'incorrect', who tended towards odd but perfectly logical decisions such as, one winter evening after a snowfall, taking the subsequent snowball-fight indoors into the Mess because it was warmer.

In the end, however, the rest of my life was resolved by a New Zealander I never met and whose name I hardly knew.

I wanted to learn to drive. This was something that the Army had shied away from, possibly because they knew that young officers far preferred to be driven around in 'tillies' by the good-looking and amenable ATS girls who were traditionally assigned to every driving-pool by understanding PSOs, labelled "Subalterns, For the use of".

Few undergraduates had a car, even though half of us were ex-Forces. Travel by train was so much easier, cheap too, and prior to the Beeching Bloodbath in the sixties one could reach almost any town, and many villages, by rail, even if it was only the early-morning 'milk-train'. Those little branch-lines, now only hinted at by a roadside fragment of bridge or by a suspiciously straight double hedge beside a field, supplied a safe and relaxed journey everywhere, gentle enough to allow even the most obstinate town-dweller to absorb the grassy essence of the countryside, to the soothing background of that hypnotic che-cha-cha we all remember so well. (A long-playing record of che-cha-cha, without even a hoot to break the lullaby, might be great for insomnia: perhaps it would sell to fraught examinees? Aha, at laundr- No, forget it). The wonderful Flanders and Swann lament for 'The Slow Train' will forever bring tears to the eyes. Mine anyway.

Mind you, there were exceptions. The infamous Tidworth Flyer would lurch along its single track the few smutty miles to the main line junction at Andover, then back again, serving just a couple of grim Army camp 'Halts'. I don't think it even carried milk. What it did carry was a steady trickle of disgruntled soldiers. Late one January night I had settled into my corner, the whole compartment full of leaking steam, when as we began to pull out from Tidworth I was joined by a wheezing sergeant from the depot. He threw two huge rucksacks ahead of him, scrambled aboard, huddled down into his greatcoat and at once fell asleep. I spent the twenty minutes scraping uselessly at the ice on the inside of the grimy window. As we drew into the remote platform at the far end of Andover station he woke up and gathered his baggage together. "Well," he said as we nodded goodbye, "That's the worst of it over." I asked where his posting was.

"Borneo".

★ ★ ★

So I wanted to learn to drive. My friend Peter from OCTU (he who had been thrown into nettles on Dartmoor) was now up at New College, busy bragging to everyone that it was only his College which must always have that word included: you never, ever just said "New" as you might say "Magdalen" or "Exeter". We all knew this already, which sized him up, or down, we thought. But he also wanted to get his driving licence and reckoned that he was more than halfway there after his smattering of lessons in Primary Training with the RASC. (They were responsible for all supplies of perishable stuff like food, so most of their recruits were shown how to drive a lorry) I was less than comfortable about this, but Peter knew a New Zealander, charming chap, who was about to return home and wanted to sell his car.

"Is he rich? What's the car?"

"He's pretty well-off and not bothered about the money, he just needs to get rid of it. It's an Austin."

"Austin-tatious?" We went to look. No.

Back in Nairobi in the mid-thirties my maiden aunt had spent her first teacher pay on an Austin Seven, third-hand at least, like a scarcely-mechanised pram with a flapping soft-top, and as it came puttering around the corner my father had looked at the number-plate – T.1415 – and said: "Ah, Agincourt, wasn't it?"

The extraordinary machine we found at the end of Norham Gardens must have been still earlier off the assembly-line. It put us in mind of an off-centre downtrodden matchbox. But we got it cheap. Peter had handed over £10.

The owner had reluctantly agreed to meet us and give us a trial run and some lessons, but by then he had pocketed the money and didn't turn up. A call to his College Lodge informed us that he was already on his way back to the Antipodes, so renowned for their original colonists, so we had a quick conference, standing alongside this relic from the past.

Time was short... We had essays and tutorials ahead of us, and the pubs opened in a couple of hours. Peter had in his past briefly manhandled one or two lorries along a straight bit of road... We drove into the countryside on our own...

... And at the top of a hill running down into Witney, we found a policeman.

And he found us. I was driving at that point but we reckoned we ought to change seats as Peter was more experienced. Mistake. Motto: When in doubt, brazen it out. But that didn't work either.

We now faced an unpleasant appearance in Court which we had to confess to our Tutors; and the Proctors would be alerted, too. Peter and I had to cast around for help.

And that, children, is how I got into the insurance business.

★ ★ ★

Jerry Morrison was an ex-Marine Commando, he told me. He once showed me on his leg the five bullet-holes which a German machine-gunner had given him on the St. Nazaire raid. I knew him as an Insurance Broker only because, having just set up on his own, he had run a small ad. in the Oxford Mail. Early in my first Term I had responded to this because I had given up my part-time job down in the steamy basement of the Agricola Restaurant in George Street. (Even today I feel sorry for Mr Thompson the owner of the Agricola, having in my first week talked him into appointing me as a storeman to work my own hours, and paid by the hour, so that I used to take my papers down there and write my essays hour after hour alongside the vats of baked beans and spaghetti which were always topped-up at the end of the day, and never – so far as I recall – delved to their hideous depths).

Jerry's advert was offering part-time work at a generous rate of commission, evenings or weekends, the hours flexible to suit. But commission only... Nevertheless to an eager innocent this had sounded better than the fumes from those vats, and in any case poor Mr Thompson had begged me to come in less often.

It turned out that an enterprising insurance company, one of those with which he had established an agency, was bringing out a special policy to insure television sets (which were then still quite a novelty and were not included automatically in one's normal household insurance). I, or else someone, or maybe crowds of respondee hopefuls for all I knew, had to hawk these leaflets around the houses, approaching only those which sported the telltale H-shaped aerial. It wasn't a bad idea, and he may have had some successes, I never asked afterwards because of my own cringing experience...

I had taken a bundle of the forms around a well-to-do village the far side of Boar's Hill and found scarcely any aerials (later, Jerry corrected me on this incredulously: "Everybody knows the only people with televisions are on the council estates"). But at last, through the evening gloom I saw what I thought to be the H atop a splendid Queen Anne house. Somehow I had the gall to ring the doorbell. The owner, a trim gentleman in his eighties, listened to my spiel, nodded understandingly, patted me on the shoulder very kindly, and told me he was a Lloyd's Underwriter.

So I hadn't seen Jerry for a few months. I did remember though, that he had told me he was a favourite drinking partner of the city's Chief Constable. Coupled with our pressing need to get motor insurance, if possible backdated (it was not possible, of course, even through him), everything pointed to this being a visit I ought to make.

His office was a narrow slice of an ancient terrace in Pembroke Street backing on to that College and just down the road from Tom Tower. He had two rooms on the first floor, and above him on the decaying second landing was a mysterious bearded God-botherer who churned out tracts on a hand-wound Gestetner duplicating-machine, which sent throbs through Jerry's ceiling and raised a flock of pigeons from the windows whenever it was used. There was also a ground-floor storage room that was damp.

Peter was sitting exams, so providentially it was I who went to see Jerry. (Supposing somebody had timed Peter's exam differently, what would the rest of my life have been, I sometimes wonder!)

"Hello, old boy, how can I help?"

I explained how we needed cover for the car; and I also came clean, as I had to, about our Witney crime and its likely consequences; and to be sure, it may have helped in the back corridors of local power because when the case came up, we were treated far more lightly than Peter had expected and I got a drink out of him on the strength of it.

I warmed to Jerry. That afternoon we drifted into a long and amusing exchange of experiences; as we chatted I looked around his office. The sixteenth century irregular walls, maintained and replastered by generations of Pembroke's workmen, and the inward-leaning window with its ledge and the pigeons, had been well compensated by the neatness and the careful fittings within the room. Jerry's desk, I noted with a touch of admiration, had no drawers and was in fact a very elegant rosewood fin-de-siècle dining-table with angles at each cut-off corner and standing on chunky pedestals two feet square. There was a sectional bookcase in dark oak with glass fronts closely-leaded. On the walls were large framed photos of motor torpedo-boats; and there was a Peter Scott, but – no – not a print by Peter Scott but a signed photo of the man himself in Navy uniform. There was also a Salvador Dali print, unsigned and thus, I'm told, rare. A small oak side-table at elbow height carried some nice Waterford crystal glasses and two choices of Scotch, a siphon and a carafe of water, but no dry ginger.

Here was a man I could trust.

He was asking what I'd got up to on National Service and I told him what I could; I noticed he didn't probe. Then where I'd done my schooling and what my father's position was in the Civil Service.

"When's he going to get his 'K'?"

I had never thought of it. I replied that he hadn't even got a CMG yet, and under the present neurotic levelling-down government, probably wouldn't. (And no, he never did).

After a lot more of this – Jerry had been at Clifton, then gone out to the Far East in the thirties with Jardine's where the insurance connection had been made – he neatly led me into the matter of Life Assurance. As a student I could qualify (no, wait a minute, give him salesman's credit, he said 'would' not 'could') for a lifelong premium discount through a Scheme he was about to launch, backed by a leading Company. This was based upon sound actuarial evidence about one's prospects, upbringing and hence life expectancy... By starting now whilst a student, the discount would (hang on, I think this time it was not 'would' but 'will', give the old devil his due) also be merited on any future increase or additional policy started before age 35.

Did this apply to all university students, I asked, as I emptied my second glass. My mind was busy jettisoning record clubs and laundrettes.

"Absolutely, old boy. Why do you ask?"

★ ★ ★

I suppose this must have been the crucial moment of my life, though I didn't recognise it at the time; and I often doff my cap to the old Austin Seven, nettlestung Peter and the disappearing New Zealander. And thank the police for arresting me, come to think of it.

I sensed that Jerry's ambitions were large but local. He saw his embryonic Brokerage as getting him among the upper crust at the county gymkhanas, regattas and rugby matches, which would naturally bring the well-heeled and at least the sub-gentry from Lambourn and Woodstock, with their rated-up premiums, into his office. (That office, I was sure, would soon need to be rather better relocated: I was right). It also strikes me, now, that Jerry may well have been a little hesitant, as a non-university man, (which did matter at the time) to try to market a brand-new student-only scheme when he was an outsider to that world. He was only hovering on the edge at that moment when he came across me, and raising the Life Scheme tentatively to people like myself who happened into his office.

But we were still talking…

★ ★ ★

"I'm asking," I suppose I must have said, "because I think students are going to be a big market. Just here in Oxford alone there must be nearly five thousand of us, half of us back from National Service, or even from the war: grown-ups," and I went on to spell out all the points Bill and I had made to each other while counting rabbits in Wiltshire, bulling boots in Aldershot and getting bombed in Devon.

"There will be masses of students, everywhere," I ended.

"What about teachers?"

"Oh yes," I assured him, "there are twenty training colleges and of course their future income is pretty well – "

He looked at me. "No," he said, and waved a bottle. "What about Teacher's – the Black Label's run out."

We sorted that one. Jerry went on thinking, then reached behind him, surprisingly, for half a loaf of bread. He went across to his leaning window and pensively fed a few pigeons.

"They don't get enough from the Pembroke kitchens these days, you know, it all goes off as pigswill, so a Top Local Councillor told me." He stayed at the window, staring into space. "If we can make it really worth a student's while to start a Life policy before he leaves – er – gets down – goes down, isn't it? – then what's the best way to tell them all?"

"All?" I echoed. I was getting him on to my wavelength.

He sat down again on the leather swivel-chair behind that lovely table. "I suppose an article in the papers. Isis, is it, and Cherwell?"

I was doubtful about that. I didn't reckon the great mass of my intake of students, having been out in the real world for two years or more, would place much trust in the waffle pages of student newspapers, especially after I'd met Alan Brien of Isis.

"Most of us don't actually *buy* them, we just skim through in the JCR to see what's on at the pictures. Anyway, an article is gone by tomorrow, you need repetition. A small running advert would be a better idea, but it's a big message to get across. You have to present this as a Big Deal" I said in the capital letters I sensed he would warm to…

Jerry shrugged. "All I can really do here, is talk to them when they come in."

I felt, all at once, a breakthrough. "So you shall," I said, excited. "Direct mail."

"Too much cost – think of the postage." But by now I was way ahead. I had pondered direct mail, along with the laundrettes – there wouldn't be any cost. This mail could be really, but *really*, direct.

"Listen." I settled more deeply into my chair while the pigeons burbled on their ledge. A sparrow alighted beside them very cheekily and was at once chased away. "I've looked into this. Of the five thousand or so of us, half live in College, the rest out in digs. But – " I paused, as they say, for emphasis; it usually works when you're selling something. "For everybody, there is a postal box at the Lodge. What's more," triumphantly, "there's a list up in the Lodge anyway, of all the student names and addresses."

"I say!" He was sitting forward. "Are you able to write them all down, or will the Porters want a bit of cumshaw?" I wasn't up to that Orientalism and had to ask him. "You know – baksheesh – a tip – for getting the names and addresses?"

I didn't see any problem, perhaps a ten bob note when I delivered all the envelopes to be put in the pigeonholes. There was only one problem, and it was fleeting. "We'll need to enclose a reply-paid card so you must get a licence from the Post Office."

"Done, old boy," and he held up a card. Licence OF173. Still ours sixty-two years later.

I carried on for a while about the need to draft a letter, print 5,000 copies, sign, fold, stuff into envelopes, address all those envelopes with name only, then take a bundle to each Lodge presumably with the ten-bob note, perhaps held behind the back unless requested or demanded – and I very soon got to know which Porters matched which of those alternatives (I have seldom in my life met a more arrogant and unpleasant person than a certain Lincoln Porter of the 1950s, who seemed to have set a standard for subsequent years. More than once, I very nearly wrote to the stationmaster at Windermere – (See Note 2 end of book).

"So when a few students reply," I told him, "I could go and see them, give them a short talk – "

"Chat them up – "

"Sort of pass the time of day, student to student – " I painted the tempting picture, "And then send them in to you here, for you to do the actual hard work of signing them up for the Life policy."

Jerry was trying not to look too happy. "I'm still a bit worried about the costs you're going to run up," he shook his head. I would be hearing that for the next fourteen years, sometimes in cables sent back to me from his Caribbean cruises; but my reply set my life in stone for those years.

"I can handle that," I said.

The sparrow had come back, perky like Hugh Lofting's Cheapside, and recklessly chased away the whole pack of pigeons. I nodded to it fraternally.

★ ★ ★

We had the ground-floor cleared, cleaned, and to a certain extent damp-proofed. I moved in a desk of sorts, and found a veteran Remington typewriter (which, in retirement and gathering dust after 63 years, is by my feet under my desk as I write). We also bought the thundering Gestetner duplicator from the man upstairs who, a cleaner said, was being run out of town by his disillusioned erstwhile converts.

We drafted the sales letter which would bring to all Oxford students the glad tidings about SLAS, the 'Student Life Assurance Scheme' as we would call it. It was, in all honesty, a very good offer indeed. We reckoned the name would serve well, being clear, quite straightforward, and 'SLAS' rang well. (See Note 3).

It is very tricky, choosing a trade name, especially if you plan to sell in other countries. A few years later I tried to translate our scheme into French, and with the words emerging as *Projet, Assurance, Universitaire, Vie,* and *Etudiants* we were heading dangerously towards marketing something called PAUVRE, which wasn't the idea at all. But then, worse things have happened: Marmite, in French, isn't just a big cooking-pot but a nickname for a prostitute; and who can forget arriving at Orly to be greeted by a poster showing a huge bottle of fizz called Schiiiittt? (The worst of these lapses is far more recent: an Italian household machine calls itself 'Smeg'. What it performs in the house, I'm sure is splendid; but that word, as we addicts of TV Comedy space sitcom 'Red Dwarf' will know, refers in real life to an affliction of the male genitals known only to the uncircumcised: could it be, just possibly, that the admen down in Turin are all Jewish and oblivious? I search in vain for another explanation).

Between my lectures and tutorials and essays in the Camera, I sat alongside that old Remington and the Gestetner. I typed out the stencil. I churned out 5,000 letters, scaring away all the pigeons round the corner to the greengrocer in St Ebbes. Madly extravagantly, in retrospect, I signed every one personally in blue ink; and folded them; and stuffed all the envelopes; and was about to seal them down when I remembered we had omitted Jerry's essential reply-paid enquiry card. Finally I delivered them all into the individual pigeonholes at all the Colleges – except my own because part of me was still a little ashamed at becoming an insurance salesman instead of continuing to pursue Higher Things and perhaps the ultimate CMG… But I was still canny enough to carry out the entire delivery late on a Saturday, because there would be little else in anyone's pigeonhole on a sleepy Sunday morning, giving them all a better chance to digest my SLAS message along with their bacon and eggs.

I visited Jerry a few days later; he was opening the post, and in front of him was a pile of sixty-two reply-cards requesting a visit to discuss SLAS. This was just one post, and not the first.

I sank into the chair alongside that rosewood table. Jerry looked up from his counting. His eyes had a certain glow. "My God, Tim," he said. "How are we going to spend all the money?"

★ ★ ★

He would find a way.

★ ★ ★

When I paid my introductory call on a respondee to our SLAS letter – and there were soon over two hundred of them – all my remaining diffidence about being a salesman evaporated quite fast. (Note 11). I was doing people a good financial service and was well received; and after all, I told myself, that nice old fellow in the Queen Anne house was himself "an insurance man" just as much as the unfairly derided "man from the Pru" in the adverts. It had also helped, to browse in the St Giles offices of the University Careers Department where the Secretary, the esteemed Mr Escritt, assured me there were many head-hunters prowling the Colleges every Spring on behalf of well-known Insurers. Curiously, I was even able to educate him on a minor point of English usage.

He was reading out the names of some of the Companies. "Wait a minute," he said, "Some of these are Insurance and some are Assurance. I wonder what's the difference?" It just happened that I had wondered the same thing, and when I checked in Fowler's 'Usage' it seemed they didn't know either; very vague and non-committal. But after some thought, it became clear: you insure against something, but you are assured of it. So with Life, which is certain to end one day, your payout is assured; but with – say – Fire or Accident cover, the risk may never occur: you are insured just in case.

Feeling very proud of myself I wrote and told Fowler, and I think I am right in saying they amended their next edition. I also wrote to a newspaper but they didn't print it. I told my philosophy tutor, too, but he just smiled thinly and set me next week's essay. I'm not sure philosophy was his strong point.

★ ★ ★

Early on, non-Life risks had raised their boring heads. Many of my Life enquirers were asking if I could insure their expensive oboe or camera or golfing risks. At first they were all waved down to Pembroke Street for Jerry's full Black Label treatment; but very soon he explained to me that the profit margin on these little 'GB' policies (GB = General Business as against Life) would hardly pay for the fading light-bulb on the stairs, never mind the juice for the Waterford glasses. He gave me a quick lesson on each of the proposal-forms and sent me back across Carfax with a wad of them and a receipt-book. I had indeed become an insurance salesman.

It was fun. I made many lasting friends as I went round. More to the point, it became a very useful lead-in to selling SLAS. One spectacular evening I visited a cellist who not only signed up himself but called in the rest of his quintet from around the quad., and I got them all, first for the instruments at a few pounds apiece, but then for the SLAS appointments with Jerry as well. That was at Jesus in The Turl and it had come from a recommendation by my original oboist in Exeter across the road. I began to see a promising network taking shape.

The next development, and a momentous one, I realise as I look back, though at the time it just drifted in, was prompted by someone I never knew: a student with ground-floor rooms in the front quad at Trinity. One Saturday teatime he had been listening to the Test Match when a hand came through the window and coolly took his portable Roberts radio, while it was actually playing! The student had dashed out, but too late. I was asked by a friend to go and see him, but had to explain that there was no way I could insure the replacement, no policy to cover small items, only All Risks cover for *specified* items of individually stated value. Therefore, I regretted… And then I stopped. My mind clicked back to Aldershot. (Note 12).

We had been offered that 'Officers' Kit' insurance which I chiefly remembered for two reasons: first, it was so simple and needed hardly any explanation; and secondly, it covered all one's kit without the items needing to be listed. Surely we could do this for our students, as a very speedy sell?

"And," I added as if Jerry hadn't thought of it too, "it'll be the perfect mass-produced lead in."

He was dubious. "Well, it needs presenting in person, then, doesn't it," and he looked at me meaningfully as usual. I knew at once that my essays on Politics, Philosophy and Economics would shrivel even more towards the feeble and perfunctory over the next two years.

But in my view, something was still a bit wrong, and one more adjustment was needed before we went to print. The Insurers were happy to buy the idea, and were wanting as an evident but to them acceptable loss-leader a very modest seventeen shillings and sixpence (87.5p) for the whole basic package, which most students would be happy to pay. Belongings, bicycle and third-party indemnity were all included. But the price was wrong.

"The price won't do," I told Jerry.

"What? It's jolly cheap. Good God, do they want jam on it?"

I shook my head and waved my arms about. "We can't possibly mess around with handfuls of silver and giving change. Besides, if we start to advertise this, nobody is going to actually send us that sum of money; too fussy, too much like hard work, especially if at the start of Term their grants haven't come yet. But they'll send a banknote. Make it a pound."

And we did: nobody minded because nobody knew. We accounted to the Insurers for the seventeen-and-six and got our commission on it; but we made an extra half-crown clear, on every policy sold. It paid for all our printing and went a long way to cover our other marketing costs.

I seemed to have found my niche in marketing to students at last, and looked around for someone to tell, from the past when I had been chewing over the possibilities. Richard was away touring in a play. Matt had written to me, but only once or twice and it had stopped and anyway I wasn't allowed to try writing to him. So then I realised I'd never properly responded to Bill's greeting letter when I first came up, only sending a postcard of the Camera saying "Try to pretend this is real". I sat down and began to enthuse: I suspect it ran to five or six Remington pages full of self-pride. It provoked a swift reply. A telegram, no less.

His style had always been somewhat staccato, but now he was clearly under the influence of persuasions that were very foreign to a simple Englishman. Was this alarmism just West Coast, or did it in some way reflect the American 'Panic Politics' one was reading about:

"Tim be careful – Times Index 1947 10 entries re commies – Times Index 1948 to September 90 entries – Talk to your FO man Pollack – IUS control most Europe. Our NSA going in. Do you know about Copenhagen – Mark private. Avoid 'hot water' – (Keep in jug?) Bill."

I was hopelessly naive about the outside world: I think most of us were. What on earth was I supposed to know about Copenhagen? I knew very little beyond Abingdon, though a bit more, alas, about Witney. Sadly I decided that my old friend had been sucked into the wild-eyed US view of the Old World and was lost to me. Who was Mark, and why was he still a private? It just didn't make sense.

I put the cable on my desk and it got filed away with some essay notes. I only found it in 1967, by which time the CIA had turned it into a great deal of sense.

★ ★ ★

I was now drawing up our plans for marketing the Life scheme on an annual basis. Instead of haphazard mailings into those Lodge pigeonholes, we had to be systematic, and only approach the different Years at times when they would be happy – or at least less irritated – to listen. (Note 13).

Meanwhile, I suggested to Jerry, some student agents – on commission? – could tour all new freshers as soon as they arrived, with the Belongings scheme on its single sheet of paper, at its single one pound premium, cash. Folding the banknote into the signed form as I left the room, I would say: "We'll be writing to you next Term about the main Scheme, so look out for it in January", and that SLAS reminder would also be inside the policy document a few days later, straight from the Insurer. And again, note, each time the annual cover was due for renewal.

Inevitably, I was getting more involved with those SLAS applications, and soon I was talking the students through it myself, and sending down to Jerry only the ones that were in some way 'non-standard', to use the actuarial vernacular (and what a lot of it there was!). A bad health history, whether personal or in the immediate family? An intention, or, more relevant, an actual commitment to live or spend time in the tropics? Service as a regular in the Forces? For those we had to get a special quotation. Things were likely to change very rapidly: in the early 50s if you had had TB (quite common) you were practically uninsurable. By the late 50s you were acceptable at almost normal rates. (My GP down in Sussex in the 60s used to run a big expansive TB clinic full of fresh air and paying patients, but he woke up one morning and found he was out of a job, he told me). I reckon he needed be-happy pills just as much as he said I did. On the whole, though, and unsurprisingly, our student clients were a first-rate risk, and I was endlessly trotting down St Ebbes, that wonderfully crummy street that our stony-faced developers have wiped off the map.

There was a second-hand art shop – what else to call it? – just before you got to Pembroke Street, where there was a very believable landscape, signed in that recognisable scrawl, 'Sisley'; I must admit that I almost paid the ten pounds being asked. But I hurried on to Jerry with my pockets bulging with completed applications. He processed them and did all the consequent, apparent hard back-up work, as he explained to me just a little bit too frequently.

★ ★ ★

My second undergraduate year was, like most at that time, completely free of exams. Oxford was funny like that. The Summer was therefore notoriously the time for everyone's extramural pursuits. Some wandered lonely as a cloud and wrote their 'dreaming spire' poetry; some like Richard went off again on tour, taking dubious drama to the provincial masses; most of us whiled away the hours punting up the Cherwell seducing each other. I began to think about the possibilities of Cambridge: should I go over there and spread the gospel amid its lovely windswept quads?? No, no, 'quad' was Oxford. In Cambridge, they were 'courts'. Do get it right.

And if Cambridge, why stop there? I felt the need to talk the possibilities through with people within my academic world. Jerry was all very well on office management and deep liaison with stuffy but Important Underwriters, and the bank, and our accountants, but when it came to marketing to these students, frankly I was on my own.

Bill, too far away in any case, had evidently gone 'far away' in a different sense, and he knew nothing about British students. (Gee, how mediaeval). So, one day after a lecture, I dropped in again on our Senior Tutor, taking advantage of an open invitation to tea and sandwiches in that history-infested room with the dusty window overlooking our famous gardens.

I must tell you that he was a delightful and much-loved man, and a splendid story attached to him. That window was set back in a recess which was covered at night by a thick curtain; and he always left the window open. In those days it was forbidden for a student to be out of College after ten o'clock at night, when the gate was locked. Miscreants could ring the bell and be let in but reported; or they could do it the clandestine way. At the far end of the garden, at the top of the jagged broken-glass-lined wall, was a gap; also a friendly lamp-post… This being surmounted, a quick sprint across the lawn and up the wisteria, and one found the welcoming open window of the Senior Tutor.

One night, a student named Harry clambered up the wisteria as usual, and silently squeezed inside into the recess. But – horror! – peeping through the curtain he saw the Don working at his desk. Harry had to stand petrified, no room to sit, turn or relax, until six in the morning; when the Senior Tutor got up, turned out the light, and left the room saying: "Good night". Harry dined out on the story for years, but so, I suspect, did the Senior Tutor. And yes, several other Colleges claim the same story.

"Insurance!" He spilt his Earl Grey.

I told him that Mr Escritt was in favour, and had spoken about the probity of the profession, and how all the best Britons in the Far East were involved in it and boosting our Invisible Earnings (having just learnt the phrase from George Richardson the Economics Tutor, who was shortly to go off and run the OUP over in Jericho). I pointed out the urgent need for students to find protection for their Roberts radios… Let alone their bicycles. I sensed that he didn't quite like the word 'protection' and perhaps he secretly used to watch gangster movies at The Scala in his spare time.

"We are really trying to do students a big favour," I ventured. Would he buy this? "A lot of us have been in the Forces and were able to cover our belongings then," I drew him a picture of all the thousands of young undergrads with their wives and children who were and for years would be flooding into Oxford, desperate for security. Oh, and Life Assurance too.

"Well," he conceded, "I suppose there's some truth in that. And when you go down, you're saying you'll be taking the same ideas and message to some other universities?"

"All of them," I replied confidently, and I recall at that point, a glint in his aged eye.

"You know, Tim," he said, reaching for a reference book, "we aren't short of student establishments. "Let's see… " A flurry through the pages. Then: "If we include the little University Colleges – they'll soon become autonomous so we can count them in – we're up to nearly thirty. If," he added with a mischievous smile, "you take the rough with the smooth."

I appreciated his turn of phrase and smirked across my cucumber sandwich. "I intend to start with the smooth ones."

"Tell me." He sat for a minute, hunched and thinking, while I imagined him just like that at four in the morning with Harry holding his breath behind the curtain. "What exactly is involved when you're interviewing – what d'you call it? – a Life prospect?"

I ran briefly through the usual sales patter, "… then we fill in the form".

"What, you mean details of the chap's health and so on?"

"Yes, everything. Name and address of course, date of birth, family medical history, their own state of health, previous illnesses and operations if any, a whole list of possible diseases or physical defects, when they'll graduate, are they going abroad… " I felt like Ratty in the boat before his picnic. I showed him the form: I always carried a couple of spares.

"Family history, d'you say? Can I keep this?" Of course, I told him. Why?

"Oh, I've an old friend up in Summertown whose daughter is going to the Far East and he thinks she ought to insure herself to protect the mortgage before she goes."

"I'd better make sure you get some commission," I nearly said, and we went on to discuss the possible sales potential, or rather lack of it, at certain provincial learning establishments he didn't think very highly of.

Two hours later, my weekly tutorial commitments discharged, I went down to that tumbledown ex-LNER station, dwarfed by its ex-LMS neighbour, and chuffed off to Cambridge: 90 minutes, change at Bletchley.

CHAPTER V

The only way to make a fair comparison today between the two Oxbridge towns is to walk around very early on a Sunday morning, before the streets are thrombosed with traffic, and the pavement blocked by nubile Japanese photographing one another amid fat locals trying to limp about their businesses.

It was very different in the early fifties. Plying to and fro weekly, I was often asked which place I preferred, and the answer had to be in sections: for overall 'ancient atmosphere' I favoured Oxford which had, hidden away, some romantic crumbling old corners in remote quads, for instance at Merton; most of the Cambridge courts seem just a bit too well-behaved, although bits of Corpus and Queens' are pleasingly decadent. As for the surrounding country, it has to be Oxford again, sitting between two ranges of hills and straddling two rivers, one of which wriggles through the town, or indeed under it, in five separate streams, none of them properly appreciated; Cambridge's flatness is an acquired taste – everywhere around it is like living on a tablecloth, and in the centre, Castle Hill is such a surprise you almost suspect it was man-made; (I write this remembering how things occurred to me as a cyclist, hurtling around on appointments), but even motorists used to confess they were tempted to change down when, out of town, they approached the Gog-Magog Hills. As for the friendliness of local people, it's Cambridge, I regret to say; presumably in Oxford the local politics, filtering acidly down from the Cowley motor works, have, over time, turned nearly everybody sour, and at ease only with their own kind. Such a pity.

Shopping? In those days, on the whole I preferred Cambridge, but as we all know, most High Streets are now caricatures of each other, and in any case, most of them you can't drive to, let alone drive through.

Jerry, though, drove at great speed through everything in his Jowett Javelin, when he insisted on visiting Cambridge with me shortly after my initial fact-finding trip. I had ascertained that they published a very useful Resident Members' List, so all the primary work of envelope assembly could be done at home: the car was loaded with them, and we would drop them off at each College Porter's Lodge, with the important ten-shilling note (or £1 for the larger ones – I remember the Head Porter at Trinity accepting it disdainfully).

Travelling with Jerry had been nerve-wracking: he cut every bend from Kidlington to Madingley, glancing across at me: "That's what we call a racing corner, old boy." We stayed with a hotelier friend of his, rather posh by my standards, downstream from the town at Clayhithe – "The Eights come here all the time, you know"; and while I toured the Colleges in my now well-developed role as spreader of the Personal Belongings Gospel, he sat in the Blue Boar holding the consequent SLAS interviews, in the hotel lounge admittedly but down at the end nearest to the bar.

We were there for four packed days, but it wasn't all work, that Summer Term. One hot afternoon we looked at each other, said "Sod it" and hired a canoe from that place at the bottom of Silver Street; in our business suits and with our briefcases we paddled along the Backs past crowds of students sitting on the grass. Jerry was wearing his bowler. Clients waved...

By the next year, Cambridge was left entirely to me, while Jerry handled all the administration and accounts, concentrating on his horsey clientele around the gymkhana belt, and soon moving house up to Boars Hill and offices to Carfax, right next to the tower.

"I was chatting to a Very Important Broker the other day," he would say, "and he absolutely agreed that one must keep up appearances." Jerry's business friends all had those capital letters.

"Do you think, then, that I ought to stay at the Blue Boar in the centre of town," I might ask, "instead of that little Spread Eagle B&B on the Trumpington Road?" It was a friendly pub run by a young couple just across from the Leys School, and one could imagine Mr Chips unwinding there after a hard day in the classroom. But at least it was, just about, inside the town; my first temptation had been to use the nice old inn out at Trumpington village, mainly because of the prospect of rubbing shoulders with the famous landlord: Charlie Shadwell, lately the conductor of the BBC Variety Orchestra and butt of many ITMA jokes. Sadly, too far out for my frantic zigzag appointment purposes.

"Depends what you can afford, Tim," was the inevitable answer. "You know your expenses come out of your commission."

My commission on SLAS policies was set at £4 per every £1000 of the sum assured, and throughout the Fifties the normal policy size hovered between £1000 and £2500. Few students ventured anything greater, for obvious reasons: they knew they could add more cover when they went down and into a job, or when – as was usually the intention – the policy was used for house purchase. At the time I was given to believe that our firm received from the Insurance Companies £10 per thousand, which would have made my remuneration for 'acquisition costs' an acceptable fraction when all other marketing and processing was taken into account. It would be many years before I discovered we had been getting not £10 but up to £20…

Yes, I know: I was thick. But despite it all, Jerry was a very likeable character so long as one made sure to keep the saltcellar handy. For instance, I was sitting waiting in a student's rooms one day when I saw on the shelf an alumni register from Clifton College. Of course I looked, but of Jerry, no mention. However, in that area there are other schools, and it turned out that Jerry had been just about correct – geographically. He blustered a bit, though, when I told him.

His business standards for people other than himself were very strict, too. Once in the early days I woke up on a Monday with a really awful dose of flu or something similar. I struggled out to a phone-box.

"Oh, you've got this forty-eight hour thing. Be here 8.30 Wednesday."

★ ★ ★

I moved across to live in Cambridge in 1953, taking with me the whole marketing side of the student business. My first office was behind the Corn Exchange, a microscopic cluttered room at the entrance to a Building Society, now buried under a car-park, and so small initially that if anyone came to see me, I had to move out to make space for him. This was put right after a few weeks when my Halifax landlord shifted several boxes full of mortgage leaflets, so that I no longer had to use them as a desk; and I went down the street to a distressed auction-room – now also buried – and bought for £5 the big old Victorian oak desk I still sit at. There was even room now for a secretary, so I was joined by Joy – for several years, thank goodness, unconfined.

One of my first visitors was a young man I knew vaguely from school. Ben wanted to insure his nice old MG. I did it for him although motor wasn't really my thing… believe this or not. Just a week later, I drove up to London for a meeting, and at the Finsbury Road traffic-lights someone ran into the back of me. I got out and said to the goggled driver: "You'd better give me your insurance details." Yes, you're ahead of me. Ben said: "They're in your files, Tim." As his Broker I had to handle the claim and I think I did it rather well.

★ ★ ★

I was sending a constant flow of application-forms over to the new Carfax offices, or clumping upstairs with them on the three-days-a-week I usually spent on my old stamping-ground. We were clearly on to a winner but I was still worried, because I didn't want anyone else muscling in and perhaps stealing the rest of the student market. One day we received out of the blue a reply-card giving the address as simply: "The Castle, Durham" and at first we thought it was one of the inevitable hoaxes that free postage always brings. Joy and I were used to 'W.T.Pooh', 'U.R.A. Nutt', 'M Hatter' and 'Master Bates', and all the rest who thought themselves so original, but some escaped us and then it would be a real time-waster. Worst were the cards referring to real students, sent by a 'friend', perhaps at Kings College London where I might have trekked all the way to their Hall on Champion Hill, only to be angrily rebuffed. On the other hand, sometimes such a hoax resulted in actual business – "Well, anyway, now you're here, come in and tell me about it" – and on those occasions my occupational smile, that precaution as I walked the client-filled streets, would be more genuine than ever.

But "The Castle, Durham" had us foxed until I woke up to the fact that this was one of the Colleges of Durham University. Here was a place of high esteem, as the Senior Tutor would say, run on collegiate lines, and it ought to be brought into the fold. I nipped up there by train to 'case the joint', fell in love with the cathedral and the university area around it, but found a difficulty which we had already encountered at other places: no such thing as a List of Members; nor would the stony-faced staff at the Lodge, or in the College Office, release any information whatever. (I never did concede that students' names – let alone addresses – were so sacrosanct everywhere except the two leading places, where the very reverse applied and they were published for anyone to see. I still don't accept that secrecy was necessary despite the political explanations I was later given). We had been getting a steady trickle of enquiries from distant universities, I suppose referred by a friend or sibling, and as I have just indicated, I had already done some off-the-cuff mailshots around London colleges, to test the market: I simply took unaddressed envelopes, ready stuffed, into the larger Halls of Residence, wrote names which I copied from the room-lists, and stuck them in the pigeonholes.

I might spend a whole day covering those Halls around Bloomsbury. The response was quite good, and I often stayed overnight in one or other of the little hotels in Gower Street, meeting my enquirers at my usual rate of one every half-hour. Dealing with King's College in the Strand, I discovered a slim little hotel just round the corner full of chorus girls… I tended to keep away from the London School of Economics even though it was just across the road – I suspected they knew much more than I did, even in their first Year. My economics had never got much further than Samuelson, and my tutor George Richardson would often shake his head sadly as we sat in the College garden contemplating my latest lifeless essay.

But going national…? I tried to talk it through with Jerry but he was busy judging a Palomino Event in Woodstock. "Go ahead and give it a try, old boy, you can sort out all these studenty people. Must go, they're waiting for me at Blenheim."

As before, I needed an outside opinion, and being by now a relatively well-earning graduate of my College, I bought my late Senior Tutor a drink at the Turf.

"Have you thought about taking your ideas to the National Union of Students?" he asked after listening to my sketchy plans towards world domination.

"Not really – aren't they all tied up with Leftie politics?"

"Well, there's always that threat, but I'm told they have broken away from the Communist crowd. I believe there's a new Western-oriented group being talked about, with our cousins across the water. Maybe you ought to look into it?"

I briefly recalled Bill's telegraphed message. I didn't want to get tangled up in student politics and their petty squabbles, little 'leaders' puffed up with their silly self-importance: a few visits to the Oxford Union had been quite enough for me, and that was the higher end of the market. I'd rather go it alone, I said, certainly for the time being, and try to set up the provincial universities one at a time, as I was doing in parts of London.

"Anyway," I added, "this is a red-hot scheme we want to keep to ourselves for as long as we can. I just need to gather student names and either their Hall or their home addresses, without raising any dust at NUS level, or any other level for that matter."

He looked a bit doubtful. "Unless a university sanctions it, you aren't going to get anywhere with home addresses, or even term-time ones. You're up against an absolute brick wall. Here and 'The Other Place' we bring out a list as you know, because we've done so for ages and can get away with it; but the Government is in a panic about infiltration by the Communists. Between you and me," he blinked confidingly over his Mackeson, "we are all very nervous. We keep being reminded about Burgess and Maclean and all those Cambridge spies just before the War – "

"Wasn't there an Oxford group too?" I put in, rather rashly.

He wriggled on his chair.

"A man called – Dutch, was it?"

"Well, Deutsch, yes, family owned cinemas, he was sort of recruiting, used to meet his prospects outside cinemas too, very odd, and – yes again – one or two others, but it's all long gone and we never talk about – "

"I've been told there's still a lot of it about," I pursued him. "Isn't there a woman down by Holywell Manor who – " but this time he determinedly shut me up. "Tim, I must be getting back to work."

I was due to go and see *'Bal des Voleurs'* performed on the island at The Trout; he was heading for Duke Humphrey's musty shelves, as he was writing one of his books, this time I think about the true origins of the Dark Age invading Jutes, but who can be certain? So I walked him along to Bodley; at the steps he suddenly remembered (how suddenly, I now wonder): "That friend of mine with the travelling daughter – he wonders if you could call on him to explain some of the policy conditions. Here's the address." It only now occurs to me that he had it on paper, already written out. Walking away, as an afterthought: "He's a bit ancient, even older than me, but very well connected in certain circles around the country, he might be able to help."

The play on The Trout island had been timed perfectly by my ex-laundrette friend Richard, who was still around from time to time: the final act started just as night fell, with all the peacocks calling from across the river. It brought to mind that famous

'Tempest' a few years earlier at Worcester, ending in enchantment as Ariel ran across the lake. Richard was splendid and we chatted later alongside the swirling waters full of fat chub; but he didn't want any insurance.

★ ★ ★

I went up the next afternoon to a large sleepy Victorian house, just off the Banbury Road, at the point where the don-infested district of North Oxford, (built to accommodate the late 19th-century flood of the good and the great in Academe, newly released by a change in the rules from their enforced celibacy, and thus swarming with children and staff) merges into that later development, Summertown, which although very attractive and comfortable, perhaps hints at an origin more in successful commerce than in suave good taste. The cream of The Town, maybe not quite managing to upstage The Gown?

The daughter came to the door and showed me into a study that looked out on to a terrace of York stone, mossy and sprouting some weeds which could easily have been hand-picked if anyone cared; beyond that, after green lichened steps, a lawn with a weathered bench and an irregular border of mixed and rather untidy bushes. The grass had recently been mown but erratically in wavering lines. I wondered whether the daughter was a bad driver.

The room itself reminded me of the well-known reconstruction, above that pub near Charing Cross, of Sherlock Holmes's study. Only the violin was missing – and presumably, the cocaine, or maybe not…

The man I had come to see on the Senior Tutor's earnest recommendation was indeed pretty old, he must have been the wrong side of eighty, and I had been mildly surprised that the youngish woman at the door had not in fact been a grand-daughter. She left us alone after the introductions, and I shook his hand. It was a firm clasp but as he half got up, it was difficult for him and I gestured so.

He waved me to an upright armchair, in fact a Windsor, in yew, covered by a travelling rug. Surprisingly comfortable, and I would occupy it often.

I am going to call him Dr. Oxdon. There are reasons for this.

"I see you've moved up to Carfax." This was the first thing he said. Did the 'up' imply we had promoted ourselves, or was it just he was a Christ Church man? "And your colleague's bought that big place off Hinksey Hill." Jerry was referring to it as Boars Hill but admittedly it was only just on the boundary.

Alarmingly, we were being watched.

Two minutes gone at the most, and no wind left in my sails – I'm sure I showed it; but I had to sit out this curiously gentle interrogation in the hope that something helpful would emerge the other side.

"Yes, business is coming in pretty well now," I nodded. "Jerry certainly knows lots of the right people."

He looked at me thoughtfully over his glasses. "And you're scooping up plenty of student clients over at The Other Place, eh?"

I thought I detected the faint hint of a mid-European accent, a touch of rough grain beneath the High Table patina.

"How do you happen to know all this, Dr. Oxdon?"

"My dear chap, everybody tells me everything, don't you know?" When he smiled, the glasses went sideways and back again.

"We are doing well because it really is a good opportunity. Now, about this cover for your daughter – "

"Ach," he said or something like it. "Never mind about that, I'm fixed up with my Brokers in the City." He spotted my salesman's disappointment and I guessed he had been looking for it. "I want to talk about something else – your plans for the other universities – all these 'redstones' – "

"Redbricks," I corrected him, and noticed at once that he didn't like to be put right.

"Whatever, whatever. Places like factories with no colleges, no – vapour?" He was looking around for the words. "No atmosphere – no ivy – a big square Degree Machine," he ended up. His glasses shifted again, as he peered at me and added conspiratorially: "… And

74

no published Resident Members' List, eh? Will you have tea or coffee?"

After last night's late drinking at Godstow, which had ended with a couple of bottles in the Nunnery ruins after the show, I chose a coffee, black, and he called for it to the daughter, somewhere deeper in the dark house. Then he went on. He wanted me to explain exactly how I planned to get our mailshots post-free into the hands of all those Redbrick students. Some Halls of Residence had perfunctory lists pinned up, but only with room numbers by the name. In any case, the great majority of undergraduates would be living in digs somewhere away from the actual university grounds. "Off-campus," I told him.

He rejoiced in this, one didn't hear it in Oxford. "Ah, ja, a new word!" and he actually reached for a pencil and wrote it down. He really was out of touch.

A large shaggy cat slid past his legs and with a gurgle of welcome jumped on his lap and settled itself, circling meditationally with its paws treading. He totally ignored it and I sensed that this preliminary aloofness suited them both.

"So, then. These – off-the-campus students, you won't have any way to make contact, will you? Have you found an answer to that?" He picked up a piece of scribbled paper and read from it, steadying his glasses as they began to slide. "From the figures my colleagues have sent me – mark you, these are a couple of years old – in London there are about thirteen thousand student undergraduates, many ex-Forces, and only ten per cent are – on-the-campus you say? – that is, living in a Hall."

"Yes, I realise we can only cream the ones who are easy to reach."

"But why?" He spread his hands out and widened his eyes expressively. "Everywhere then, so many redbricks, so many possibilities but so many unzu… " he thought for a minute and I could see him flipping dictionary pages through in his head, "unapproachables," he ended with a slight sigh of relief. He put the paper down and gave his attention at last to the cat. "Unless – " he then added, looking calculatedly anywhere but at me.

This was beginning to get interesting. I waited while a purr filled the room. Then I couldn't wait any more.

"Am I to understand, Doctor, that somehow you have an answer?"

Now he did look at me. "Drink your coffee, Tim. May I call you Tim?" The cat was getting heavy and he shifted in his chair. "I am a founder member of a – a study group, you might call it. Obviously I'm now retired from everything else, but one must keep the brain active. Little white cells, doesn't Mrs Christie call them? Well – "

"Grey," I said.

"*Bitte?*"

"Little grey cells. Agatha Ch–"

"Whatever, whatever. But listen. We, my group, are researching. We look at undergraduate details from everywhere. What area students come from, and which place they go to. How they perform in their degrees, for example, compared with their age, background, if or not they have done National Social– er – Service… "

I seized the chance, as he took a sip of tea, to tell him of my own observations when visiting the rooms of students; how I often arrived before they were back from a lecture, and whiled away the minutes by looking around the room and its contents. I had found it possible almost always, from the evidence of the bookshelves alone, to guess accurately whether this was a third-year who had come up straight from school, or a first-year who had been out in the world in the Forces. I used to have bets with myself and nearly always won. I once wrote about it to a newspaper but they didn't print it. Doctor Oxdon wasn't really listening, I think he was contemplating life and the stripes on his lawn. But I had to know what he was getting at.

"Let me get this right – " I began, but he shook his head.

"No, no, I must go on. I gave you just one example – London, thirteen thousand. We must analyse so many more. Given a full list of student names and addresses we want also to study where they live in relation to the courses they take, and their success-rates. Ach, dear me, so much… So many things to be studied… "

"But if I can only get small partial lists off the notice-boards – "

"Aha!" He wagged a finger and the cat bit it. "Suppose, on my group's official notepaper, with all our academic members' names and titles and qualifications along the bottom, I were to give you a letter to show at each university you go to?" I must have looked very bewildered. "An introduction. A letter in much confidence, saying this is a highly secret study, and their co-operation will be valued very much by – well, by us."

I couldn't see how on earth I fitted into this.

"But Doctor, why not contact the Registrars yourselves, direct?"

He twitched, no other word for it.

"No, no," most emphatically this time. "No. We must work freely because the data are needed at a higher level, even perhaps as a report upon a Registrar, you see, or an exposing. If he knew, a Registrar or official could boil the books." I knew better than to correct him. "If any university got wind of our researches and what we are studying, our group here in Oxford, they could spoil our results, change their selection procedures, alter the intake balance between faculties… "

He went on like this but he'd lost me. I had to wait.

Then: "No, no, not the Registrars. You must show my letter to all the local Student Union secretaries, only them, the permanent Union officials, absolutely them alone. When they read it they will be very pleased to help, they will be flattered by the confidence in them, you see. You tell them how secret and important it is, yes? And then they read the letter. You will get the names and addresses."

"But if they refuse?"

He stroked the cat upwards instead of soothingly down the back, and it bit him again: they both seemed to enjoy this. "Tim, we are talking about allowing you full access to tens of thousands of the country's future high earners. Nobody else has this. A few non-results you won't miss."

We drew up a plan of action. After using the lists once a year for our own purposes, they would be delivered to the Doctor. Together we drafted the letter he would give me, to take to the Union Secretaries.

As he walked me to the door slowly, sometimes taking my arm,

I was partially intoxicated by the vision of unimagined rich pickings, and at the same time filling with alarm. I stopped, worried.

"Suppose this gets queried at a high level – who can I refer the Union to?"

He beamed at me. Had he been a fisherman one could tell he had me firmly on the hook.

"Nobody, my dear chap. You're the one getting the full benefit. You're on your own. But then, you like to be, don't you?" How did he know that?

"Should I tell a Union officer to ring you or write, to confirm this is genuine?"

"You can say whatever comes into your head, dear boy, but they'll get no reply because there won't be a number on the letterhead and the address won't help either. Just vaguely Westminster."

I persisted. "But if I really do get into trouble – "

His sliding glasses smiled at me again as he reached the front door. "Then," he said, "You'll be like Isiah's daughter of Zion: Desolate – as a lodge in a garden of cucumbers… "

I knew the quotation from something I had published in my school magazine years ago – a brilliant nonsense verse written by one of our teachers.

He then really scared me. Looking at me mischievously he added: "You'll have knitted them socks, but you've knitted too late."

"My God," I said, "Do you even know Mary Scrutton?"

"Tim, I told you, everybody tells me everything." And he shut the door.

★ ★ ★

As I drove back that night along the usual bunny-run towards Cambridge, I grew more confused than ever: was all this good news or bad? The potential market for SLAS had suddenly become enormous, but what was I getting involved in? Research, indeed! My background had been probed very thoroughly, almost to a ludicrous extent. Whoever they were, they knew me.

I stopped off at The Swan in the centre of Newport Pagnell to gather my thoughts with the help of a couple of Laphroaigs, a favourite Scotch so peaty and smoky in those days, it was like licking the back of the fireplace. This was always a good halfway point to break the journey, and Marian behind the bar poured the first one as she saw me come in. I took it into a corner and sat staring at it.

Four thoughts were tangling to and fro, and gradually I unwound them.

First, whatever was behind Oxdon's offer, on the surface it was exactly what I needed and if I didn't accept it, somebody else would; and to have chosen us first was a considerable compliment.

Second, if the letter didn't have the desired effect at every Union, it surely would at some, maybe many: which could well be sufficient for us.

Third: we would have the opportunity to take the Belongings scheme into every Union on the back of the SLAS, and get postal sales enclosing a pound note each time: the Insurer could then invite renewal every year and that letter could enclose more SLAS sales material, just as I had been envisaging for Oxford and Cambridge.

Fourth, those renewals would eventually be reaching graduates after they had left: we ought to design a sort of 'senior' Belongings policy. And after all that, one more thought – ought I to report all this back to Jerry? He had memorably told me to take care, myself alone, of "all my studenty people".

When Marian pointed out to me that I had gone through more than one refill it seemed a good idea to stay the night at The Swan, and get some rest from the brainwork. They put me in a pleasant room but it was about six inches away from the next-door church. The tower, to be precise. The damn clock chimed every quarter, right in my ear. Do you know what it's like, telling yourself all night long that you have exactly fourteen minutes to get to sleep?

★ ★ ★

In the morning, with all the night hours still ringing in my head, I lay in bed, not yet properly awake. When I am published and famous, and they ask me about the one luxury allowed on my desert island, I will request a constant supply of hot soapy flannels: place it, very hot, on the back of the neck, and under the ears, and I'll swear you can feel yourself waking up, right down to your toes but chiefly in the brain. I didn't have a flannel with me, so I just lay on, despite the enticement of breakfast smells from the kitchens below.

I thought about where I was. Newport Pagnell lies close to some of England's most venerable cross-roads. Nearby was the Romans' Watling Street, along which so many generations had bumped and cursed towards the 'stony street ford' over the Ouse, among them a thousand years later the two little princes hopelessly fleeing their nice Uncle Richard; and then an endless procession of coachmen buying drinks and swapping tall stories and the latest rumours at the Cock and its neighbour the Bull. Just a few miles south, the beeline towards London cuts across the oldest road of all, the literally prehistoric Way trodden by flint salesmen from Norfolk going west, and the tin and copper merchants coming up from the west-country mines. One can imagine the entrepreneurs setting up their stalls: "Insure your axe-heads here. Costs only a copper."

It was certainly time I got a move on. The bacon was as good as it had claimed to be through my window; and as I drove on, I again pondered the good Doctor from yesterday, whom everyone tells everything. I could well believe it – they had certainly done a thorough job on me. Not only the latest update on my company, but even back to my schooldays. Oxdon had quite deliberately let me know this, I supposed as a hint – a threat – that I was in his – their – hands, whoever they were.

I had edited the magazine in my final two years, and Miss Scrutton was a Classics teacher who had been brought in as wartime replacement for the normal master who had been dragged away to the battlefields, or down a coalmine or something. As everywhere else, we had lost a lot of staff that way, and I remember in 1945-6 they all came back with suede shoes and limps. We in the upper sixth, lounging at the back of the Hall, smugly knowing that the fighting was over before we had to get there, used to try guessing which limp was the most impressive, which a probable sympathy-fake.

(More recently, Jerry had introduced me to an Insurance Company Inspector who did a lot of business round the villages because of his blazer, the undecipherable striped tie, and the heavy limp which was in fact due to a drunken drive into a ditch near Swindon in 1938).

The verse, which Miss Scrutton gave me for the literary section, had never been published anywhere else so far as I knew, and I expect still hasn't. It was inspired by that curious bit of Isaiah (i.8) and I love it:

I dwelt in a lodge in a garden of cucumbers
Silently watching the cucumbers grow,
And for many a century, rain falling steadily
Fell on the roof, but the wind did not blow.
I gathered and ate of their leaves in the twilight,
They sprouted again ere the morning was grey
And at Christmas in leap-year the eldest slug sometimes
Would bring me some worms for my tea on a tray.
But the cucumbers grew (though their reasons were few)
And strange was the light of their stalks in the gloom,
Till – well I remember – late, late in November
One looked down my chimney and started to boom.
Resistance was useless. I quoted Confucius
And gnawing a breadknife, lamented my fate:
I had known, I had known, but I'd left them alone,
I had knitted them socks – but I'd knitted too late
For the lodge floated wide on the crest of the tide
While they swam and blew bubbles through holes in the floor,
And with jubilant screaming their eyebrows were streaming:
They shouted in Welsh: Nevermore, nevermore…
But we passed by the Cape and I made my escape

Crying 'Vive La Republique' and 'Auf Wiedersehn';
Yet the things of this Earth have no manner of worth
For I never shall see my cucumbers again.

Mary Scrutton, you of the wartime Classical Sixth, a genius.
(And see Note 4).

Two immediate developments followed that meeting in North
Oxford, though it was only the start. As soon as I received the
Doctor's precious Letter of Introduction (and I fleetingly saw myself
as a latter-day Victor Lazlo, clutching his Letters of Credit), I made
my first tentative approaches to Student Unions. This had to be in
London, for several reasons. It was the most convenient place to
cover many substantial universities quickly; it was the greatest
accumulation of potential clients; and rather more subtly, it was the
likeliest place for me to hit problems, if this sort of approach had
been tried before and rebuffed, so that I would know pretty soon if
the whole thing was, despite the Doctor, a non-starter.

There was a more significant long-term reason: I had been trying
to take a nationwide view of our business and I felt that, given
Oxdon's deal with me, I must start planning to carve up the whole of
the UK. It seemed ridiculous, like Hitler fiddling around with Europe
and treating the Rhineland and Austria and the rest as if they were
bits of a jigsaw; but to be sensible, if I explained to Jerry – No, wait a
minute, I wasn't going to tell Jerry just yet – if I was about to get full
lists and therefore a flow of enquiries from, say, Exeter, Durham,
Liverpool, Swansea, Nottingham and Belfast... I must start looking
right away for a Life Assurance salesman. And, first, for London.

Jerry accepted with pleasure the fact that we were going to get
an increase in enquiries, without wanting to know how or why; and
he approved my idea for a Manager for London, agreeing that this
new recruit should receive the same commission as myself and I
would have a small over-riding on his production... As I was
envisaging a few more such Managers, there didn't seem to be much
of a problem. I ran an advert in one of the less boring insurance

journals. And all along, I hadn't the slightest idea what the CIA was up to: yet.

As far as I remember, only Max replied. He had worked for ten years for a Life Assurance firm, one of those Canadian ones that used to leap out at you from Readers Digest; but he wanted to have an area of his own to build on, and a wider choice of policies to recommend: he would get this with us, as we were independent Brokers. I met him in a large and ambitious coffee-bar at the Swiss Cottage end of Finchley Road.

You could park almost anywhere in those days, despite the growing traffic, and I had left my car round the corner, opposite the Central School and its gorgeous stage hopefuls who had recently started to inhabit the old Embassy Theatre after expanding from the Royal Albert Hall. Max arrived shortly after and left his more expensive car right outside on the main road.

He was older than me, and more experienced in terms of his number of years in the insurance business; but I trumped him noticeably when I mentioned, and proved from my notes, the enormous number of policies I was writing day after day on our SLAS scheme. I had his full attention after that.

"So you supply all these leads?" This is the first overwhelming question put by anyone answering a sales small ad. Their life will be bearable, enjoyable, only if they are fed with 'leads' from interested prospects: 'cold calling', as I had discovered on the wrong side of Boars Hill back in 1950, was hell. To succeed in cold-selling you need to be (i) thick-skinned, (ii) a brilliant actor (knowledge of the product is secondary), (iii) preferably a flirt, and (iv) financially carefree because you probably won't sell a thing. Given all that, it can be enjoyable – just.

I explained the way we operated, and especially the way I personally followed up the reply-card enquirers: the full three-page information pack direct from Cambridge, with a copy to him; then his visit, and the call-back note to be left in the student's room. A few more refinements.

While he listened to this I was sizing him up. He was presentable, probably more so than me; but would he perhaps be a bit too business-like and consequently rather off-putting for our somewhat unorthodox clientele?

I always played the prospect in a jocular manner. When I steamed into his rooms I tended to chat away and be like a student myself, blessed with the gift of spreading to him our sensational SLAS gospel he had heard about, no doubt, all over the campus. Student, in fact, I still almost was. When it came to filling in the form, I would turn the 'state of health' questions into a bit of a joke. "Do you spit much blood?" I would ask before entering a 'No' against the question on TB. When we came to the final question: "Do you suffer or have you ever suffered from... " followed by a gruesome list of unlikely diseases, I would get up and back away with the form to the far side of the room, covering my mouth. Things like that.

Was Max too stuffy? How would he handle these radical and often anti-Establishment youngsters? Did he have a sense of humour, or more important, how was his sense of the ridiculous?

He was telling me about himself. He had been through the later years of the war in the Middle East, where he had originally come from in the late thirties. At one time he had served in the Aegean, attached to the prestigious – though scruffy and nonconformist – Long Range Desert Group. This was a comfort: the vision of him in such an unruly outfit reassured me. But – "

"Desert Group – in the Aegean?"

"We were being retrained for mountain combat."

I knew this to be a fact, from discussions in the Army in my last year.

I tried just one test: I knew by reputation a certain Brigadier who had been comfortably based in Cairo at that time, very reluctant to be sent anywhere at all.

"Did you come across" – I mentioned a name – "in your time there?"

He smiled, gave me a look and shook his head. "From what we

heard, he was firmly attached to the Short Range Gezira Group."

Gezira Club was the nesting-place in Cairo of all those well-fed Staff Officers having a Good War. It was the perfect answer, and I had no further worries about Max. He would do…

So I now had an assistant covering Greater London. Who next?

But meanwhile I had the rest of the UK to tackle, and I must waste no time.

★ ★ ★

I was driving in my chunky old Humber Hawk down to Exeter where I intended to carry out my first raid on the provincial redbricks – although as I knew, Exeter was a cut above, even then high on the chosen list for well-to-do students preferring to avoid Oxbridge, though only a 'University College', its degrees granted rather sniffily by London until very recently.

On the way I had to call at Glen Eyre Hall in Southampton, quite small at that time but more recently outgrown its strength; and I decided to bed down somewhere. On the road to Romsey was an inviting little place which Jerry had told me about: basically an intimate restaurant by the roadside, but they had rooms.

Every day of my life, every single day, I have remembered this. And it will not stop. I don't want it to, in all truth, ever.

I was the only guest, and after dinner I was invited to have a drink with the family in their own cosy sitting-room. We chatted for a while, but across on the piano was a large photo of a young woman, perhaps twenty, with such an unattainable though desirable, lazily dreamy-eyed sincerity about her that while we talked, I was quite unable to take my eyes away. This was their daughter, and soon after, Sarah came into the room and joined us.

I haven't, now, the faintest idea what, with the family, I talked about. It is immaterial. I suppose, looking back, that I was willing the parents to just go away. They might as well not have been in the room. I am not going to describe Sarah because we all have our ideas of perfection, and whatever yours is, that will do. Just be sure to include the direct but humorous look of those blue-grey eyes with their sideways glance as she brushed aside with a laugh her long mid-brown hair; the confidential smile that lingered on the lips when we found a belief or an opinion that we shared or could amicably debate; the poetry we threw across to each other, my Chesterton, Housman and Betjeman, her Frost, Thomas, Eliot and all those others... Oh, and Yeats, both of us.

But with that side-sliding grin, the lovable tilt of the head and all the stuff that Astaire used to sing about, added to the wonderful slim fencer's figure. Oh, what's the use. As he put it, they can't take that away...

And before long the parents did leave the room. We talked and talked into the small hours. What about? Everything under the sun. Sarah mined out of me all the buried aesthetics which had been overlaid by the drabness of storekeeping, then economics and now the bloody insurance business. I was back in the sixth form, the Debating Society and the school magazine, the Literary Club, even the chapel choir: I have just looked up 'aesthetics' in Roget because I don't want this to sound stupid or pretentious: I find there are three sub-headings in the index – sensibility, beauty, and good taste. Help yourself.

She had just left a London drama college and was killing time until the autumn. Meanwhile she was looking around for a vacation job... At this point in my somewhat stressed life I had been married for seven years (yes, I know: it's always seven, isn't it, but I couldn't for the life of me help that). This instant bond was too powerful and had dragged to the surface submerged parts of me, despite myself. It was on another plane.

At last I went up to my room. Sarah followed to get a towel for me from the bathroom. I said: "I'm afraid I'm going to have to kiss you goodnight."

"I've got a terrible cold."

"You must learn to share these things," I said...

★ ★ ★

I had to visit all those universities and sit in their Student Union, having produced Oxdon's letter, to copy hundreds of names and addresses from their card-index. At this distance it sounds mad, but remember, we were in the Fifties when carbon-paper ruled; and we really did use it, needed, in our case to make the second copy for the Doctor. Sarah had a pleasing round handwriting but if she had been a claw-fisted dyslexic I think she would still have got the job. Over the next three months we drove in that comfortable old Humber, all leather and tobacco-smoke, to Exeter, Bristol, Birmingham, Sheffield, Nottingham and Leicester. ("Not Manchester" Oxdon had said, "We have a connection there.").

Everywhere, his Letter of Introduction (centred around some abstruse statistics labelled 'Westminster' which, I was sure, were taken from thin air but sounded most impressive to a student union officer) achieved its purpose. Back at the Cambridge office, the subsequent mailings, the reply-card response, the follow-up by Max or by me, all worked. At intervals out in the provinces I would descend upon the respondees in a three-day blitzkrieg, as I describe in Notes at the end.

But the list-making was just the necessary soil from which grew my short-lived paradise. For those three brief months, my life was a dream. Even the simple fact of sitting side by side with that delicious girl at a strange desk in strange surroundings right through a day, and then two more days, sharing all that time the most banal happenings, was enormously sensuous; but add to it the excitement of visiting new places – and such places! – and again side by side in our explorations, in a friendly old car ("Above us the intimate roof… "!) with good meals at good hotels… I made sure to plan our journeys to those universities so that we took in a chain of wonderful stop-offs. We went to Exeter by way of Old Sarum and Corfe, Lulworth and the Abbotsbury swans, then Lyme Regis. Our Bristol job included Bath, Wells – oh, Wells with the four-poster (and more swans, come to think of it) – and Cheddar with the Wookey Witch, and we thought of poor Monmouth in his Sedgemoor ditch, and wondered whether that nuisance from Porlock had been an insurance salesman.

On the way to that epitome of genuine old Victorian Redbricks, Birmingham University set so beautifully in its grounds and with its student newspaper rejoicing in that title, we went into the church at Stratford. At that time, two things struck us: first, one had to pay to go in; and secondly, it seemed they were in some danger of worshipping the wrong bloke. I wrote this:

> They bought their entry, led him in
> To see the sacred view.
> In awe, they tiptoed through the Shrine
> Towards the altar, where recline
> Relations of The Bard, in line;
> They paid the homage due.
> He noticed, as he raised his head,
> The Figure on the Cross. He said:
> "Is that one Shakespeare, too?"

I sent it to a newspaper but they didn't print it.

★ ★ ★

We visited the Blue John mine beyond Sheffield, and were entranced by Little Moreton Hall. I showed her the Chesterfield spire. In one timber-framed town I remember immense old cruck-beams and a creaking floor. Oh yes, I still nurse every little detail and I must have re-played them in my mind almost every day.

But, you know, though still together through every night, close, holding, we never made love, in the accepted meaning. I never even asked, because that would have spoilt it. However can I explain this?

I think it was off the agenda, as one might say today. Probably for Sarah (she was more or less engaged to a graduate who was away somewhere and due back in the autumn); and clearly for me. I knew that our fleeting relationship was deeper and more important, though it had to end. We were being, physically as well, extraordinarily close (and you can imagine my urges). I have never known such an anguished temptation, but it would have been so wrong... I'm not just talking about morals: to upstage the distant boy-friend would have been so simple...

But suppose: if something ecstatic has to end – has to – and simply *must* be warmly remembered, and yet its incidental and less important lovemaking has turned out, as so often, to be less than utterly perfect, how terrible. I dared not take the risk of, I suppose, shattering the more intense and longer-lasting image of – what can one call it without sounding stupid? The 'intercourse of minds'?

Much later, when my wife came to know about those magic months of mine, though she was forgiving over what she naturally assumed, I couldn't possibly tell her the truth. "Of course we did," I told her. "What else?"

The truth would have been too cruel.

CHAPTER VI

To the tune of "For he's a jolly good fellow": "Oh, the bear climbed over the mountain (repeat twice), to see what he could see." And as I'm sure we all remember from our palmy days of innocent singing round the campfire, "All that he could see was the other side of the mountain."

This depressingly negative outcome of the adventurous bear's curiosity was destined to symbolise the Fifties. But wrongly, I assure you. Although many writers, who weren't there or even born then, insist on it being a negative and unimaginative decade they don't know what they're talking about. Nor did that late-developing Hull librarian, who seemed to think that life as we know it only began in the mid-sixties: for him, maybe, yes, up there, I can imagine that...

But the climb up the mountain of post-war Britain had an air of purpose. I remember first our enthusiasm for the 1951 Festival (it was my father, at the Board of Trade, who first suggested the slogan: "Britain could take it: Britain can make it"); and then, distressingly soon after, but reassuringly emotional, the awakening of the public with the 1953 Coronation. As we headed up the mountain we still had food rationing; down the other side towards 1960 a galaxy of intimate little clubs and restaurants was springing up, all over London and soon in the provincial cities too. It could be captioned 'The Prawn Cocktail Emergence' or perhaps better 'The Maryland Revival' in memory of that splendid chicken dish, now quite lost. Whatever happened to those happy little dining clubs?

In popular music, which inevitably concerned my students far more deeply than my suspicious and agnostic self, though I had to keep up with it, the trend was moving from balladeers like Pat Boone and Michael Holliday ('The Finger of Suspicion... ' – oh, Sarah!), to performers who actually got in there and performed the song as well as acting it out. No more did you just listen to Elvis, or Lonnie, Tommy or Cliff – you had to go out and buy a guitar, and join in; no matter how ghastly you sounded, the folk around you were a wild cotton-wool protection against the reality of the critics. Don't let them in.

Frivolity on the surface often conceals a disturbance underneath, and as the Fifties progressed I think this can be detected in the behaviour of young people, growing up in the uncertain shadows of the Cold War. Quite apart from the overt activities of protesters, a seriousness was developing in the Arts – especially in the theatre where, almost overnight as we all know, the drawing-room sofa and French windows had been replaced by the kitchen sink, snuffing out all the fond aspirations of hopeful young but old-fashioned playwrights: instead of "Who's for tennis?" it became "Who's doing the fucking washing-up?" And in musicals too: that dreadful man Leonard Bernstein began the decade with the innocuous 'On the Town', but ended it with the grimness behind 'West Side Story'. (A little later I watched his TV concert celebrating, wildly over-the-top, some birthday of Beethoven's. I wrote to a newspaper: "If that was Beethoven's birthday, God help us on Bernstein's" but they didn't print it.)

The ways in which students were absorbing and reacting to these changing undercurrents, began to open up a slight gulf between us. In visiting them in their rooms I was very aware of this. Yes, I could certainly still identify with the older ones; but National Service was coming to an end by 1960. If they were fans of trad jazz – and many had been in the mid-50s – I could enthuse about Chris Barber and throaty Ottilie who was so much undervalued, but the tangled paths leading off into modern jazzes of various subtle differences were quite beyond me. The life-size cutout of delicious Brigitte (and wasn't BB so much more enticing than the overblown and over-obvious MM?) which I encountered in so many student rooms thanks to 'Reveille' magazine early in the decade, was as exciting to me as to them, but it was steadily becoming more difficult for me to say so: from being a contemporary I had become a sort of older brother and would soon be a young uncle to my student clients, themselves so much more immature now. Also, I now understand as I look back, my whole attitude must have shifted a little: the Dong had lost his Jumblie Girl… "Far and few… ".

I realised that my future was depending more and more on recruiting some more Maxes; but no, they must be much younger than him or myself. I should look out for likely Area Managers from among our own soon-to-graduate clients, and I asked Max to do the same.

★ ★ ★

Meanwhile my peripatetic visits to student unions had become far more simple, thanks to those two benefactors Mr Rank and Mr Xerox. The loss of Sarah had threatened to leave me with that soul-killing job of wading alone, all, all alone, through those dismal miles of index-cards, with of course the carbon-copy to the good Dr Oxdon. But the lifesaving photocopier had reached those offices in the nick of time. The humming box in the corner very soon reduced my annual visits to a swift formality.

Continuity had also become simpler with the rise, in the larger unions, of a permanent Manager or General Secretary, who clearly ruled the roost although technically subordinate to the pompous but ephemeral student officers. Usually, on taking up his position he would have found our Oxdon-inspired arrangement already in place, and in a growing majority of universities the release to me of the sacred Full Student List was becoming automatic.

Mr Jones at Birmingham, Mr Brown at Liverpool and the fearsome Mr Blood at Leeds came to accept me as a normal part of the annual routine. Not only did I get the lists, but in many such places the distribution of the letters was also facilitated and I was allotted an interview room when I later came back to round up the applicants.

That would set the pattern for the rest of my visit, so I went to the cinema quite a lot, if there was one locally (Note 14).

This was because my quietest time was the afternoon of Days Two and Three, when so many of my prey were on the sports field or involved in some other unspeakable sport of their own which I hesitated to barge in upon (my belated apologies to that chap in Magdalene and his girlfriend). I soon became an authority on all the crummy side-street picture houses which gave a spark of life to most inner suburbs in those days; they were immortalised in that wonderful Launder and Gilliat film 'The Smallest Show on Earth'. On looking it up now in his indispensable reference book I am surprised to see that my old friend Leslie Halliwell didn't think much of the film. I would have thought it right up his street – literally, since when I knew Leslie he was running just such a side-street cinema on the edge of Cambridge for that great man George Webb (great indeed, he needed two seats even in his lorries); on many a sunny afternoon, chatting to them at the back of the empty circle, I appeared to be the only paying customer (though it now seems that Michael Winner may well have been sitting, equally solitary, in the more expensive seats below me). I do believe that Leslie, who knew the ropes far better than his boss, used to run good old films mainly for his own benefit; and later events in his too-short life must only add to the suspicion.

As one may well imagine, Leslie gave plenty of screen-space to the wonderful Hitchcock, but I remember he agreed with me that the man's genius for suspense ought not to overshadow his good touch for comedy, neatly inserted into death and disaster: I never fail to chuckle when, in "The Trouble with Harry", the old retired seadog is invited to tea by the demure spinster, and they are both on their best ultra-genteel behaviour. I write from memory so I don't have the exact words, but she mentions that her father "passed away" at some time or other. He says how sorry he is to hear that, and trusts the old man had a peaceful end. She: "He was dragged into a threshing-machine". Lovely! But is it in the original book? If so, well done, Trevor Story, I must look it up.

★ ★ ★

It was Max himself who found me a potential Area Manager for the North, a recent graduate he had first signed up and then enthused. I reckoned I could continue, for the time being, to handle the Midlands, but further up, from Liverpool in a zigzag across the Pennines via Sheffield to York and Hull, was a bit – literally – over the top despite the lovely views. I would keep Durham because I liked the place so much (those fantastic Cathedral columns, however did those little men do it, all that time ago!) and, being Collegiate, it was easier to handle in brief visits.

Sid was graduating from somewhere in inner North London. He was due to meet me at our office across the road from the Round Church in Cambridge but it was smelling of cabbages after some mysterious disaster in the greengrocer's downstairs, which was threatening to be bad for our business as well as his; so I changed the appointment to London instead and we met in the bar of ULU (University of London Union) on Malet Street.

Max arrived first.

"Something good ought to emerge from this," I told him

"That's what Mr Freeman said," he replied.

"Mr Freeman?"

"To Mr Hardy, when they went to meet Mr Willis."

Max introduced Sid, then left us. I looked him over: a powerful build, perhaps a bit heavy, but he seemed energetic. I asked what he would like to drink.

"A large one, of anything."

"Well," I began while he rather quickly got his glass down to halfway, "we've already fixed you up with a SLAS policy, so I don't need to waste time telling you how good it is… "

"You're right," said Sid. "If there's any nasty surprises behind Max's sales talk, I'll find them soon enough, simply by joining the firm." He was looking around the room, crowded with the liquid lunchtime clamour from UCL. "Christ," he went on, "All these thousands. What a challenge."

"You know it's the North I want covered."

"I can handle everything north of Watford."

I told him my idea of a wide northern area, centred on Manchester. Not only was that the largest accumulation of students, but it was central; and secretly but even more to the point, it was the only large university where Dr Oxdon had asked us to withhold his letter: I bore in mind that he already had some sort of deal in place there. Our Manager would do well to be locally based not just to establish our own connections, both with the genial Union Manager George Carrotte, and the numerous other student nuclei that were starting to develop a Higher Education status, but to keep an ear to the ground and in time perhaps find out more about the Oxdon connection. On top of that, Sid's job would involve building contacts with the specialised Colleges such as the Northern School of Music just down the road, the Poly, and further down, those many Halls of Residence towards Victoria Park, crying out for us to go and convert a few heathen...

"How do you feel about living round Manchester?" I ended on the steps outside, after our talk had led to me offering him the job. Sid's enthusiasm suggested that he would only be happy if he found himself surrounded by potential clients, no matter where. He shrugged. I thought he was going to ask about rail or road connections with his native East London, or perhaps the cost of housing, or how bad the weather really was...

"What are the women like?"

★ ★ ★

I walked him back to Tottenham Court Road Underground, then wandered on through Soho. Not long ago, Bill Haley had been performing live at the Dominion, and already that seemed as dated as the nearby Wimpy Bar. (The Wimpys had started over here in

95

1953, and they met a need – of sorts – a good place to take the kids on Sunday morning, fill them up and shut them up while you read the papers, and back home while the good lady was making the dinner; but their kiss of near-death would come very soon, when in 'Beyond the Fringe' their unique aroma was, they said, "like sniffing your armpit". Dreadfully cruel, but one could not deny it).

Mentioning The Fringe immediately takes me forward a couple of years to that sublime but short-lived Establishment Club founded by Peter Cook, he who sent me a Life Assurance enquiry-card but was never in his room – and no wonder. My best memory of the satire show is from 1962 when the enormous Graham Sutherland tapestry first appeared in the new Coventry Cathedral, to the horror of nearly all normal people. These were the earliest days of The Two Johns, Bird and Fortune, in their brilliant duologues. "Yes, but it's quite representational, I believe?" – "Oh indeed, people know at once. They all identify it: as they come through the door and see it, they all say "Jesus Christ!". (And incidentally, I heard of a delightful Japanese lady, very much a stranger to our shores but an admirer of Sutherland, who thought she was looking at Winston Churchill).

That new Cathedral at the beginning of the Sixties was also the time and place for the first performance of Britten's (apologetic?) War Requiem. He and Peter Pears had attracted much opprobrium by sliding off to the States in 1939 when war threatened: I seem to remember that nearly everyone was aware of this and saw it as a bit of a national letdown. When the pair slunk back a few years later, I heard somebody say it was "with their tails between each other's legs".

Skiffle, too, had come and almost gone: the 'Two-Is' was as crowded as ever, at that time of day they were mainly out-of-towners, hoping to get a glimpse of Tommy Steele, but as one might have told them, misinformed. 'Heaven and Hell' for coffee was to be avoided also, in daylight, because Hell downstairs didn't open yet, and Heaven on the ground floor was as boring as the shoe shop it probably used to be. So I went into the nearby 'Necro', which briefly existed in imitation of the better-known and better-run

'Macabre'; and I sat at a coffin nursing my sad cappuccino in its cloudy see-through cup.

Guitars were everywhere. Even Sid played one, he had told me... Then I stopped short. Why did I think: "even" Sid? I ought to be glad I had taken on somebody who would identify with our student clients: it was nearly 1960 now, and with the end of the military call-up, we would be aiming at youngsters, more than ever. Had I erred in employing the older Max – even older than me, and I was worrying about my own suitability. As I scooped off my froth, I reflected that among today's young, the 'acceptable' changed so quickly, unless you were really "in there with it", you couldn't win.

Last month's slang phrase is even more dated than last year's clothes fashion. To use a dated in-word was the surest way to guarantee yourself a social body-bag and no sale. We must, even Sid, be sure to avoid that sort of faux-pas; and we must in future, whenever appropriate, recruit young people and insist they keep in touch. Perhaps on short-term contracts so that we could replace them every few years? But then they would set up in competition? Needs looking into: perhaps I could do a deal with the manager of an insurance company's salesforce, to pass our men on to him after we've trained them up for a while?

But thank God, I reflected over my second cup of the filthy stuff, (One more of these and I'll be in the box, not sitting at it), our students all over the country, brought up on splendid idiocies like the Goon Show, could usually be relied upon to soften their views, upholster even their basic dislikes, by wrapping them in good-natured irony and a sound sense of the ridiculous. I thought of the dry exchange I had recently had with my elder son, who was about to get involved in setting up what would soon become known as a pop-group.

"I've got to get some plectrums," he had told me as we drove to the shops. "Plectra," I corrected him. And a while later I asked: "You've got two guitarists, but what does your other pal Tony play?"

He looked at me. "The dra," he said.

★ ★ ★

I drove over to Oxford as usual the following week, and checked in to my hostelry at that time, the Isis Hotel on Iffley Road, where by coincidence I had earlier been on that 1954 day when Roger Bannister did his four-minute thing across the road. I went into town, parked in Cornmarket Street, and went into the Cadena cafe for breakfast, where in the afternoons they held thés dansants (I never know how many 's's there should be in that, nor whether tea in France is feminine). Then, planning ahead for lunch at my desk, I called at a cake-shop just down Queen Street where the Co-op sold coffee-iced buns. Where did all these places go?

Up the two flights of stairs, at our office on the corner of Carfax, cosily next to the tower, Jerry had a surprise for me.

"It's a matter of continuity, old boy, just in case anything happens to me. You've been with us for quite a time now, and I think our Insurers and the Bank and so on would be happier... "

So I became a Junior Partner, with a one-third share in the business.

"Of course, there's no money or extra income involved or anything, but it'll look good on our letterheads and of course it'll help you as you go around your colleges. Some Very Important Brokers I've spoken to think I ought to charge you several thousands for a partnership like this, but I said no, not a bit of it." He went on: "Come to think of it, while you're here you can sign below me on these forms – I'm applying for a lease on some better offices at Ellistons up the road, the top end of George Street. Far more room, we're so cramped here now."

I signed my name proudly where it said 'Partner', and walked up to look at the new offices. They were indeed better, on two expansive floors, right on the corner. Jerry would have a superb room, soon to be full of light oak furniture and leather desk fittings, a 'genuine Regency' cocktail cabinet, a framed letter of thanks from somebody-or-other, and a two-way view including the whole stretch of Broad Street. We would be accommodating about a dozen staff (notice I say 'we' – I'm a Partner now, aren't I?) mostly in the

Accounts Department dealing with new and renewal premiums as they poured in daily.

There was a small room on the lower floor which peeped out on to the side-street through a sort of misted-up arrow-slit which the cleaners never managed to reach in their time available. This was the overflow filing room and it contained on rough wooden shelving, the forty or fifty massive Kalamazoo ledgers which recorded in painful longhand all the activity on every policy we were administering, as Brokers, for our clients on the one side and the Insurers on the other. In among all this was a desktop, used mainly as a breathing-space for whichever distressed and puffing girl had the job of lugging the ledgers around; and alongside the desk I found an unexpectedly Art Nouveau chair which I recognised from the old pigeon days back in Pembroke Street. It was my office, for use on the days – usually Monday and Tuesday – that I still devoted to Oxford students when not ploughing around other parts of the country.

My usual plan, you will recall, was to visit SLAS applicants in their rooms, but in Oxford I occasionally had appointments in the office and I remember the young Winston Churchill coming in to arrange ski insurance (as did one of the Gloucester princes over in Cambridge). Nobody else, anywhere, was offering special insurances for students throughout the period 1950 to 1965. I was making some very useful contacts. Among them was a charming chap at Keble with whom I started tentatively to discuss developing a business interest miles removed from insurance, just in case, in trying to build up a national sales team, I should find myself squeezed out somehow between Jerry and the Area Managers at some future time.

The Keble man, with whom I got through a great deal of sherry and coffee in his room just along the corridor from the Porter's Lodge (Keble was the only College to have corridors, in all other quads the arrangement was vertical staircases) was heir to a soap manufacturer, and full of promotional ideas for their brand. We worked out a brilliant plan to produce small 'visitor' squares of the soap in a distinctive wrap – probably tartan to please the Americans – to be given away by top hotels, by Cunarders, perhaps by attendants at the London clubs, theatres and golf courses, and inside each one, or printed on the wrapper, there would be a voucher offering a full-size bar at half-price. His father's Board turned it down, so there was another good idea gone. But I went on thinking. I wonder what became of the Keble man... I can't even remember his name, and judging by the amount we drank, I don't suppose he can either.

There were plenty of other students in those days, interested in SLAS or the Belongings cover, whose futures are no mystery at all. I am forever reading about Cabinet Ministers, writers and comedians whom I first (and last!) met on those visits. Very few made much of an impression on me at the time, but one man who did – and we spent what to me was a memorable evening, long past midnight, in his Peck. rooms in Christ Church – was Andrew Bertie; a delightful man, a connoisseur at the time of Algerian wine, who ended up at the head of an immensely distinguished international religious Order: no, not the Pope but you're not far off. We chatted, I remember, about various religions, and intriguingly he turned the whole approach upside-down simply by quoting in full that delightful verse, surprisingly by Rupert Brooke, called simply "Heaven", to demonstrate how different our beliefs and desires can be. (Note 6)

I was pleased to meet J J Cooper partly because of his graceful handwriting on the enquiry-card, but mainly because his father, Viscount Norwich had made such a brilliant broadcast I listened to as a schoolboy in 1939 when he was Duff Cooper and later Our Man in Paris.

We also, as I've said, had a card from Peter Cook in Cambridge, but he was working on 'Beyond The Fringe' and understandably he soon reckoned that he was unlikely to need the security of an insurance policy for his old age. I didn't get the chance to persuade him otherwise, although I could have made a good case for it, in retrospect...

But it was in a room close to Cook's that I sat one day, waiting for my client to get back from a lecture. As usual I looked along the bookshelf, and found a gem. It was an anthology of poems compiled by an Army General – indeed a Field Marshal. We think of our top commanders as being men of blood-and-guts, but this made me realise (as I should always have known) that they have a private side, too. This is what I found: it is by Mervyn Peake, the man who wrote 'Gormenghast', and dedicated to his wife Maeve. It is exquisite and I love it.

He tells her: "You walk unaware of the slender gazelle that moves as you move… ", a beautiful thought. It goes on in that way for less than seventy words, but like a string of pearls.

Yes, I'm sure you're ahead of me. Mervyn Peake must have loved Maeve very much; but for me this was the distillation of my Sarah: the loose-limbed slimness of the fencer, the poise of that unattainable gazelle… What a great little poem. (See Note 7)

★ ★ ★

Doctor Oxdon sent for me.

I don't suppose that brief statement strikes much fear into you, but into me it certainly did. Since that fruitful first meeting, several years back by now, I had met him only twice, and that was briefly when – unusually – I had for some reason to deliver his copies of our lists personally, to that slightly sinister North Oxford house. Yes, I do remember why: there were local strikes by our surly and unreliable postal workers, most of them escapees from the Cowley motor-works who had deserted to the Post Office and brought their ill-judged truculence with them. Oxdon had merely received the envelope at the door and nodded thanks, suggesting that our arrangement was still best kept secret.

I had three days' notice of this new meeting which the Doctor had set for five-twenty in the afternoon. The precision was surely designed to alarm me. As it was Autumn, was he intending to chat in general terms until twilight seeped into his study, and then paralyse me with some new rapier-thrust which would once again demonstrate that he knew all there was to know about me? It had been most unsettling over the past few years to be aware that, however benignly, I was personally being watched, but there was nothing I could have done about it simply because we had needed those lists so much. I could see no alternative until now; but I felt I had to break away from this reliance if there was any way, now that the lists simply rolled off a machine. I would have to be tactful...

I had to decide what suit to wear, too, stupid though it now seems. At that time, a businessman wore a business suit, full stop. When I first started with Jerry he even insisted that I carried a hat: he took his with him everywhere though I rarely saw him wear it when he wasn't paddling a Cambridge canoe. Nowadays we smile at the old black-and-white films where the detective has a homburg, and all the Men from the Ministry are in bowlers, let alone the goodies and the baddies in Westerns, identified by their hat-colour! But as I was dealing almost entirely with young students, I had to some extent rebelled against Jerry's ideas of formality. Most students possessed just one suit which they kept in the wardrobe at home, ready for interviews and funerals and those pompous university occasions one had to sit through. So I tried to play down my appearance.

I did have two fairly recent subfusc suits, one dating from the Oxford matriculation ceremony and the other made for me by Castells on Broad Street when I graduated (tailors got rich in university towns as they did in Aldershot). I forget why I felt it was necessary but no doubt Castells had convinced me: I only remember the price and the eighteen months it took me to pay the bill. Come to think of it, when I starry-eyed joined the Oxford Union Society in my first Term, I bought a dinner-jacket with the money I got for selling my Army dress uniform and my Sam Browne. But since I never attended the Union because I didn't much like the people who did, and since I was never invited – least of all by Jerry – to anywhere 'suitable' (now there's a pun!) for getting dressed-up, it hung and mouldered and gradually went green like an old schoolmaster's gown.

But my life-saver was a much-loved old tweed suit from my Army days, on which I had always relied when instructed by the Mess Secretary that some event was to be 'informal'. I had bought it cheaply somewhere on the Welsh border, and even there it was old-fashioned: it was in a very solid Harris that was halfway between heather-mixture and – I suppose – the tired-broccoli colour of rain-forest. After several years of overuse I began to make excuses for it and called it my 'sympathy suit' for that is the reaction it aroused in nearly everyone I met. It baggily brought out a nostalgic benevolence everywhere and I slowly realised this was to my advantage. I wore it for Dr. Oxdon.

★ ★ ★

He met me personally when I rang the bell. Whether he had been hovering in the hall since five-eighteen, I never knew, but the sudden face-to-face didn't help. I almost expected him to say: "Nice old suit, how are those tailors off the High Street in Church Stretton?"; instead, and leaning on a stick, he was in a floppy cardigan above the most awful yellow corduroy trousers within which he had shrunk, and defensively secured them around himself with an old college tie, probably Balliol. I felt over-dressed.

"My dear fellow, Tim, do come in."

I came in. He shuffled me into the study, ushering me into the same chair as before, where his cat grudgingly made room. I looked at the animal and wondered how old it must be; it looked back at me, probably thinking the same. After a few minutes of small-talk: "You seem to be expanding your business very creditably," said the Doctor, pleasantly but without the glasses shifting this time. "I imagine my letter must have helped a little?"

I told him that, of course, his Letter of Introduction had been crucial to our development, as he and his colleagues must have deduced from the regular copies he had been receiving. But I added: "Things are changing, Doctor, and most of those old contacts are becoming irrelevant."

I shouldn't have said it like that. Oxdon reacted quite violently. He spluttered and the cat ran to the door, only stopping to lick itself when it got safely into the hall and round a corner.

"Irrelevant! My recommendations have *made* you, Tim. Without them you would have got nowhere – nicht – isn't that so?"

This was very unfortunate. He was glaring and had gone red. Was he ill? I felt I owed it to him, to take him gently through the changes brought about by technology. He was clearly very much the wrong side of eighty now and far detached from everyday academic affairs, let alone modern business.

"Of course," I said, "all our progress in the redbrick provinces," I thought he would like that, "has been due to your letter – "

"Well then – "

"But you see, Doctor, a new invention has come into use. This means we no longer have to write out all the student data by hand," I explained gently, "but we can be given full lists now, of all the names and addresses, in just a few minutes. It's called a – "

He indicated towards the far corner of the room.

"I had that put in two years ago," he said, and this time the glasses did slide, while I absorbed the huge grey machine smirking at me from the shadows. He even told me what make it was. I was surprised he didn't quote the serial number.

There was a short silence as I crawled back under my stone and he quietly enjoyed the situation. The he went on:

"Let me tell you, Tim, what our problem is. Of course we've noticed you are sending us photocopies. But you see," and here he bent down and swept up the cat who was being solicitous, "These printouts aren't giving us sufficient information."

I didn't follow, and said so.

"We have completed our study of mere names and addresses and the geographics and so on. What we have to do now is analyse the full background of those students who have been sufficiently forward-looking to take an insurance on their lives; we want to follow up, from the details you can give us, their family situation, the health element, etcetera; and when we have identified, from your data, which students we think are interesting to explore in more depth, then our own people can do this by a whole battery of deeper researches."

As he had calculated, I'm sure, it was now getting dark and I could scarcely see him across the room, where he was blandly smiling at me while the cat purred "get out of that, then".

"So what we now require instead of those lists, is a photocopy of every Life proposal-form." He sat back; I sat forward.

It was my turn to splutter. "Confidential," I managed to say. "That proposal-form is completely confidential"

"My dear fellow, almost everything in our lives is confidential, but many outsiders still have to get involved in it. The postman knows what bills you can't pay; the newsagent knows what you read; the chemist knows what you need treatment for… "

"We get all sorts of – "

"Of course you do, dear boy. So do all the junior staff in your office, and all the staff at the Insurance Company you send it to. Do you imagine their bosses insist they all sign a Secrets Act? You aren't in the Army any more, Tim."

"We've got – " I cast around for examples, while he watched me amused. "There's the bastard child of a Minister of the Crown… There's the son of a famous poet who's got VD – "

"All famous poets have had VD throughout history, it's an occupational hazard, and most politicians have bastards like themselves." Then he got serious. "My associates are insisting that you owe us this favour. We gave you entry to those Student Unions for your personal profit. You still have this unique facility. Our new requirement, copies of the proposal-forms, will in no way complicate your normal business activities, will it?" I had to admit this; the copy would simply be built into the system, a minor routine for a junior girl. "So there we are," he went on. "That is their final word on the matter. I suppose your Xerox machine – " he pronounced the word very deliberately as if it was new to me, " – is able to cope with copying your five thousand forms every year, or perhaps I can recommend a better one?"

Whether he then pressed a hidden button, I don't know, but at that moment his daughter came in.

"Hello dear. Tim is just about to leave us, could you see him to the door, my leg hurts and anyway I'm stuck here under the cat." So far as I remember I simply followed her out. I don't think I said goodbye to Oxdon, let alone shook his hand. But what I do remember, very clearly indeed, is his parting shot.

"I gave you a very helpful letter, Tim, years ago. We can very easily write again, countermanding all we said before. It wouldn't take more than a few minutes to photocopy it to every Union, would it, with all this new – what d'you call it? – technology… And I suppose we could include the Oxford and Cambridge Colleges, don't you know, Tim? I must have a chat with my people."

As the front door closed on me, he called: "So don't let me down."

CHAPTER VII

I went in a daze from Oxdon down to the Randolph to pick up my suitcase, and there were three messages for me. At the time I little knew how they were about to turn my life upside-down.

First, our Accountants would like me to spare them a few minutes, next time I was in town. Secondly, Max let me know he had found me a very promising man for our Midlands position in or near Birmingham. And third, Jerry had a spot of good news and would I get in touch?

This could all wait until tomorrow; and so on the bunny-run back to Cambridge I drew up outside my Newport Pagnell pit-stop for the usual welcoming Laphroaig, and sat over it – OK, them – pensively. Never mind those Randolph messages, I thought, I must get clear in my mind the way my future was heading, and how I should play my cards. We would have to comply, for the moment, with Oxdon's demands because we had to have our access to lists. After all, I nearly convinced myself, he was right: all sorts of people see those forms and we had never been told to maintain secrecy, much though it might be implied. Any young clerk in my office, or the insurance office, might go home and shout: "Hey, guess what I know about so-and-so in the headlines." But other than that, what were my main worries? I coaxed some scrap paper out of Marian and scribbled a list. (I still have that bit of paper, yellow now, crumpled into the cardboard box under the back seat, into which I have always dumped the contents of the glove compartment when selling car after car: God knows why, I never seem to sort or replace the stuff). I can still just read it. It says:

1. Get an income apart from Jerry. Students Europe? Just me?
2. Oxdon. Who behind him? Can we bypass?
3. Talk to NUS – share?
4. J spending. Can I tell him?

It was getting late but I couldn't face the fourteen minute drip-torture of the next-door chimes, so I decided to head for home. I went over and told Marian about W C Fields and his legendary health advice: "You should always carry a large bottle of whiskey in case of snake-bite," he had said, "and also carry a small snake." Suitably protected, my list of problems being my snake, I headed on in my wonderful old aerodynamic Sunbeam Talbot 90…

Driving through Bedford, as always I thought back to the wartime occupation by the BBC Orchestras, who had come there after being bombed out of Bristol, and used several local halls as studios, notably our school's Great Hall. Along with a few others, I became a devotee at their rehearsals; I used to sit at the far end of the Hall, quite close – as it happened – to a half-concealed pointer to the toilets. I was always being asked directions: Constant Lambert… Granville Bantock… Vaughan Williams… York Bowen… Guy Warrack… I must have sent more composers to the lavatory than any other schoolboy in history.

Like most wartime schoolchildren, I suppose my first real introduction to classical music was the oft-repeated Myra Hess, 'Jesu Joy', at her lunchtime concerts at St Martin's. At first we all thought that 'Bach' was just 'Bach': it was much later that I realised there were about eighty of them! After that I finally stumbled upon the brilliant Peter Schickele's creation of the presumably-prestissimamentic 'PDQ Bach' (whom you really must look up if he has evaded you so far!); my own modest contribution to this harmless conceit – at least, I hope it is original – is the little-remembered 'NBG Bach', who became, of course, a music critic…

I never, myself, learnt to play a musical instrument; but I did once, at school, compose a short piece when pushed to it by the arrogance of a friend, Giles Roche, who was annoyingly competent.

It was scored for piccolo, cymbals and tympani, it lasted for three bars, and I called it 'The Lark Descending'. It went down quite well with most of my circle, except Giles.

★ ★ ★

The next morning, and thereafter, a lot of things began to happen, not least in Moscow and Virginia, and to develop right through to the end of the year when the crisis came. Much of this was concurrent and I find it impossible to weave it as a single pattern, without causing confusion. I must thread the happenings one strand at a time so that when we reach the crucial date in November, the position will be understandable without any further embroidery.

Those Randolph Messages.

1. I called on our accountants the following week. Apparently, being now a Partner, albeit so much the junior one, I was required to add my signature to the Accounts. Ollie asked how things were going. I enlarged enthusiastically upon our student marketing and my plans for further expansion. He was intrigued. He asked then about how well Jerry must be doing, judging by the new offices and all his reported activities around the County Set. "Great friends with all the Right People, eh? Is he around just now?" Not at the moment, I said, he was looking into a big polo-related scheme which had taken him to the West Indies.

2. Our new Area Manager for Birmingham was introduced to me by Max, who had found him as a student policyholder somewhere in Essex. Maurice was just out of his finals year reading Languages and enjoyed using them in conversation with his monoglot friends. Knowing my background, he tried it on me when Max brought him up to meet me in Warwick, a brand new university he would be covering. After learning that Max had already explained what would be involved as Midlands Manager, I asked him: "Do you think this

is a job you'd like to build on with us?". Ah, he replied, *"Il ne faut jurer de rien."* I seem to remember him smiling while I tried to think of a response.

3. An astonishing thing happened the next time I went over to Oxford, Jerry having returned. I asked him what was the 'good news' he had referred to in his note?

"It's brilliant, old boy. I've got some money for you."

In view of the enormous amount of business we were doing, our main Insurer had paid us a very substantial bonus. There were no strings attached because their Directors and Jerry were now on such good terms: as my Junior Partner share, I was to receive £10,000. Here it suddenly was, now, a cheque in my hand; but we could talk another time because he had to get over to Lambourn.

My Sunbeam was up in St. Giles, so I walked, bemused, to the Lamb and Flag where I sat in front of a Guinness, a pork pie and £10,000. I had never in my life seen that much money in one chunk, let alone with my name on it.

What to do with it? I got out an old envelope and began to scribble helpful notes to myself, but didn't know what to write. Also, my pen didn't work. It occurred to me that I could afford a new one. I went home.

My Newport Pagnell Notes.

1. Magically it seemed, with all that money I would now be able to protect my future by putting some eggs into a different basket, and buy a little independence from Jerry. With a good London-based friend called Jeremy I found a flatlet house in Pimlico; there were six letting bedsitters, a basement flat also for letting, and on the first floor a two-roomed flat which would be my London HQ, as I needed to be at the centre of things. I would not only have rental income but save on hotels.

But first, I must complete my personal independent plans for taking student insurances into Europe. I decided to treat myself to a fact-finding fortnight, and booked a round-trip air ticket via Paris and Zurich to Rome and home by way of Madrid and Lisbon. At each stop I would seek out the Commercial Attaché at our Embassy and sound them out on the local structure of the national student organizations. I tried the first two, and they knew absolutely nothing, as became clear over excellent lunches.

However, my real target was Rome. Back in Cambridge I had made the acquaintance, a few months before, of a delectable young Italian language student, whose intelligence had impressed me almost as much as her vivacity and considerable other more personal attractions: dark tempting hair; deep, deep brown eyes; that Mediterranean colouring, a hazel-brown figure to dream of, lying back alluringly in some Trevi fountain…

Anyway: I would suggest to her that she might like to work for my Company as my assistant in the European venture.

In short, for whatever reasons, Olivia did. I had never been to Rome, and fell in love with the city as much as I did day by day with her: a lovely and lovable little Roman and – thank God – a staunch Anglophile. She took me everywhere; and when she was busy at her temporary job with a British airline, I delved on my own into the more hidden and less likely backwaters. One of the most evocative must be the extraordinary Monte Testaccio, that little hill beside the Tiber made up entirely of ancient broken pottery, one piece of which would cause excitement if found in an English field. I was reminded of that equally romantic pile of Tyrian purple shells, over 100 feet high, at Sidon. Or, coming depressingly down to earth, the modern version at the Teufelsberg in Berlin, a mountain of rubble from 1945, topped by (what else?) an American listening-post. O tempora, etc.

It is the small unlikely things that one remembers. The languid cats in Largo Argentina… The dishevelled but proud old lady who wandered on to a seat close to me in the almost-empty Forum, and at once, while feeding a pigeon, began to speak in clear cultivated French about some long-distant problem she had endured in, I think, Antibes, and had now come to tell the Pope about it… The cobbles in the Appia Antica, but also the pieces of ancient statuary sunk into the tarmac alongside them... The whole thought of '*Quo Vadis*'...

Also, one glistening evening along that evocative road, Olivia and I dined under the stars amid a surround of empty tables, the only other occupied, pleading boomingly with some producer for extra backing for a film project, by Orson Welles. I hope he got it but I doubt it.

★ ★ ★

I stayed for a third week. We talked about the various countries in our sights, and the likelihood of their student unions being interested in mass insurance of belongings. I already knew that Life Assurance would be problematical due to financial restrictions. We decided that the Swiss and probably the Germans were likely to be well-organised already, so we would keep well away from them for fear that they might be tempted to pre-empt us in other countries.

At the other extreme we dismissed Spain and Portugal as being not yet ready for our gospel. So we settled upon first the Scandinavians (I remembered Matt's comments), then the French and Belgians (where British insurers were already well established) and finally I asked: "What about Italy?"

"Bo?" she shrugged. This, I soon learned, is a typically Roman expression and I suppose it is related to similar noises that accompany a shrug all around the Mediterranean. I don't think we have it in England but perhaps, if I do a British shrug, it can be joined by a 'pouf' and a puff of the cheeks? Same difference.

We agreed that Italy should be included but at the end of the list.

I cancelled the rest of my tour, and reluctantly dragged myself back to the world, arranging that Olivia would join me in September at the Pimlico flat; and I returned to my tangled agenda.

2. "Who are behind Oxdon?" I had written, in my memo to myself,

but did I now really want to know? If he needed the data for research purposes – and presumably such research is done – who was I to interfere? Passing on the copies of every proposal-form might, on the surface, seem a bit naughty but, as the Doctor had pointed out, the information was already lying about in various offices and we had never been told it was 'classified'. Above all, I simply had to have those lists, and not allow Oxdon to carry out his threat: with a third Area Manager joining us, we now had more than half the country covered.

Ultimately, I managed to tell myself that we were justified as we were bringing a great financial benefit to students everywhere, and they all deserved to know about it. Rather than rock the boat by putting our flow of addresses at risk just now, I therefore resolved to set aside my ethics for the moment. Plenty of time to see Oxdon again and renegotiate once we had all our facts on Europe lined up. After all, Edward Heath was tacking to and fro across the Continent as only he knew how (and with eventual results he certainly did not know), and I felt we ought to get in there with him.

3. Talk to NUS? At this time, student politics were a minefield. The previous President had been a moderate, and he went on into our Foreign Service and had the distinction of being listed in an East German propaganda book as a member of MI6. His successor was, I think, only slightly Left-inclined; but as always, those who were pushy and up-and-coming behind him hustled him into their camp. It would get worse.

Since we were the only insurance firm making a speciality of designing policies to meet the particular requirements of students, it seemed pretty obvious that we ought to aim to link our service in with the various student-friendly facilities that NUS provided to its members, through their hundreds of local unions.

I had got to know a brash, but charming and roguish young Yorkshireman who had fairly recently graduated from a Northern university, where – understandably – he had been Union President. His first job had been in advertising and it suited him well. His name was Robin, and I met him for a couple of drinks at The Bedford pub just off Tottenham Court Road, close to ULU. We both knew that this chat may well lead to him joining me in some capacity or other, as soon as the time was ripe.

He thought we should seek to establish a proper liaison with the NUS and offer a full insurance service to all students, suggesting to each Union separately, or better, to the NUS centrally, a commission-sharing deal in exchange for them supplying the lists, as soon as their Freshers arrived. He arranged a meeting.

Student politicians were, at their lowest local-college level, merely arrogant and stupidly obsessed with the Holy Grail of fishpond power. As they moved up their tiny hierarchy, they changed. Almost always male, they had already enjoyed the adulation of nubile young Freshers, and now they would savour the heady joy of issuing wild instructions to the union's weary permanent staff twice their age and with ten times their experience. The final step up their ladder, to National level, was practically always hopelessly beyond their range… But those few who did make the grade, unless they had done – or overdone – something stupid, were a pretty intelligent bunch, whatever their politics.

The cream of these people, deep in suspicion of businessmen, were the ones for whom I several times provided a pleasant supper: once at my friend Jeremy's new bistro 'Grumbles' in Pimlico; once or twice at 'The Pheasantry' on King's Road. I proposed a jointly-owned company; Robin hovered with drinks and made all the right noises. The NUS people – delegates I suppose they would have called themselves, even at an off-the-cuff private supper – went away with pages of notes, to think about it. And with pleasantly full stomachs.

The only positive outcome was their recommendation, as an aside when I mentioned Europe, that we might go to Holland and talk to COSEC, "Combined Secretariat", the unifying organisation of all the National Student Unions of Western Europe. This was a spin-off that paved a way forward for Olivia and me, entirely unexpectedly; it led to some odd happenings and it had a very, very odd background… But that emerged later.

4. My last scribbled note had asked if Jerry was getting too extravagant. You will have gathered that my Senior Partner, semi-transparent phoney though he was, had considerable presence and was a thoroughly likeable and charismatic man. But he had been socially sucked into the vicious vortex of 'The County' at a higher level than he could cope with. He would not have admitted it for a million years but he was out of his depth. I was always kept at arm's length from his Insurance Company relationships: indeed, amazingly, it later transpired that the Directors of our main student insurance schemes had no knowledge of me whatever; they seemed to think all the business we had been introducing (and for several years it represented over three-quarters of their entire production) was somehow originated by Jerry himself, and he was just being very coy about his secret. I enjoyed seeing their astonishment, later, when they saw the light – and even more, my appointment diaries – and subsequently invited me to all their functions.

But all these scribbled worries were suddenly overtaken by events that wove the strands together, that November.

★ ★ ★

Olivia had come to London in September, all ready to work on our Europe plans. We indulged ourselves for a while at the Pimlico flat. I drove her around town. The usual places. At the 'Prospect of Whitby' one Sunday lunchtime, as we got out of the car, a three-foot moppet asked: "Shall I guard your car, sir?" What against, I asked him. He said that the big boys would come and trash it otherwise. I paid my shilling and Olivia was intrigued to experience the Mafia Inglese.

As we drove through Trafalgar Square, she looked up and said: "Ah, Horace Nelson" and I decided I couldn't argue with that, and told her so. She then commented that Nelson's Column could act as a giant sundial with its shadow marking the hours right round the Square: this had never occurred to me or so far as I knew, to anybody else.

She didn't like the Albert Memorial. I do, but I could understand her slight distaste, imagining it in the middle of the Forum, as someone who was used to the pompous austerity of the old Romans (but then, just look at their 'Wedding Cake'! – happily she didn't approve of that either). I used to threaten her: "If you don't behave yourself, I'll take you and show you the Albert Memorial; and she would cry: "No, no, anything but that!"

Getting back to Horace Nelson for a moment, I have always felt that for years he'd had his famous last words all prepared: "Kismet, Hardy" would have been ideal. I like to think that when Hardy messed it up, Nelson's actual famous last words were something like "Silly bugger," and that he died laughing.

Olivia was very observant: from studying her A-to-Z she unearthed the strange fact that along the river, Chelsea Reach appears to be in Battersea and Battersea Reach in Chelsea; we worked out that 'Reach' must mean 'the right way to reach', as Oxford Street points the way to Oxford and Edgware Road is just the road to Edgware.

Those early weeks of settling in were a great joy. She made me all the traditional pastas and wondered, after a while, why I kept talking about two in particular: tagliatelle and conchiglie, especially with aglio. I had to confess, in the end, it was nothing to do with the food, just the marvellously sexy way her mouth and nose moved when she did the 'gl' sound. We don't have it in English: 'glamour', paradoxically, does nothing for us. When we try to pronounce it in the Italian way we just slur and look stupid, though Olivia quite liked it on me. I suppose we were having a 'gl' relationship. It worked for me and that lovely little Midi-brown signorina (yes, 'gn' is quite nice too).

One strange memory I have, about her keenness to make me pasta dishes in the flat, is that I had to drive into Soho in order to find a bottle of olive oil at a specialist shop in Old Compton Street

– otherwise it was tiny bottles in the local chemist's. Looking back today, that seems utterly impossible.

There used to be an organisation, both sides of 1960, called the London Visitors' Club. If your home was outside London it gave you membership of a host of the intimate little Dining Clubs which have nearly all faded away. With my Cambridge home address, I qualified. There was the 'New Yorker' at the top of Curzon Street where it joins Park Lane; the one in Shepherd Market down the other end, where Stirling Moss was said to hang out. (Oh, and between them and absolutely not on the list, that window where reclining ladies advertised 24-hour French lessons). Halfway down Fulham Road was the dusty and deliberately decadent place whose name I forget but it seemed to be full of broken guitars; but probably our favourite was 'The Little Elephant' just off Piccadilly, where you went down the basement stairway opposite De Souza the resident pianist, who would play your favourite tune as soon as he spotted you. (Ours? 'Moon River', it wasn't corny then.) And somehow it was all so 'laidback', though I don't think we had the word, we just lived it.

Summed up by the story of the chap who rang Ronnie Scott's to ask what time they opened: "What time can you get here?" asked Ronnie... Not just me but surely everyone from those days must ask: where did those good days go?

★ ★ ★

I had a call from our Accountants. Please would I come and see them. When I rang, Ollie said: "Tim, the Bank Manager wants to talk to us. I've made a date for tomorrow afternoon."

I replied: "Quite honestly, Ollie, I don't really know anything about our banking or accounts –."

"Exactly," he said.

"Wouldn't it be best for him to talk to Jerry?"

"Absolutely not," ominously.

I checked with my Cambridge office to ensure that everything was OK. Yes, they said, the new business was coming in well. No adverse messages from the Area Managers. No problem.

I rang the Oxford office and asked for Miss Robey, our gigantic cuboid Chief Accounts Clerk. No, premiums were coming in fine.

At the appointed time, Mr Perkins the Manager said Hello; he was a man I had never met, never had any reason to meet since Jerry was the chap who looked after all that stuff.

Perkins and Ollie sat looking at me, coughing a bit. "Tim," they said, very quietly.

Oh Christ, I thought. I'd heard that tone before, from Bank Managers in my private life, though not recently. Not since I bought that new pen.

"Tim, you've got to stop Jerry." Stop Jerry?? "He's out of control. Look at these last few payments."

He waved some cheques in the air. "A week at the Dorchester, over £1000... A camera to take to the West Indies, £900... " (This, in the days when you could, as I did, buy a three-storey house in Westminster for under ten thousand).

I tried to drag up some residual loyalty. "But surely, these are business expenses and he has to mix with lots of Important People?"

The capital letters didn't impress any more.

They exchanged another glance, and Perkins cleared his throat. "One way and another, your company bank account has steadily dwindled and now it's gone into the red."

I laughed, but not much. "Good heavens," I said, "I'm sure that can easily be put right –."

"Tim," said Ollie gently, "That account also holds all your clients' premiums, waiting to be passed over to the Insurers. Or should do."

It was Perkins's turn. He had more papers in his hand. "And those premium collection accounts are up to five months in arrears. Jerry has been spending clients' money for years."

The situation, or anyway the shady outline of it, was beginning to sink in. We apparently owed the Companies over twelve thousand; plus, now, an overdraft; plus yet more because Jerry had run up a tax liability of several thousand; plus, he had recently borrowed to buy a spanking new Rolls Royce and special handmade tiles to stand it on in his garage… I began to feel rather sick.

But something didn't add up, and they were waiting for me to spot it.

"How can this be," I puzzled, "when the Insurance Company has just given us a great big bonus? They must be happy with things, to give us all that? You know, my one-third share alone was ten thousand!"

Ollie sighed and Perkins shook his head sadly.

"Alone?" he echoed.

"I'm afraid you've chosen not quite the right spelling," he said. "The entire deal was a loan."

★ ★ ★

Somebody brought tea in. "One lump" I said, "Must cut back." I nibbled at a biscuit. I was utterly naive, no businessman at all, just an energetic salesman… I was only in my mid-thirties and had never even met any of Jerry's 'Important People', let alone our creditors.

Perkins said: "Only one person can stop him," and they both looked at me. I stared back.

"As a Partner," Ollie explained, "although you've never made use of it, you are entitled to sign cheques. And countersign, too. Now that you're in overdraft you have the right to insist on it. Our suggestion is that you talk to Jerry, or better still," he added sensibly, "under the circumstances, write to him. Stop him. Then you must go and throw yourself – "

"Off Folly Bridge?" I suggested. It is the main Thames crossing down past Christ Church, but the name had never been so appropriate.

" – on the mercy of the Companies. After all is said and done, you're a splendid producer for them, with all the Area network and so on."

"No other way," Perkins agreed, dipping his biscuit gloomily.

119

I drove back to Pimlico in my shabby old second-hand Sunbeam Talbot 90 which might have to last me for years, and wrote a long letter to Jerry, signing it with my new pen. I knew that I had to reason with him and step very gently around his self-esteem. I had no experience whatever of this sort of diplomacy but had to do my best with the likeable and charismatic man who had, anyway, given me my great opportunities before landing me in the closest ditch to bankruptcy.

I told him I knew how much we owed, how it all had to stop, wouldn't it be a great idea if he retired and let me take over? I was going to countersign all cheques from now on, otherwise the Bank would bounce them.

All being well, I, as the Company, could give him and his wife a decent pension. If we wanted to talk this through, of course I could see him at the office anytime.

He never came to the office again.

It was going to be my Company, my Sole Trader status... *My* debt.

CHAPTER VIII

I remember that I smoked rather heavily all the way back to the flat. Not only was I now ridiculously in debt, but the traffic was terrible due to a rail strike. Postal strikes were also the bane of our lives and this was about the time when the Duke of Edinburgh was driven to exhort workers to "pull their fingers out." I, if nobody else, was inspired by the incident; and I wrote a verse, to be sung to the tune of 'Onward Christian Soldiers':

Onward British industry, marching as to death.
Strike! A blow for freedom with every second breath.
See the British working man, finest of his class,
Fashioning our future with his finger…

I sent it to a newspaper but they didn't print it. (Finally, years later in our joint old age, I sent it to the Duke, who was kindness itself in his reply).

Once I had written that final letter to Jerry, I got out the bottle. No, no, not Laphroaig any more but the cheapest I could find without actually taking the enamel off my teeth. I had to 'come clean' with our Insurance Companies and make the most of our continuing high production; but I dared not let our office staff know what was going on, and even less my – now three – Area Managers. If at this point they got wind of my troubles, I might well lose them, and see them getting together to set up on their own in competition; after all, they were free of personal debt, while I now had the additional problem of fighting a long-drawn-out legal action against Jerry unless I handled the matter very tactfully.

Nor could I allow the NUS President and his sidekicks to get the message that I was in trouble. Nor Oxdon, for that matter (to whom 'everybody told everything'). The hand-over from Jerry to me would have to be presented as a straightforward agreement, allowing the older man to retire gracefully after all his years of hard work building up this flourishing business, so that he could sit back and spend more time with his garage tiles.

Jerry didn't see it like that. He fought back at first, vigorously, until I persuaded Ollie to go and spell the situation out to him. I had to outplay him inch by inch, and as the months went past, clause by clause. I was very lucky to form quickly a close friendship with the Managing Director of our main Insurer, who pulled all the necessary strings to transfer the arrears into a long-term loan and also absorb into it the 'bonus' Jerry had delighted me with... Hugh was one of the old school who ran his firm with quiet and relaxed bonhomie: perhaps significantly, it was based in an a rambling old mansion, tucked away in a lazy country town and far away from the increasingly frantic life of the Big City. (There was a popular drift in the Sixties, of large businesses away from London and into country houses; but Hugh's had always been 'out in the sticks' and he was proud of it).

He struck me as a most unlikely Insurance Impresario: away from the office, he delighted in any little-known classical music, especially around the turn of the nineteenth-century, but only the little-known. He had a record collection of remote symphonies and concertos, and we enjoyed comparing notes on people like Hummel (not that trumpet thing, but the piano concertos, especially the one where the piano stays asleep for several minutes); I'm sure our business relationship was largely cemented because I worked steadily on this mutual music interest – I brought him subtly into the twentieth century by a late-night chat, down among The Pantiles, about "Wit and Humour in Music".

Of course, he started off by countering with Haydn, both the audience-awaking shock of the Surprise Symphony and the non-too-subtle rebuke to his Esterhazy employer with the Farewell Symphony, where all the players, unhappily far from their homes, gradually leave the stage because they want to go back to Vienna, each blowing out his candle as he goes.

But I think I won over old Hugh in the end. Not just with the sardonic overblown lead-in to 'Variations on a Nursery Rhyme', that lovely joke by Dohnanyi, (which surely takes the mickey out of the start of Brahms's First Concerto?), but also by some delights from Malcolm Arnold. A truly witty man, he must have been: look at his "Cornish Dances", where as a Cornishman myself, I must confess I secretly rejoice in the superb tease of the Methodist Chapels, with tambourines included – I wonder whether my 'strict' Grandad would have appreciated the satire, he who didn't allow me any radio on Sundays (except the wartime One o'clock news, Mr Middleton's gardening half-hour, and – after I protested so that the neighbours could hear – ITMA)?. And there's more: just listen to his "Padstow Lifeboat March", which could surely be by Berlioz. I was once nearly blown away by that very foghorn, booming suddenly out of the darkness a few yards away. I wish I had heard Arnold playing the trumpet in his Cornish dance band, after he ran away from College with his Welsh redhead.

Apart from all those, the best wittiness in so-called Classical Music must belong to Rossini. Everything points in that direction, not least that he wrote over forty operas, many forever famous, before he was forty – and then, almost nothing, we are told... But the little snippets he called his "sins of old age" are still a delight, and have been put together both by Respighi (the 'Pines of Rome' man) and by the rather unpleasant Benjamin Britten who seems to have been claiming the music as his own, to judge by the constant attributions made by his devoted BBC announcers – sorry, presenters – who insistently seem to deny that Rossini had anything to do with the brilliant music.

But then, they're an odd crowd at Radio Three, aren't they? For ages, some of them with their Celtic pretensions would talk about Clara Schumann's friend as "Bramms" until I wrote to point out they had no trouble saying "Mahler"...

Anyway...

With the need for caution, economy and secrecy, I asked Ollie what I should do about my plans for Europe. He advised that so long as we kept the costs down, "Er, it might be – er – tactful, Tim" to keep to my plans, in moderation, so the recent past with its explosion of expenses was not seen to stop too suddenly. I took the point: it made sense.

It also opened up our exciting new venture, and into it was dovetailed something else. With all this secrecy, whoever could I really talk my worries through with? Apart from my legal and financial professionals like Ollie (who after all, had their own agenda and charged by the hour), nobody must know. But there was just one; she was happily humming in my mini-kitchen, and as I churned this great mound of fragmented worries over in my head like a mental Testaccio, amid a scatter of cigarette-butts and the beginning of a twitch, there she was, calmly making us a *spaghetti al burro*. I sank back and relaxed. I will let her, for a little while, take over, and maybe edit it later…

★ ★ ★

INTERRUZIONE

Goodbye, I am Olivia.

I am not clever at your English humour but that was a joke:

it is what many of our young Italian girls say by mistake when they first come to England and ring the doorbell of their landlady. I did it, too. But now, friends tell me it is done sometimes on purpose, to establish a friendly – *come se dice*? – relationship? – I have lost my dictionary…

I must try to tell you about our Europe insurance visits, and do it well or else I will be shown that Albert statue thing.

Tim in these days is very *sconvolto* – out of his head I think you say; and so he tells me that he cannot fully remind himself of all we have done, and I have promised to register, from my diary, this year of 1963. Our year – I say 'our' because Tim really feels there is no other he can confide with – has to be cut into divisions as he did in the chapter previous. The timing does not have to be seguential.

I must first forecast that you will, you English, expect me to write constant silly phrases like *'merda'* or *'Mamma Mia'* but my writings will soon be well corrigated by Tim, and I hope also editioned by his publicazion person, (if he ever finds one to make a book about all this). So, better now I hope.

★ ★ ★

Yes, now corrigated, as you will see:

1. Europe. Scandinavia is cold in January. Tim – *stupido* – came to Copenhagen without a greatcoat, but bought a very good one at the British Shop. I too bought some clothes, but not at the British Shop. In each country up in the snow we made an appointment with (i) the Commerce Director at the British Embassy; (ii) the Sales Director at an Insurance Office chosen by Tim; then (iii) the Presidente Director of the Students.

We visit, after Denmark, Oslo, everyone skiing right in the middle of town; then a train to Stockholm, nice clothes; on the train we ate some reindeer and met a real Lappman, simpatico but rather hairy, perhaps to keep off the cold. From Sweden we flew to Finland, very many lakes. Helsinki was a very nice town and people. Big, tall, fair men. Here too I bought some clothes. (I copy all this from my diary). We flew back to Heathrow and Tim had to pay some extra.

(After this I go back to Language lessons near Hanover Square, nice teacher, and soon my diary reads better. After this, Tim has corrected too).

He was busy then until the start of Summer. We did not find any business chances in Scandinavia except in Finland they wanted us to insure the teeth of all the students, thousands of them, all nice with nice teeth too (not fully covered by the health policy they had with their government). Tim went to Lloyd's to see a friend called Mr Kidd but I think nothing resulted.

Then in the early Summer we went, like above, to Brussels, to Paris and to Milano. The insurance man in Milano was stupid, I was to be translator for Tim and this man talked to us for twenty-five minutes but said nothing: but you see he was *Milanesi.*

Me, I am *Romana.*

In Brussels and Antwerp there was a nice Englishman, Mr New, but we could not get a permit to work except by including Belgians as Directors, and officials said to us after a very long time that "it would take very too long". In London the Belgian Consulate is close to Pimlico and every time Tim drives past now, he spits at it, but it is only a joke, I think.

In Paris, it was better. The English 'Ocean' is a strong Insurer there and very close to the best shops. The Director was very sympatico. His name was Ali Baba but that must be a – how say? – *soprano* name because he was properly an English gentleman and quite old: he raced horses at Longchamps, too. He liked our ideas and they created a student belongings policy for us with thirty thousand leaflets. I sent them – or took them even sometimes – to many of the big universities: Lyon – Bordeaux – Toulouse – Grenoble – ready for the Autumn. Afterwards, Ali wrote to say they got six replies. We didn't see Ali again.

But meantime, Paris was good and I had stayed there working for some weeks and bought some clothes. Tim came over a few times and one night we door-crashed a little cinema on the Rive Gauche where Jacques Tati was showing the premiere of one of his funny films with new colour, and we met him and shook hands; he talked with Tim in English and French. We also went one evening to a special restaurant based on Rabelais and called 'Le Mouton de Panurge' which was very funny and naughty like Rabelais is: the waiter played with a big pepper pot and stroked it and looked at me very naughtily – I liked that, but I don't like it when they do it in Rome.

Another time we found a wonderful Armagnac called *Arbellot,* and Tim said he asked me to order it each time because he wanted to watch me saying the 'gn'. I don't always understand English humour.

But at the end of that year Tim decided Europe was not really ready for him, and anyway he was getting much too busy.

2. NUS and COSEC. Tim had talked quite a lot at dinnertimes with the Directors of the NUS in London and so he usually came home quite happy; they asked him to discuss co-operation with a man who used to be at NUS, but he was now running all the Western Europe students at this COSEC office in Holland. His name was Gwyn but he wasn't a girl, just Welsh. We wanted to visit him there but he was always flying all over the shops; we did meet him once in Paris, and another time at the restaurant on top of the Atomium in Brussels, where the food was very good. Tim paid. Tim always paid but the accountants said that was OK and Tim said it was because we were the ones seeking favours so it really was OK. Well, he thought so.

By the end of the year Tim had told the COSEC man, and the NUS people, everything about selling insurances successfully to students and they said it all sounded very good. (Later on, our Robin Yorkshireman told Tim that the NUS President Geoff had described him as 'a benevolent cobra' and I wasn't sure that was a nice thing for an important student president to say, but perhaps they are not very nice people; or else I suppose it was English humour again).

3. Area Managers. At the start I met Max and that other one, Sid.

Max was quite nice, old, like an uncle who you kiss hello but don't much warm to. Sid was simpatico but not like an uncle exactly, more like that man down the road who looks at you, if perchance (I just learnt at my college that word by Ivan Novello) – if perchance at a party you do have to kiss him you stand back quickly, you know?

At Easter when Tim got to meet for the first time the new man Maurice for Birmingham, Max was with him; and I was there when they talked; I noticed that Maurice had already met Sid, with Max, somewhere else. I thought this was a little *sospetoso,* you know, a little worry?

But, all accounts done, Maurice was quite nice: very young, didn't seem to understand much, but very wanting to sell and make a lot of money. He talked a lot to me about cars: Bugatti... Ferrari of course... Maserati... Hispano-Suiza... Especially Hispano-Suiza. He tried to talk with an Italian accent, but then said things in French. I couldn't understand them though my French is good. He didn't mention Fiat.

4. HQ Men. Very soon Tim began to realise that with all his worries, he had to employ some Managers inside the office. I heard Max say to Sid that this was not a good thing, but they didn't say that to Tim, just shook their heads when he wasn't looking.

I asked Tim if I may join in when he was finding all these HQ Men, as my psychology has always been quite good, I have read some books, and people are interesting to me. The meetings were at the flat in Pimlico and you see I was there already. (I am not Jewish but have unlaid my dictionary and cannot find another word. We have jokes about Jewish people saying 'already' all the time, but the only one I like is the Christmas one where the Holy Mother says to the Magi: "The gold is nice but myrrh and frankincense He has already." That is really funny, not just English funny, and I think God would like that, so all the other Jewish should as well).

a) The first HQ Man was Tony. He worked for a big Insurance Company up beyond Cambridge in the marshes and told me he was a Fen Tiger: I think, if I understood correctly, that he lived out in the swamps like in the Pontine Marshes near Rome, and I said he must be careful about the mosquitoes and getting malaria. I still don't know why he laughed, the world is getting hotter. I know those Fens. When I first came to England and was at that Language School in Cambridge near the Catholic Church, we went once for a picnic in long reeds and grasses near a windmill and a big ditch, and we saw a swallow-tail butterfly which everybody got excited about. I told this to Tony but he didn't seem to get at all excited: his big hobby was shooting. I understood this very well because in Italy we have many such shootsmen. Tony said we were bad shooters on the Continent and down in Italy because we shoot everything that moves, including Mussolini. I have been trying to analyse this because I have read books: do you in England shoot politicians who do not move? (I have learnt in English History that it did happen once, but that was back in the time before Horace Nelson I think, because Voltaire wrote about it, no?). I must further explore the crania of the Englishman: did he want to shoot the swallow-tail? More study will be possible because Tim has appointed Tony to manage all the insurances, at the Oxford office where Jerry used to be, which are not Life Assurance. (I must also find out why Insurance is different from Assurance: my dictionary which I have unlaid was stupid on this. Tim says he knows but it will take too long to tell me).

b) The second HQ Man was Ron. He was quite old but simpatico. He said he had been a war prisoner in the East and I asked him sometimes about this, but I felt he was happier not to talk about those things. I understood this from my own uncle who had been captured in Tunis, although he was only a prisoner in Eastleigh, growing cabbages. Ron had then been working, what they call an Inspector, for many years for a big Scottish Life Office (he taught me those words of correct description) as their man in Cambridge; but now he wanted to have the freedom to recommend to his clients the best policy for them, not just the policies of one Company. This was very sensible and showed how thoughtful he was for the people asking for his advice. He was the first one to explain to me that was what a Broker was, I don't think we have them in Italy yet except for big businesses, and I liked him and am grateful to Ron, to this day. Tim wanted him to be in charge of all the back-up (that's a new word, Tim likes me to say 'sostegno', I can only guess why) supporting the Area Managers from Cambridge, especially now that those in the Areas are talking of recruiting young students to be their assistant salesmen. I am asking myself sometimes if this recruitment will escape Tim's hands… Max and Sid, with Maurice, are now very close I think.

c) The last HQ Man was the young man from Yorkshire: Robin who had been a Student President somewhere up there. Yorkshire I cannot understand: it is all over the place. I think there are three real Yorkshires, and a fourth one that doesn't exist except in a book they say – or perhaps on television, it is too complicated. (And there is something curious about the growth of – *rabarbaro* – I wish I could find my dictionary). Tim and sometimes the others would talk about Robin the same way we in Rome talk about the Milanesi, but I didn't think him particularly stupid. He was often very funny, with jokes he made especially for me, and I could properly enjoy them: this was kind and simpatico. I felt that perhaps he needed to be looked after while he did all his advertising. When we ate in a restaurant, and he and Tim were thinking hard about business, he would sometimes –(*pensierosomente*: pensivally, yes?) lick his knife, forgetting where he was and who he was with. I began to carry bandages for him in my handbag, one of those I got in Paris. Robin was to be in charge of all Tim's marketing. He never knew or needed to know where the student address-lists came from, because Tim just gave them to him; but apart from that, we were placing many advertising reply-cards in student handbooks and newspapers all over the country, to be given to the new Freshers when they arrived or at their homes before they travelled to their university. He was kept very busy but he and Tim had much fun, were very close, and laughed a lot, until the end of the year.

5. The debts. These were terrible. Tim had managed to make the Insurers agree, also the Bank, for him to continue; but also these big strong companies were sitting – Yes? No – leaning on him and wanting more security. And this could only happen if he made the business into (I have my dictionary now, it was in the kitchen underneath Signora Beeton – I am learning the English cookery) – into a Limited Company, he must no more continue as a 'sole trader'. I understood the reasons for this, because those Insurers and Bankers were wanting to get back a lot of money. But I went to the Library on Buckingham Palace Road opposite the Air Terminal place

and found out that the Limited Company would want more people to be Directors or Secretaries or so on; and I remembered how his three Area Managers had spoken, and exchanged looks, and I feared that Tim might be – what is your school word – like *'tiranneggiato'* – as your politicians say about your Public Schools – bullied, yes. (But in London I saw many schools as I walked about, and there was much bullying, and it was not Public Schools, so your politicians are not good. I saw Tim's Public School often and it is a very happy place, and has been since 1552.)

6. The Lists: student addresses and names. Here is a thing which I said, which can help Tim very much. I did not ever meet the Doctor Professor that Tim calls Oxon, but I could see the problem. Tim had first found him because of an introduction by his College Tutor, Senior one I think, and I think he over-respected him for that reason. It seemed to me that the facility given by the Oxon man, the access to all the private information, was too much depended upon; and one day I said to Tim: "This old man, this *'sorpassato'*, even if very nice, how important is he? Is there not, now after some years, a better way to get these names from the universities?"

He replied, as I remember: "I need to keep getting the details for other reasons too, and I cannot discuss it." I did not understand this, but perhaps Tim was in some complicated situation, perhaps a blackmail: in Italy we are accustomed to this, and we don't have to go to Sicily to learn about it. So I went on:

"Tell me, are there any other people – *c'est a dire* competitors, for your student insurances?" (Sometimes French comes out automatically when you've been there for a while, as useful go-betwixt, is it not, *nicht war*?) That is a joke because *nicht* – " Tim has told me to shut up, or he will take me to the top of Exhibition Road and I don't want that.

But yes. He told me of another Broker, older than him and working at Lloyd's, who had been sending similar letters to students about Life insurance; but he had not met this man.

I then suggested to Tim that they should indeed meet in case they could make a *collaborazione*, especially if there might soon be official interference from NUS – I do not think he had seriously thought of this. So Tim did go to see this man at Lloyd's and he will tell you about it.

7. Jerry. I never met him, but I am sorry for him because apart from all his terrible faults he must have been a nice man. Not good but nice – I'm sure Tim found him a good friend for all the early years, when the business was growing, and I think he was unfortunate to be carried away mentally by all the money swimming around him, you know? I have read books and I can understand. I think he wanted to be liked, and to be thought more important than he really was: like some Milanesi? When Tim came back to me after his Bank man and Ollie had said he must take over, he was distressed. He had loved Jerry who was, of course, much older, a war-wounded veteran, and very charismatic (*carismatico* – why do all you English put a silly 'h' into so many of your words you take from us? It is an irritation; and you can't spell '*cocodrillo*' either).

But then, Tim suddenly knew that for all those years he had been taken – for a journey? – for a ride. It was a big shock for Tim. *Poco a poco* he had to fight his friend through all the legal negotiations: he would buy the business… He would take over the Company debts… He would arrange a pension for Jerry, paid out of the Company's income… But Jerry must go, completely. No more expenses. This was at last agreed, but only at the last minute when signatures were needed. Tim and Ollie and Simon the lawyer would have to drive, through thick fog, across to the far end of Norfolk where Jerry had gone on a fishing holiday with his son. Even then, at the last scheduled minute of Tim's ultimatum, Jerry pleaded illness and went off to bed. So, cleverly, Tim asked the concierge to book everyone an early call for six o'clock in the morning; and went to Jerry's room at half-past, agreeing to let him keep the Rolls-Royce he was mostly worried about. So eventually it was all signed and sealed over breakfast. And a very nice breakfast too, said Tim to me back at the flat.

He would now be 'an Important Insurance Broker' like Jerry had always claimed to be – but broke, he said. Tim's friend Jeremy came round to help us celebrate and I made spaghetti but Jeremy laughed when I said "Eat them up". He told me it should be "Eat *it* up,"

I had already had that conversation at the Language School, so I won by asking him: "What about baked beans?" Then I said English is much more silly than Italian because wheat and barley and rye and corn are all 'it', but oats are 'they'. He went home quite early.

We opened that cheap and nasty whisky. *Mamma Mia!*

CHAPTER IX

As I hope you will have gathered, despite Olivia's fractured English, I came out of 1963 still in business; and overall with three Area Managers, each of them building a sales team and selling like mad; and three HQ Managers who were – so far as I could tell – devoted to my ideal of a business that was available as a free and independent advisory service to all students.

The company was giving out, as one might have said in those days, 'very good vibrations'. The debts, though they might well have been enough to buy an entire smallish university, were under control, and the Companies happy to accept a long scheme of repayment. One obvious change that ought to have happened fifteen years earlier, was to have separate bank accounts for clients' money – nowadays that would be legally essential. It was beginning to look as if, one day decades ahead, I might actually be that 'Very Important Broker' Jerry used to talk about – certainly if my plan for a shared scheme with NUS came to fruition. But if not?

Olivia had suggested that I might find an alternative approach to students, as a hedge against the risk of my present arrangement drying up, due to negative action by either the NUS or Oxdon. "You told me once," she said, "that another firm is writing about insurance to students everywhere?"

"Yes, but only about Life. I've never met him but he's a Lloyd's Broker I think. We often come across his adverts, in competition; but it's all very gentlemanly, as Lloyd's always seems to be. He's an Oxford man like me, and we've never had to cross swords – "

"Why would you have to do crosswords? *Mamma* –."

"No, no, we don't – er." I gave up on that, but I'll tell you about Olivia and crosswords in a minute.

She waved a finger at me. "Never mind these games you insurance people play – I think it is too much the public school heritage. But, Tim, you must meet and talk with this man. In case you have more Oxdon troubles, it is imperative, no?"

So, halfway through 1964, I did. I met David in the lounge of the Great Western Hotel, Paddington. It happened to be the London rail terminus suitable for both of us and they did good coffee. He had gone down from Lincoln the same year I came up to my college, he being a bit older and a survivor from Bomber Command, into which he had been steered by a malicious stepfather (and his brother into the even more perilous Fleet Air Arm), with an eye on inheritance possibilities, he told me. Apparently, when both had survived against all the odds, David had then made a crash-landing into insurance via other, rather more amenable family connections. We chatted; then:

"Tell me," he said, "Back in 1950 when you started, were you mailing the undergrads at the whole of Oxford?"

"Well yes," I replied, "except – come to think of it – I left out my own college because I was still up, and a bit touchy about being seen as an insurance salesman."

He laughed. "I was new in insurance, too, and when I suggested selling to students, my people asked me to do a test. I chose your college quite by chance and found nobody else in the field, and we got lots of enquiries. If I'd chosen any other, and found you there in strength, I'd have been put off the whole idea."

"So," I suggested, lighting a Stuyvesant, "you owe me a favour."

David put down his coffee-cup, leant back and took a deep drag on his Benson & Hedges. "Say on."

I said nothing at all about the Oxdon connection of course, but told him briefly, without giving away anything vital, how our access to students had lasted for more than ten years but was now at risk. I also said that the NUS may well in future move into the market: maybe on their own, I told him. Was there any viable alternative approach that he knew of?

"Tim, I've always been aware of that risk, so I've never relied on – never even used – your ways to source the names. I've developed an entirely different approach which is foolproof, but – " looking up mischievously as he leant forward to stub out his cigarette, "I'm not going to tell you, as well you must know". He coughed. "God, I wish I could give up these coffin-nails."

"Me too," I said, "I'm on about thirty of them a day."

He looked very superior. "That's nothing," he wheezed, "I'm on – "

"My father," I told him, "says he can't take the risk of giving up, because coughing is the only exercise he gets."

He then trumped me once and for all. "My father, and his father, died of it." I couldn't possibly beat that; but insurance brokers can be very competitive. I sat puffing away, and thinking quickly because I had had an inspiration.

"I'll tell you what, David, let's have a bet." He had started to re-open his packet, but I stopped him; and very ostentatiously I thumped the life out of my own cigarette even though it was still very young.

"That's murder," David exclaimed, staring bewildered at the corpse with its filter tip in the ashtray.

"How about this? The next one to smoke, as from this minute, must pay the other a thousand pounds and open his company's books, including all marketing information."

He grinned at me. He liked that a lot. "Make it five thousand?"

Lloyd's Brokers are, after all, experts in the risk business. But I had to be, too, and I knew that as I was already so deeply in the shit, what the hell. Nevertheless, I told him, I was only a poor provincial insurance man, not at Lloyds like him, so keep it at a thousand.

"Done", and we shook hands on it. We gave both our residual packets to the surprised Hall Porter as we went through the swing door into Praed Street. We took deep breaths of the Paddington air, to prepare our lungs for health.

★ ★ ★

136

I trotted back to the flat, so pleased about the bet that I walked the whole way, still deep-breathing: past the medical students' hostel for St Mary's, awash probably with our leaflets; past Tyburn at Marble Arch where, no doubt, a few hundred years ago I might well have been hanged for my hopeless financial situation; and then in consolation, past that cosy little dining-club The New Yorker at the bottom end of Park Lane but top end of Curzon Street, where, as I've told you, Olivia and I were then quite well-known, and the lederhosed owner Yoji (or however he spelt it) would wander all night between the tables, remorselessly and ungrammatically singing "Thanks Heaven, for little girls", while grinning lecherously at every man's companion to indicate that it wasn't the little ones he was after.

When I got triumphantly back, Olivia found it hard to share my enthusiasm for the deal I had struck.

"It is uncompro.. *Non e... Ma, stupido*," she scolded. "You do such a gamble? You are – " She was searching for the ultimate put-down. She thought she had found it. "You are like schoolboys."

"Absolutely," I said proudly. It didn't go down well.

"This is how we are," I tried to explain. "Anyway," I pleaded, "I can't lose. I've wanted for ages to stop smoking. And if I did lose, my own marketing will hold no secrets as we're likely to be wiped out anyway". I gritted my teeth.

"But I will stop. Now. God knows, I have an incentive."

Olivia frowned. "How do you trust this David?"

All I could do was shrug, tell her "Bo?" and add: "It's just, he's – well– one of us."

There will be some, even after all the recent years of down-sliding, who understand what I meant. But Olivia shook her head bewildered.

"I cannot understand you English so-called businessmen. Your silly trust."

I became rather pompous. "In the insurance business, and certainly in the City and the London Market like Lloyd's, there is an understood standard of ethics, sealed by a handshake and accepted by everybody, and we call it *'uberrima fides'*, which is –"

"*Crotte de bic,*" she exploded, "I am Roman, you don't have to teach me Latin!" But with that I had gained an unexpected bonus point.

"Aha – now you, a Roman, are swearing in French!" I picked up a new packet of Stuyvesant and put it down again.

"Si, I know. I learnt it during my three weeks in Paris. It sounds better than saying it in Italian, it is more staccato, no? But perhaps," she considered with that tilt of the head, "not too bad in English too? Goat-shit? You like?"

I tried it out. Yes, quite expressive and rewarding; but it reminded me of food. That might disgust you, until I explain that I had once found, in Nimes, a wonderful and practically masochistic cheese named *'Crotte du Diable'*, The Devil's Droppings, indeed! (And it's still available, they tell me).

Olivia went on about her distrust of 'utmost good faith', and I again reached for a cigarette, then retracted surreptitiously – this would not be easy.

"How can business be done this way, on trust, on *'fiducia'*," she wondered. "In Italy we must have guarantees – "

"But," I reminded her, "insurance started in Italy. Think of 'The Merchant of Venice'."

She shrugged with the puffed-out cheeks.

"Anyway," I went on unnecessarily, "you've only been a country for about a hundred years, until then like Germany you were all in bits and pieces, so now, many of you have local rather than national loyalties. Locally, surely you have trust – as if within an extended family? Look at Sicily. In the City many of us are like that sort of extended 'family' I think."

She was still shaking her head.

"In Rome," I pressed on, "with all your history, you despise the North for being brash and arriviste: look how you spoke about that manager in Milan: 'Twenty minutes and he said nothing'. Then in the South, you despise them too: you think they are indolent. You call it the *'mezzogiorno'* suggesting they only get up for lunch. You treat it like a sort of Italian Colony: Italian Domaniland?"

I had hurt her feelings, as I now admit. I was merely being shallowly 'clever', and if she is reading this, I apologise, Olivia. I was pretty tense at that time, and besides, I wanted a smoke.

★ ★ ★

Beneath the surface and despite the flowing progress of our sales, there were eddies of discontent. Around Easter 1964, while I was still entangled in negotiations with Jerry and his lawyers, I began to sense that the Area Managers were starting to circle around me, sniffing blood in the changing tide. I had a meeting with the three of them, at our usual Cambridge mid-morning watering-hole, the Kenya Coffee House just below the Pruhaus. (This was my favourite place for a quick break and I used to meet friends there. I remember two of them, each believing he was a reincarnation of Oscar Wilde, and they didn't much like each other. I was sitting chatting to one, when the other came in and said Hello. "Hello, dear boy," said the second one, " what a lovely overcoat with all that fur. I've adored them for years, ever since they were so fashionable.")

Our Area Manager get-together over the coffee went like this:

Me: Business is coming in very well and I'm glad you've managed to service all these enquiries. If you are achieving this by recruiting sub-agents, I need to vet them, and be quite sure they have our loyalty.

Max: Oh yes, to us, absolute loyalty.

Me (to Maurice): Does that apply too, in your case, since you've joined us so recently? Are you settling in?

Maurice: Oh yes, I'm tying in completely. Max and Sid have explained their systems fully. Will we be getting enough enquiries for the Autumn Term?

Me: I understand Robin's got enough Student Handbook inserts booked, as well as our mailshot letters going out as usual.

Sid: This new clerk Robin you're taking on. He was a Union President, wasn't he, somewhere up North? Can you trust him to work for us and not just waste time swanning around the Unions like a failed prima-donna, and waffling? He was in Advertising, last year, yes?

Me: Yes, and I'm sure he's got the right ideas. We get on very –

Max: Tim, forgive me but we must know this: If your war with Jerry turns out successful, I suppose it will just about justify you now taking on at HQ these three Managers –.

Sid: Three clerks.

Max: To do the work you've done yourself for years? But why now?

Maurice: What are they producing, net, for the business? Up there in Nottingham or Birmingham or everywhere, I just sign up students, send down the forms and the cheques; why do you have to have these people at HQ to process them, just one clerk would do.

Me: I'm afraid none of you are showing any understanding at all of the paperwork and my need for back-up at a high level.

Max: We're just worried, Tim. We three are now in complete, or nearly complete, control of all actual business production. We think – .

Me: That brings me on to something else. I, personally, can no longer do the interviewing and selling for Oxford and the Southwest – . Or Wales and Scotland too…

Maurice (very quickly): I can get to places like Bath and Bristol –.

Sid: Anyone can. From Manchester I can fly anywhere in no time…

Max: I would like to know what Tim is getting at.

Me: Max, thank you, I think you are ahead of the pack as so often. I need to look forward. Each of you now has an area crying out to be developed. You mustn't waste your energies by swooping on to other areas and picking off the easy cherries. You must concentrate on your own orchards, and I must go on looking for other Managers for the rest of the country. For a start, I'm now looking for a fourth Area Manager to cover Oxford and the South-West from Reading right across to Bristol and down to Exeter. And beyond, too, because you see, one day there will be Plymouth, they say. There's going to be expansion in all your areas, don't you see?

(long pause)

And all in good time, I intend to make my three HQ Men Directors of the new Company as soon as I've formed it.

(slight sensation and some puffing by all three)

Max (heavily meaningful): I think you need to think this through very carefully, Tim. When this new Company is formed – and I gather the main Insurers are insisting on it – they will want to know there is a secure relationship with us as the actual business producers – .

Me: You, though, have to accept that just calling on students who have already been referred to you after our HQ marketing efforts, gives you a pretty cushy source of income. You three, or four, or five, or whatever, are only one cog in the machine.

Sid: A broken cog will stop the machine.

Me: If the machine stops, for whatever reason, and whichever cog – and we are all just cogs – we could all starve.

Maurice (to me): '*La mejor salsa del mundo*'

Me: Is hunger, yes, but when did you get into Spanish as well as everything else?

Max and Sid, together: Probably still going to night school.

Maurice (ashamed): I can't help reading Cervantes.

Sid: Or perhaps the ODQ?

Me (must control the conversation): Can we talk about Directorships?

(instant attention)

Me: The Companies we owe money to, currently supporting me in a big way, are adamant that all our 'top people' both in the Areas and at HQ level, are Directors. This is, basically, in case I should fall by the wayside.

Sid: You mean die?

Me: Not just that. If I go bankrupt, they want to know the business will continue.

Sid: Why should you go bankrupt but the Company survive?

Me: Well, I've acquired a whole lot of debts and I am also guaranteeing Jerry's pension.

Max: And the Company isn't?

Me: No, I don't think that has been written in – but Ollie our accountant can give you all the details, once you have been appointed.

Sid (to Max): Have you looked into this? (to me) How many Directors are you planning to have?

Me: I reckon there will be nine, your three – four – at present, in the Areas – and the HQ three, plus myself of course, and Ollie our Accountant for the time being, just to steer us through all the formalities.

Sid: Christ, it's like signing up the crowd at the turnstile – "

Max: What about shares?

Me:?

Max: If we are all going to be invited – *if*, I say – to be Directors, we will also, I suppose, be offered shares in the business. This will be our only incentive to stay with you and build.

Me (out of my pathetic depth): Well, yes, I suppose.

That was the one I had been dreading because I hadn't even started to think it through. I said I would get back to them, as Area Managers with an area to exploit and an axe to grind, after I had talked to Ollie. So for the moment I side-stepped it. much as I now needed their full support.

I did note, however, that all of a sudden they appeared to be in favour of a fourth colleague, once I had found him or her. This was out of character, but I think I could decipher why: it would presumably add another vote on their side of the boardroom table, one day soon.

They went back to their Areas, and business continued to flow well.

★ ★ ★

Max and Sid asked me, the following week, if they could very privately meet me for 'a chat'.

I suspected that this was an approach designed in some pseudo-friendly way to establish those two in a senior position relative to all my other intended Directors; and I had been expecting it. But I had to resist, especially at this precarious time. I must try to hold on to my long-term view of the business, and keep as many of the cards in my hand as possible. True, Max and Sid had been with me a little longer than the rest, but, let's be sensible, by next year that predominance would have halved, and in five years' time it would have shrivelled into insignificance. I must not let myself be bullied by this duo who had evidently found solid common ground and would use it.

So I used a bit of devilry of my own. I arranged to meet them for coffee, "I just have an hour", at the 'Brush and Palette' in Bayswater. There was method in this.

Prior to buying in Pimlico I had taken to staying, when in London, at a pleasant small hotel just down from Paddington, called Carlisle House. It was a tall detached building of that typical inner-London wedding cake style, that must have been constructed from materials left over from when they built the more expensive Belgravia; outside, there was a hint of Wedgwood incorporated in blue to the white plastered walls. Several of the letting rooms were occupied long-term by merry old widows, fondly remembering as they drank, sang and decorously danced, the departed husbands who had worked themselves to death to bequeath them this happy and hedonistic old age.

In those days one could park outside, and since I have always had a weakness for wandering city streets, I often explored westwards towards the crummy but intriguing shops along Queensway, most of them now gone in the wake of the Arab take-over of Bayswater. In one of the basements, halfway along, was The Brush and Palette, 'The Artists' Bistro'.

This deliberately seedy establishment claimed to be dedicated to local artistic talent, by which it meant that anybody was welcome to bring their paints and materials in, sit with a coffee and a bun, and work on the stools and at the easels provided, to make full use

– so far as propriety allowed – of whichever attractive girl was currently stretched out naked on the chaise-longue. Where the proprietor found these luscious models was a dark secret, but night-time Bayswater was itself very much a dark secret, popular in the Sixties and not just for the coffees and buns…

I had suspected rightly, that neither the middle-aged family man Max, nor the East London oriented Sid, would know of this intriguing place in an area of town that was likely to be foreign to both of them. So I got there twenty minutes early, around opening-time and chose a table only a few feet away from the charming girl, who was sensibly reclining underneath a warm blanket, "before the balloon goes up," as she put it.

I bought her a coffee and, in fact, two buns, which struck me as appropriate. I asked her to do me a favour, when my friends turned up, by smiling at them invitingly while fully exposed. I then sat down with my back to her…

Max and Sid came down the stairs just a little hesitantly. They had to sit opposite me, and I told them I hadn't much time, but what was it they wanted to talk about…

I never did find out. It was a very satisfactory meeting, all things considered.

★ ★ ★

Next I had to come to terms with the rest of them. Olivia having pre-empted me, you probably know as much now about my three HQ Men as I did myself at that stage. But it is worth reporting the basics of a meeting I had with them one morning at the flat in Pimlico, Olivia making the coffee, in the early Summer.

Me: Our Insurance Companies are insisting that we must become a Limited Company.

Ron: That makes sense.

Me: And that each sector –

Robin: Maurice would call it a '*tranche*'.

Me: – will have to have one of the Directors heading it.

Tony: Do we have to have all this bureaucracy? I just want to get on with the job.

Me: And so you shall, Tony. You'll be over in Oxford in complete charge of everything non-Life, just as important.

(I pointed out to him that our good old Belongings Scheme – his responsibility – was still the best possible lead-in to higher – er, different, er, more profitable – matters like Life, upon which we were all dependent for our livelihood. He nodded and shut up, to the extent that he soon apparently fell asleep. He often did this but it was an act, as he was always fully briefed afterwards on every conversation).

Ron: What are your plans for the Area Managers as regards directorships? Surely they are entirely self-employed, so they don't have any real loyalty to us, just a dependence on us for the leads?

Me: I take the point, but for the very reason they're self-employed, we need to tie them to us. So long as I – well, you all – can continue supplying all the leads they need – .

Robin: Tim, you've got this mysterious source which brings us all the names; maybe one day you'll reveal it to us. But as you know, you're also asking me to attract many more enquiries by placing all these ads and, more to the point, inserts and reply-cards in student publications all over the place. Aren't we duplicating?

Me: Yes Robin, your work is our insurance against us losing my source. We can leave it at that.

Ron: Really, Tim, how can we just 'leave it at that'? I've come to you from a big Company where I'd been their local Inspector for ten years. I'm not a youngster any more and I've a family to support. When you took me on, there was this flow of leads and that meant security, but now you aren't doing them yourself and we're becoming dependent on three unreliable self-employed –

Robin: Four, I think.

Me: The number doesn't matter –

Ron: I'm reliant on them, and now apparently on assistants they are employing, chosen entirely by them and I don't even get to meet them. I just don't feel my duties are –

Me: I intend to tell all Area Managers that if they want to stay with us, you, Ron, have to be involved in the approval and appointment of all the salesmen they want to take on.

Robin: They're not going to agree to that. They all want to build their own little empire.

Me: Is that entirely a bad thing, if they are Directors and tied to us?

Olivia (entering with coffee and biscuits): "The cat is brooding… " (General bewilderment).

All: What??

Me: This is going to take some time. We don't have a cat – .

Olivia: In Italy we say that, we say: '*gatta ci cova*'. You say, I think: 'something is cooking', no? My meaning is, there will be trouble with the beginning of your Limited Company. (Exit)

★ ★ ★

We sat and drank our coffee in an air of impending gloom; but then, in the traditional English upper-lip fashion we went round the corner to my friend Jeremy's restaurant 'Grumbles', and found ourselves very soon revived. I remember there was an E-type Jaguar parked outside and a very good-looking girl smiled at us – from the driving-seat, I noted approvingly. Life wasn't all that bad.

I have always been amazed, especially in those crisis-ridden days, how resilient people can be when everything is going wrong and disaster threatens. I'm sure this must be uniquely English, to "play your ukulele as the ship goes down". In all our meetings over the years I am describing, when many of my assumed colleagues were actively wishing to destroy me and my business, our talks still involved joking, banter, and sheer hilarity. I recall it with astonishment but it's all there in the minutes.

Amidst all this hysteria, I was concerned about Ron. Older than the rest of us, he had already told me of his anxieties, after taking the risk of leaving his secure job to join us in the unknown. But he was by far the most experienced of us all, and had proved extremely useful in introducing us to new Insurers whom he knew so well; also, to a new Bank which had already proved more helpful than Mr Perkins's bosses.

In short, Ron's presence had given the company – what can I call it? – not exactly 'respectability' because I think we had that, but I suppose a sort of 'authenticity' by comparison with certain upstart brokerages beginning to sniff at the 'youth market'. We were now getting some quite substantial help with our marketing costs, mainly from various Scottish Life Offices where, to my surprise, I sometimes found myself lunching with their Directors all around George Street. But Ron, though still on the surface solid as a rock, was now starting to show signs of lack of drive. I remember, one Saturday when the two of us were catching up on a backlog in the Cambridge office, he looked up from a heap of papers and said: "D'you know, Tim, I think I must be losing my – er – my – er – "

"Memory?" I suggested.

He was grateful. "That's it," he nodded.

I only hoped, remembering his prisoner-of-war experiences in the Far East, that his health and concentration would hold out for a few more years.

★ ★ ★

At the other extreme I was drawn more and more into reliance upon Robin and Olivia as my sounding-board, much as I dreaded trying to define the word to her. (I need not have worried: only now have I found it in the old dictionary she left behind). In fact Olivia was greatly improving her English, and her School had urged her to go to the theatre and cinema to polish up the vernacular. Unfortunately she made the mistake of going to see 'Oblomov' just when Spike Milligan was horsing around with it, which resulted in 'Son of Oblomov' and understandably she couldn't make head or tail of it. Nor did she get far with 'The Bedsitting Room', which she sadly thought would somehow be relevant to our Pimlico house and its six bed-sitters. I had to bring her down to earth, so we caught up with 'Oliver' (wonderful on stage for its changing sets and the kids); 'West Side Story' which she loved (women always do) but I positively hated (making heroics out of unpleasant bad behaviour – was I just getting old?); and best of all, 'My Fair Lady'. I had already seen it in its earliest days in the West End, when it arrived cast-and-all from the States. The curtain going up at the start of Act Two upon that sensational black-and-white Ascot Opening Day caused a gasp; and then the chorus with its perfect satirical upper-class treatment of the words: "Ev-ry Duke and Earl and Pe-er is he-re".

Lovely, and really a sort of in-joke, and I think under-appreciated by reviewers. It is almost retained in the film, too. I so admired Alan Jay Lerner: he got right inside the British character. (Look at his lyrics for Eliza in "Just you wait, 'Enry 'Iggins" – spot on). I would love to have met him, and I glow vicariously in the fact that I have since met one of his wives. She was nice, too.

It is easy to overlook the subtle timing of words-and-music in many of the 1950s musicals. Richard Rodgers (I suppose it was his idea?) is particularly good with irritated women: in 'Oklahoma', Laurey's 'Many a New Day' doubles-up the backing rhythm so that you can hear her tutting and tossing her head; and in 'South Pacific', Nellie washes her hair with a dismissive abrupt final off-beat on the first two lines. It must feel great to create atmosphere like that.

Being Italian, Olivia was also quite keen on opera, which appeals to me only when a good tune comes along, so I'm OK with – for instance – much of Verdi. She told me, one day, that she had been listening to 'The Incredible Tangerine'. I let it go, I didn't think Bartok would mind.

Staying for the moment with Olivia: when she and I were walking back from Grumbles, the others having headed off to their offices, she came out suddenly with this: "Do you notice, how different people are when they drink?"

"When they've been drinking, yes," I said, underlining 'been'; but she didn't mean that. I had to admit that I seldom wasted my time looking at my pub companions through the bottom of my glass.

"It is interesting. Now, Robin drinks in big mouthfuls so it goes fast." This I had noticed. "And he sometimes makes a noise like – like that machine in the new film we saw."

Only a woman would expect her man to know what she was talking about. I waited.

"With Virna Lisi and that man you like. A cartoonist."

"Ah. 'How to murder your wife'. Jack Lemmon. The gloppitta-gloppitta machine." Yes, I had to admit there was a resemblance, especially with the full pint mugs.

"And then," she went on, "Tony drinks much more slowly in little sips, but when he puts the glass down, if it is a wine-glass, he dips a finger in and rubs the – *come si dice* – "

"The rim. Yes, I've seen that."

"Si, the rim with his finger trying to make it sing. But Ron –."

"Ron doesn't drink."

She was surprised. "Not at all?"

"He's the only secret non-drinker I know. He tries to conceal it because everybody else in insurance drinks like a fish."

"*Momento*," she held up a hand. "How d'you know fish drink?" I didn't; but luckily we avoided an argument about it. "Tea," she said.

"Fish drink tea?" Idiotically I reflected that there was a fish called a char. We were going to be in dictionary trouble soon…

"Ron drinks tea, I am saying; and when he does, and stirs it because of the milk and the sugar, he finishes stirring by tapping his spoon on the cup. Every time. Always four taps. Is it not funny?"

I found myself after that, surreptitiously watching my own drinking behaviour and everyone else's. I was astonished how ridiculously repetitive we all are. Putting his glass down, Max would set it always in the exact same spot. Sid would wipe his mouth with his sleeve. Maurice would hold the glass in his right hand, then move it to his left, then put it down… I'm not going to tell you what I did, it's just too stupid. But anyway, if my colleagues go no weirder than that, I told myself, the Company probably has a future. This future was due to be launched at the end of the year, and it was preceded by an uncomfortable 'Board Meeting' for want of a better phrase since there was no Board at the moment, simply a motley crowd of Managers who were 'wannabe' Directors, in two mutually opposed groups. This would not be easy.

★ ★ ★

We met in September just before the start of the Academic Year. A number of new universities were coming into operation, and as it happened none of them (East Anglia outside Norwich; Kent at Canterbury; grim Stirling; Strathclyde hidden within the dark streets of central Glasgow), none at all were located in one of our Areas. This meant, as was already the case with many other places, the required sales visits were in my gift. Nobody had ever made any reference to this, and I far preferred to leave it open because it might give me a useful bargaining card to play one Manager against another.

By now, all the preparatory work for forming the new Company had been drawn up, and we were ready to go; nobody was entirely satisfied with his lot, but we all knew that our creditors demanded a united front, and we all therefore had to comply. The meeting was attended by Ollie who had with him a handful of boring documents which turned out to be the forms for Share Allotment which I had to sign and pass to everybody.

"I understand," Ollie began, "that you all have an interest in buying a shareholding, which is essential if you're going to be a Director. You will have agreed, or at any rate you will now be agreeing, with Tim, the price you're paying him for your allotment."

Various murmurs, within which somebody with a Holloway Road accent said "Tuppence".

"I myself," he went on, "am taking just one share 'ex officio' so that it will really be held by my company, which your creditors have requested."

Max was paying the closest attention to all this; Tony was dozing in his corner. "Are the creditor companies taking shares?" Max asked, and Ollie shook his head.

150

"They don't want to be seen as intruding upon you as independent Brokers, which I think is pretty fair of them." It was sensible, too. No good comes from an Insurer owning a Broker. Client trust soon evaporates.

"I'll just clarify what I'm told you've agreed about the division of the firm and what the shareholdings will be"; and here he, and I suspect the rest of them, drew a deep breath. Me? I had given up breathing, along with giving up my Company.

"Each Area Manager is to have ten per cent. It being capitalised at a hundred thousand – "

"What?" Sid was astounded. "It's not worth ten!"

Ollie frowned at him. "The creditors think ten thousand would not be enough – "

"I mean ten," said Sid. "Ten quid, top side."

Ollie went back to deep breathing, while the rest of them stirred in our chairs. We'd been through all this. I stepped in.

"Sid, we all know that at this moment I couldn't sell up for much spot-on cash. But, one: we have goodwill and prospects; and more to the point, two: the firms we owe all the money to, want to fix the capital at a hundred thousand. It's all a matter of looking ahead. Reputation comes into it, too."

"I'll talk to you later," said Sid, "about what I'm prepared to pay per share."

"Of course you will," said Ollie. "You all will."

But Sid still wasn't very happy. "How about this new Area Man you're planning to appoint. What will he get when you find him, the same ten per cent. If so, why?"

I was getting fed up with this. "I have, in fact, already found him. An Oxford graduate with a very good Law degree in Business Studies. He starts next month and if you've got any more problems you may care to consult him."

I enjoyed saying it but it caused considerable disturbance. Max and Sid, with Maurice huffing in the rear, exploded that they had not been taken into my confidence: surely this new man would be their associate and they ought to have found him themselves, or anyway been consulted, or at least met the fellow to size him up? The HQ men, whom I had in fact consulted, sat rather quietly. As for myself, I had reckoned I could do with a manager who would be an innocent friend, not least a lawyer.

When they had settled down, Max asked: "This new man we're supposed to get pally with, what's he like?"

"Mid-twenties. Shortish, slim, curly hair, neat and tidy, that sort of thing."

"Fotheringay-Thomas," said Maurice.

"Is he married?"

"Don't think so. but he's still quite – "

"Lives with his mother?"

"I've no idea, but yes probably," I said, seeing which way this was going "But – "

Sid looked round at the other Area Managers. "Sounds to me like a bloody fairy." Which didn't help.

Ollie coughed a bit, understandably for a domesticated provincial accountant, then went on: "And each HQ Director will have five per cent, so that – "

"So that Tim has lost control," said Sid rather too quickly. He hadn't wasted any time doing his sums, I noted.

"Only," Ollie responded just as quickly "if nearly all of you so decide. And that is how all your creditors want it to be."

Max had been looking increasingly thoughtful. "When you say 'all our creditors' can you be more specific? I think we would all like a full breakdown of these debts, so we can see how they divide between the premium shortfall, the agreements for taking over from Jerry, and anything else."

Ollie looked puzzled. "Surely you've had all this in writing? But OK, I'll make sure you have a full statement again."

It had been a long meeting and Ollie began to gather up his papers, glancing once or twice at Sid and at his watch..

"Now," he ended, "you have the Allotment forms. The quantities have been written in, all that remains is for you to enter the agreed purchase price so that I can register the transfers. Post them back to me. I'll see you all here to tie things up in November as we've agreed."

"Poppy Day," said Ron. Ah, yes, that will be nice.

★ ★ ★

After his first meeting with the other three Area Managers, which they arranged privately and I only heard about later, my new man Edward, who would be looking after everything South-west of Oxford and Reading, and including Southampton (oh, Sarah!) asked me some searching questions, which I was of course expecting. Little Edward was a freshly-trained lawyer and it showed.

"If I am buying into your business," he said, "and with your recent experiences you have such a vast amount of debt, what exactly will I be buying?"

I went over, once again, the renewal income, the goodwill, the ongoing university relationship, the background support and advertising help from top Insurers. He would have sole agency for us in the whole of his vast and well-heeled area; not just current students, but those who are now graduates and want to extend their policies. I made it sound pretty good.

"Suppose you lose the student connection?"

"First – we can't. We may get competitors, but every business expects that to come along. We'll still have a share of the market and of course the existing clients. It's a big country, Edward, and you are buying a big chunk of it."

He nodded. "I appreciate what you're offering, and incidentally I'm very grateful that you're slotting me in as a Manager alongside the others. I sense that the other three resent this and I found them rather hostile when we met. I suppose that's natural and it doesn't bother me; but it might bother you." He laughed: "As you progress and keep expanding, you'll get this reaction every time you create a new Area, and I suppose I'll be in there complaining with the rest of them."

He stopped. But then: "I'm sorry Tim, but I can't stand Sid."

I didn't want this to develop and tried to say conciliatory things.

"No," he said firmly. "He has a malevolent streak. Bad thoughts fester in his head – he's just saprogenic… "

I pretended to know what he was on about, and nodded mutely, and looked it up when I got home. He was probably right.

But it was on another occasion that he described to me some wild statements that Sid made. "They are simply proctogenetic", he told me, and when I looked that one up, it delighted me.

★ ★ ★

As you know, I was now very close to Robin and we used sometimes to visit colleges together, to acquire new outlets or new lists from those minor establishments which were beneath Oxdon's dignity. We had some interesting encounters in these lesser places. At one South London college we had been received very enthusiastically by the black Union Treasurer, who was new to the job and clearly enjoying his position. However, the Union President, himself from a somewhat superior African country, was jealous of his own standing. We said: "Yes, but your treasurer, I believe from an emerging country – "

"He's not emerging in *my* union," the President said.

★ ★ ★

In view of his closeness to the people at NUS, I had asked Robin to keep his ear to the ground, (the phrase delighted Olivia), and report back when he had any news. We met up one evening at The Pheasantry on King's Road, and I also brought along as a companion for Robin, a very pleasant girl whom I had dated in the past after finding her in the window of Peter Jones – it's too long a story.

Supper was convivial, and after it, when asked if we wanted coffee, we decided to drive to Heathrow for it; they tell me it was a fashionable thing to do at that time and they may well be right. There was a thick fog and when we got there we found the airport closed.

God knows whose idea it was, but with that strange midnight logic which can follow a good dinner we all agreed to move on, not to the next coffee-place but to the next airport. Still in a swirling mist, we found Gatwick at about three a.m., also closed. We came to our senses and crawled home.

In the course of all this Robin told me: "I hear the NUS have made full use of all your ideas and are advertising for somebody to build their own Brokerage. I don't think it will include you."

In my crowded head I now had a new fog that was all my own.

CHAPTER X

I drove into town on Poppy Day 1964, you may remember, much as a miscreant bishop might have gone to the stake: fairly sure of a future of some sort, but uncertain how his good intentions were going to be reconciled with his poor performance. And was it going to hurt, getting there?

Once down the long curved slope into the Pruhaus car park, I had to wriggle into the space only just allowed me by Maurice's Mark VII Jaguar. For God's sake, would the silly man never listen? I had already had embarrassing feedback from more than one Midlands Union, on meeting the President at Western Bank in Sheffield, and also during a long evening at Hugh Stewart Hall in Nottingham, that his lifestyle was causing comment (a very recent graduate, a car so expensive, there must be lots of money in this insurance business), and I feared that if it filtered back to the NUS in London they might be further encouraged to proceed on their own. Now, it appeared from Robin's report, this was happening. It was also astonishing the speed at which these universities were growing: when I first visited Nottingham University with Sarah and her lovely handwriting, their Student Union office had been no more than a single room with a card-index in the bowels of the main building; now, for Heaven's sake, they had the enormous Portland Building all to themselves, perched above the lake, and about the size of the main University Headquarters. Student power, eh?

Next to me on the other side was a Morris Minor. That would be Edward? I looked inside at scattered leaflets about not SLAS but rain forests. Ah, yes, Edward. Tony had driven over from Oxford as well. There were some feathers on his back seat. He was now ensconced at Jerry's old offices on the George Street corner, and handling all our non-Life business which was fed to him by the Area Managers, as well as supervising all the Accounts. He had turned out to equal the ever-reliable Ron in quiet efficiency, but was scared stiff of Miss Robey, I was sure.

She had been there for years as Accounts Manager, a big square owl of a woman. In the corner of her upstairs domain, she had built herself a nest of big squared paper, all covered in sums and scribbles that only she understood. She lived with a lesser owl called Patsy, in the woods somewhere in Berkshire. She rarely spoke but, when alone, could be heard hooting to herself in a muffled baritone. I often wondered why Tony had never shot her. After all, he was a devotee of wading out into swamps and brambles and blazing away: he had grown up in the Fens and nothing was safe. Once, in happier days, when he had fallen asleep during a management meeting, the rest of us had sneaked down to fix in his rear window a sticker, designed in-house, which read: "Help Stamp Out Wild Life". They say he didn't notice it for weeks.

I have always been an aficionado of the rare truly-witty car window sticker, but there are only two I classify in the Premier League. At Miami Airport in 1985 I found and brought home the ultimate American response: "Don't tell me what kind of day to have"; and in a supermarket park recently, on a dilapidated Transit van that one would have expected a real beard-and-sandals God-botherer to drive, was this delight: "Jesus loves you – the rest of us think you're an arsehole". Some things still make life worthwhile, what's left of it.

Up in the lift, along the corridor past all those forlorn one-man businesses quietly fading away, I puffed into my offices where I was greeted, as ever, by my secretary and PA, Rosemary. She had in her hand the latest Resident Members List which must have just arrived from Heffers, the publishers down the road. It was strange that Cambridge was so ready (Oxford too) to make their student list openly available while all the others treated it with such idiotic secrecy. Nevertheless, of course, that reticence made our unique position all the more rewarding, thanks to the good Doctor. (Cambridge was really a bit blasé: a few years back I had happened to spot that one college's list of their Fresher intake, while of the correct total number of entrants, only ran from A to L, which didn't say much for their entry selection procedures!).

Incidentally, talking about lists of names, across the alphabet, have you ever noticed how nearly all the 'Mac' surnames are in the first half? In the local phonebook I found 122 from A to M, and then from N onwards only 17. Odd. But anyway…

I greeted Maurice who was thumbing through his commission statements; Edward, reading the Guardian; and Tony, who was drinking a fruit juice, and discussing with Rosemary the details of a complicated Universities' Expedition to the Antarctic to remap the entire area: would we insure it and include the maps? (Yes, we got the business via Scott Polar Research, up by the Catholic Church. One of the party was a friend of mine, who had the distinction of being proposed to by a penguin. He had made a fuss of the bird for some days and eventually it toddled up and placed a round stone at his feet, which is what they do. What sex it was, I never knew, and knowing Joe I didn't ask).

I took a phone call from Ollie, who was on his way. Bad news: they had found another Insurer we owed two months' arrears. Going back to my chair I saw that Tony was running his finger around the rim of his glass…

I took another call, from the Bank this time. Not good: they were just giving me a reminder that they would require all Directors to sign the joint-and-several guarantee. My three HQ men already had, but how the hell could I put that over to the Area Managers?

On cue, Max and Sid came in. I imagined they had met up in the car park, but maybe they had travelled here together, plotting something? Without Maurice though? I watched: they greeted him cordially enough, and threw a cool nod to Edward who looked up from his paper only for a moment. On the matter of joining in with that bank guarantee, how could I handle it – perhaps get Edward to sign, then they would feel – what? An obligation? Anger? A decision to chuck the whole thing and 'go it alone' more likely? Or demand a big reduction in the cost of their shares...

Ron bustled in from his office with an armful of files he needed to check with the four AMs, adding a strained smile to the rest of us. I wanted to get on with the so-to-speak 'Board Meeting' part of the day, but where was Robin? Then I remembered he had a meeting earlier in the day – must have been at dawn, I thought – down in Essex. Well, we must start without him, though I always felt our meetings were a bit flat when he wasn't there with constant wit and good humour. Among his habits was to arrive out of the blue, singing his own version of a popular song; and this time I wouldn't be disappointed.

But I asked poor overloaded Ron to defer his talks (about difficult Life proposals, but also, I was pleased to hear, about the assistants being recruited by the AMs – following my insistence that he should be involved at all times). I want to make this a short Meeting, I told them, there isn't a lot to get through –

"Bank guarantees," said Sid, "are quite a lot."

"Yes, of course; but there's not much else. Ollie will be here soon; and if none of you have experienced our Cambridge Poppy Day, it's time you did."

A silence, while the AMs looked at one another and the HQs shifted uneasily... The tap was dripping in the kitchenette and I found I was counting the drips.

"Where's your young clerk Robin, anyway?" asked Sid. "Is he too junior to attend grown-up Board Meetings?"

"He's going to be late," I told them. "He has been at an important marketing meeting down in Dagenham."

"Dagenham?" everyone echoed: it was so unlikely. So un-university.

I explained: "There's a publisher down there, who specialises in student newspapers and Robin is booking inserts in student papers for you in the Spring Term."

I then had to take a deep breath, again. About the Bank joint-and-several guarantee. The thing was, if the bank is going to support us, and frankly they've got to, they must have that security. It was only natural. Moreover, all our Insurers, not only accepting a long-term settlement of the overdue premiums, but giving us substantial grants towards our advertising costs, needed to know that those guarantees were in force: to show them we all were working together whole-heartedly as a team. I looked round at them all, hoping they didn't realise that the last part of my harangue had been sarcastic.

Max had met Hugh with me, a few weeks ago, at their country offices in Kent. He asked: "Does Hugh insist that we go on giving him the greater part of the business?"

I said that we really were expected to, since we now owed them so much.

Max held a hand up, I thought sadly. "Tim, that won't do any more. No matter how good their schemes are now, SLAS and so on, if any of us," he looked around at everyone and especially the HQ men, "are to put big money and our futures into this, we must be completely free to switch Insurers." I knew he was right – we were Brokers; but while I was searching for a suitable reply, Rosemary came in. "Is Robin here yet, there's a call."

"He's in Dagenham."

"Dagenham?" said Rosemary.

"Yes" said Sid. "He's having an insert in one of the local Pipers."

★ ★ ★

The general mirth did much to ease the tension; but Max returned to the subject.

"We all know the huge extent of debt. You may claim that the firm's goodwill can cover it; but what if we lose part of the market?"

Sid added: "And how about the current expenses. What have you been building in Europe? Shouldn't you and your Olivia stop fucking about across the Channel if you'll pardon the expression?"

"No," Maurice put in, he who had Languages and ambitions. "I think Tim's quite right to look into Europe. It could be enormous – "

"This is up to Tim," said Max reasonably. Sid was shaking his head, and I took a quick look at my HQ Men. Tony was dozing off and Ron said that any expansion was OK so long as we didn't lose contact with all the Unions over here; we had to keep getting their lists; he saw our UK Union connection as my main strength and the chief contribution I could make in the future, once all Areas had been covered. I was grateful to him, older and wiser than most of us in the room.

"No," said Sid, "you should stop all this farting about on the Continent."

"But – " Maurice began.

"All right," Sid went on, "why don't you and him and Olivia bugger off out there and stay there, you can insure Mark VII Jaguars against damage from falling coconuts."

This made me laugh a bit, from sheer desperation. Maurice looked across at me. "*Je ris pour ne pas pleurer,*" I told him, and to give him his due he smiled and nodded. I felt that a bond was established: perhaps him and Edward…?

"These meetings," said Tony suddenly, "Are becoming a bloody silly waste of time. I've got an office to run. You're the ones with your eyes shut."

At that moment the door burst open and in came Robin, loudly singing his version of Nat King Cole:

Robin: "When I fall downstairs.."

All: "… it will be completely."

It is a terrible judgment of small-business people in Britain, or maybe our salvation, that these sudden outbreaks of utterly inappropriate hilarity at times of extreme crisis are my most vivid memories of that – and so many other – fraught meetings.

★ ★ ★

The great redeeming quality of Robin had always been his exuberance. Mind you, he was a Yorkshireman, from the Rhubarb Triangle. His bonhomie was verging on the aggressive, and this was

161

due either to that provenance or to his Student Union Presidential debating experience. Also contributory, as he himself was keen to confess, were the other experiences derived from his mighty position at the head of a large Union.

He was fond of telling us about the two young Fresher girls: "I love our new President – doesn't he dress well?" – "Yes, and so quickly."

What is it about Yorkshiremen? I noted quite early, when we met in Bloomsbury, that he was completely impervious to other people's alternative opinions: he knew what he knew, and he had that strange physical impairment common to Yorkshiremen – when they open their mouths, their ears close up. It isn't exactly arrogance because I think they themselves recognise the weakness; but it sometimes makes the rest of us antagonistic. I remember when the TV celebrity Michael Parkinson underwent – and incessantly bragged about – his vasectomy, I wrote to a newspaper congratulating him on his decision/incision and expressed the hope that it would serve as an example to Yorkshiremen everywhere. They didn't print it.

The only time I was able to puncture this over-confidence had been a couple of months earlier, when Robin was booking a full-page advert. for 'Young Professionals' to apply for our 'Complete Plan' SLAS super-scheme, in Heseltine's splendid old 'About Town' magazine, that issue with the superb picture on its cover of the young Sarah Miles when she was delicious in tight jeans and before she went potty, and started drinking her own urine... His ad. was L-shaped and carried a message about how everybody was getting the good news about our Scheme. The main caption, big and bold, would be: "All over the country, people are Learning" – inside a big 'L'. I just happened to come back from holiday somewhere or other, and took a quick look at the proof, luckily early on the morning he finally had to OK it...

... It is amazing how proof-readers so often ignore the big headlines. The general sales text was fine, well-presented, nicely spaced, good wording, neatly argued... The caption told a million eager readers: "All over the country, people are Leering". Robin never quite forgave me for spotting it at the last moment after all his editing. But…

… But, whatever sort of typesetter at a national magazine could have happily set those words without exercising basic human common-sense to query them? And even at our most sober national daily broadsheets, are there no intelligent sub-editors any more? One finds absurd mistakes or oversights, almost every issue.

★ ★ ★

Robin's arrival encouraged us to take a coffee-break, so we all trooped down to the favourite mid-morning watering-hole, the Kenya Coffee-house practically next-door to the Pruhaus as you will remember. We talked about this and that, and the various Poppy Day events that were waiting to be explored, including a spectacular 'battle' on the Cam between rival college 'galleons', each one built on a four-punt chassis for the occasion. This was another good excuse for cutting the meeting short, I realised with some relief. But I heard a sort of quiet gasp.

A really beautiful-looking girl had come into the cafe and was standing at the counter with a sandwich in her hand. Tall, darkish, willowy, endless legs. I knew her, as most locals did, by reputation.

Sid was the main gasper. "Cor!" he said, his eyes popping out. "Look at that."

"Yes, I know," I told him. "Gorgeous. She works in a shop down the road. But unfortunately she's got the most awful speaking voice."

"Cor!" he repeated. "Who wants to *talk* to her?!"

I addressed myself to the other six, who seemed not much less carried away.

"Funnily enough," I reminisced, "the only other time I've seen a girl quite so immaculately good to look at, was when I was at school."

I sensed a general leaning-in. Even Ron stopped tapping his tea cup, after the obligatory four times.

"My final year, just after the war ended, all the old teachers were coming back with their limps; but one – quite old, well certainly more than middle-aged – came back with more than that. He had rescued a luscious young woman, really, really desirable, a member of a famous musical family, from Vienna or Salzburg or somewhere, smuggled her out and married her. He came back to our boarding-house and she came with him. She was absolutely divine, and we all fell in love." I looked across at Edward, who knew his musicians. "She was a Wolf-Ferrari."

"I bet she was," growled Sid, dreamily.

★ ★ ★

Back upstairs, Ollie was waiting for us. He had all the Share Certificates with him, and handed them out so that I saw my business and the hard-fought ownership of it falling away minute by minute. There was nothing I could do about it: I would be left with about 40 per cent of the company, but – it seemed – nearly 100 per cent of the overall debt. Ollie would await our instructions about the price paid for each person's shares.

This had to be decided between me and the AMs individually, the share price being dependent upon the extent to which each of them would agree to support the Bank guarantee. It was a complicated matter and would take time. I had calculated my offer price with some reference to their length of time with me, though clearly this would dissolve as the years went by. The main problem was Maurice, insisting that his price should be no more than Max's and Sid's. I felt I could not honestly agree this. I was tempted to impose a surcharge on the price because he had so badly endangered our interests in the Midlands through his 'bragadaccio' around the Unions and Halls (and oh! how I longed to use the word to him!), but he insisted on deferring his decision so we eventually shelved the matter as we left the office, planning to have a chat over lunch one day soon in that nice hotel in Henley-in-Arden.

I now remember sparing a thought for Jerry, no matter that he had blatantly taken advantage of my youthful over-enthusiasms and sold me down the river. After all, he had given birth to the business and now, in the retirement I had enforced, his child had been taken away, put into care, and was about to be taken over by strangers: not so much adopted, I reckoned, as kidnapped. I suddenly realised that he had never, not even once, met any of my colleagues.

It was sad.

We all dispersed in various directions, wending our ways through all the Poppy Day activities. I didn't stay with any of them, I felt deflated. I had signed away control. I decided to walk down Petty Cury to have a look at the proofs of our adverts for the Easter Term, prepared by Robin in his makeshift 'marketing office' which we were temporarily occupying in the bleak abandoned lounge, still nicotine-stained, of the old condemned Lion Hotel (soon to be the Public Library). I think we were paying about five pounds a week for it... There he employed three bumbling but charming elderly ladies – elderly is an understatement – the arsenic-and-old-lace-brigade I would call them – to process all his circulars: the envelope addressing, from our lists, the folding, the stuffing, the sealing and stamping...

From our lists...? Wait a minute! I walked a bit faster.

They were all away at lunch. As I went to open the door, I heard a shot.

Robin was lying on the floor.

Across the room, there was a zebra.

It put down the gun and took its head off.

"I told you to stay away from The Lion," said Matt.

★ ★ ★

There are a few things I haven't told you. Maybe now is the time.

MESOLOGUE

Yes, you're quite right – I could have told you everything as it occurred; but those last two years had been so complicated. With worries flooding in under every door, I had a job stemming it in all directions and learning to dodge being swamped or washed away. Anyway, I only slightly bent the facts…

… When I said the postcards from Matt had stopped, way back, around 1950 with that last one from Fiji or Marseilles or wherever, that was perfectly true.

But out of the blue and to my great surprise, and – I must confess – pride, I received twelve years later, when first starting the European explorings, not a postcard this time but a very persuasive letter, typewritten on official COSEC paper and posted from Leiden where Gwyn, our contact was based. (By now we were all aware of the 'Communist threat': missiles were about to be shipped to Cuba). It was only natural that I would comply, particularly as I remembered our background, on the high seas years ago.

My Dear Tim

It will surprise you to hear from me. A colleague has told me about the great success in building your student business, and as you know that is also our sphere, here at COSEC. The West needs your help.

It is vital for the security of our Free World, as you will surely appreciate, that we are aware of any subversive activities at the universities. To the best of our knowledge (and we have researched this at COSEC) yours is the only privately-run organisation, quite independent of all Student Union or Academically-controlled connections, which operates at all UK universities and has access to the private details of individual students. We also know that you are planning to extend your scope to certain other SUs in Western Europe.

We need to know, at certain places and times, the names of student leaders, both those in office and – more important – planning to stand for office, at the earliest possible stage. But only the leaders and only at those places and times. Please be sure to give, in detail, such persons' political alignment: you can obtain this by a study of their local student newspaper, and on noticeboards around their campus; and also by contacting all the SU political societies perhaps under cover of booking advertising.

We prefer not to seek such information from the SUs themselves and I am sure you will understand why, when the Left is so entrenched. Nor from the NUS centrally, for much the same reason. As you will know, there is infiltration everywhere and we must counter it. It seems clear to us that all the data can best be elucidated in the course of your casual conversations when you meet potential clients, thus we consider your insurance interviews ideal for our purposes.

Tim, my intention is to send you, at such times, simply the name of a University in which we have an interest; and the address of a local Post Office. We would like you, within a month from receipt of the message, to compile all the information you can, and leave it in a sealed envelope addressed simply to 'Mr Benson' at the specified Poste Restante. Please do not make any attempt to identify the collector of the envelope as this could be any one of different agents whose safety you could compromise.

You must not contact me or anyone here. I hope one day to be able to meet up with you again on the old social basis we enjoyed on the 'Illyria', chasing far more interesting prospects round the decks. But for now –

Most sincerely,
Matt.

There was a footnote asking me to indicate my willingness to help the future of Western Europe, by writing 'Yes' inside an envelope and leaving it for Mr Benson at Poste Restante, Trumpington Road, Cambridge on a specified date; which of course I did.

I agreed without hesitation: how could I not? I was well aware by now of the 'battle for the student mind' – such as it was – and of the pervasive threat from communism to the starry-eyed young. In plying our innocent trade around the campuses we had ourselves more than once fallen foul of communist student officials in all their pomposity, and been unable – sometimes for years at a stretch – to advertise our capitalist wares to their members.

I once said to a local union president, who had informed me haughtily that only he would decide who was permitted to advertise to all his six thousand members: "I thought you people disapproved of monopoly?"

"It depends who holds the monopoly," he had replied with a bearded toothy smile which I next saw on the Westminster front benches.

★ ★ ★

I wrote to Mr Benson four times in the early months of 1963 – at a Post Office near Liverpool's Halls out at Allerton; at one in Leicester at the end of University Road; down the Mile End Road past Queen Mary College; and in South Kensington, across the road from Imperial, and round the corner from Van's wonderful 'Hades' bistro with its old-fashioned horn gramophone and new-fashioned gorgeous waitresses. In the Autumn Term, Benson awaited me on Castle Boulevard, Nottingham; in the main Post Office, Exeter; and in Edgbaston. All through 1964 Mr Benson had seemed to be concerned chiefly with London (Kings, Imperial again, and UCL, always care-of a local Post Office. I was surprised LSE was left out but guessed that as it was so well-known as a hot-bed of the Left,

Matt probably had the place fully covered anyway.)

Then his requests had petered out, for which, with all my Company worries, I was not too sorry. But all in all, I suppose I was quite proud of myself: this was my very own secret service. I kept the deal entirely private, not even telling Olivia, nor mentioning Matt on the two occasions we dined with the COSEC Director. I greatly looked forward to the day when Matt and I could meet over a relaxing Scotch or two and compare notes…

From which you will deduce that I was hardly expecting a zebra, a gunshot, and a dead Marketing Director…

We must get back to that.

CHAPTER XI

I stood semi-paralysed at the door, staring at the headless zebra, getting the sharp smell of the gunshot, and shocked above all by the appalling sight of Robin's lifeless body, spreadeagled among his papers and lists on the splintery floorboards of the crumbling old drawing-room that was once the pride of the Lion Hotel.

Matt was climbing out of his zebra costume. He looked down at Robin. "You can get up now," he said, "It didn't work – it's only Tim."

What hadn't worked? I couldn't handle that weird tableau for the moment and filed it away in my head for some later time… I could well understand anybody wanting to shoot Robin, but why just pretend to?

I'd come down here for a bit of peace and quiet after that traumatic Board Meeting, giving away everything I'd worked for while being left with all the debt. As you do perhaps, when everything is piling up so monumentally, I seized on the most unlikely incidentals. "Why is the phone off the hook?" I asked lamely, not that I cared. They ignored me.

"Sit down," said Matt, in his underwear. "We must talk."

Robin was now up, and dusting himself down. He looked at me guiltily, while Matt went over to the door and locked it. I began to realise the extent to which I was out of my depth, and decided to shut up and see what happened.

"It's OK, Tim," Robin began, but Matt held up a hand.

"Let me," he said, "Tim and I go back a long way." He came across and shook my hand. It was good, very good, to see me again after all these years.

I wasn't so sure.

"For years now," he said, "my job has been involved with the students and academics all over Western Europe – "

"Yes, I know that," I told him, but he still went on about it.

"We are devoted, absolutely devoted – "

"Devoted," said Robin.

" – to student freedom. We are utterly against all the Communist brainwashing of youth – "

"Utterly… Brainwashing… " Robin was echoing, until Matt tutted at him.

"The Soviets are doing it all over Europe. We can't stop them in the East except through Radio Free Europe – "

"Radio who?" I asked. It wasn't on the dial of my Roberts Radio, and the old set I'd transferred into my new Jaguar had been stuck on Caroline for weeks until I could find the knob, which I could hear rolling under the seats every time I braked. They didn't enlighten me, but I found out about 'Free Europe' later: run by the CIA.

"What I am in charge of, back in Holland – "

Ah, I thought, here comes the 'Mr Benson' admission; but is he with COSEC or the CIA or our own MI6? Or are they all the same? And does it matter?

" – is the student population on our side of the Curtain, to stop infiltration by Moscow."

I felt I was being unnecessarily talked down to: I knew all this. I said so, and added that I'd been doing my bit to help, when asked. Privately I was a bit sour that he didn't give this any acknowledgment.

"Yes, Tim, I'm sure you're aware of the threat. But do you really understand the extent Moscow will go, to identify youngsters as potential agents: first butter them up, then recruit them as sleepers to be used years later for 'The Cause' – just like the ring: Maclean, Burgess, the others, here in the Thirties?"

"That's been worrying us," said Robin. Was *he* still here? I swung round to accuse him. Here was I, who had secretly been working for Matt (whoever he was) for over two years, and never for a moment had I allowed any hint of my activities to be seen by Robin or anybody else. Jesus, perhaps we were all working for Matt. At least Robin was looking a bit embarrassed, but he often was: he was by nature clumsy, though he would usually cover it with a bit of rugged Yorkshire crag. He sat there, typically scratching his arse. What the hell did he mean: "Worrying *us*?"

Matt stepped in. "I approached Robin last year," he confessed, and curiously went on: "I was concerned about how you were behaving."

"Good God, without even telling me?" I was staggered. I was doing all this surreptitious work after his letter; I was devoting hours to digging out the names and appointments they wanted and the political proclivities of those boring embryonic politicians, wherever they directed me. And what was this about "how I was behaving"?

Robin put in: "Tim, with the best will in the world, as they say, we really owe it to our UK students, to protect them by doing more to guard them against the Soviets. Here we are in this unique position with access to them all – "

I exploded. "Do you think I don't know that, you – " Matt saved me from the four-letter word.

"It's no good shouting at Robin. I knew I had to step in – "

"But I've been going out on a limb – "

"I'm sure you have, sure you have, Tim, within your own business world. But as soon as I realised you were so ignorant about them, I had to move on to Robin as my next best contact."

"Them?" The alien word went into me like a knife. "Wait a minute, Matt. Let me get this straight. Are you really saying this? Saying that I was passing information to Moscow as well as to you? Brilliant! Haven't you credited me with any loyalty at all…?" He pulled a face.

"… Any intelligence…?" I went on.

A much more sombre face.

"Tim," Matt said gently, "your insurance business is the only private organisation in the UK accessing all our students, which is not corrupted politically, and so with its thorough – "

I gritted my teeth, which hurt quite a bit. My words came out so firmly that for that minute I held the stage. "Listen, the two of you," I said.

"For over two years," I pronounced, "I've been doing this job for you. Scraping away at the meagre information available at all the Unions you've specified, I've religiously given you the lowdown on all those students. I deserve a word or two of thanks."

For some reason they were both shaking their heads.

"You must now have a complete picture of those student activists. It must be over a hundred of them, I've given to Mr Benson. Don't you – "

My voice trailed away as Matt sadly went on wobbling from the neck up.

"Who," he asked, "is Mr Benson?"

★ ★ ★

We sat and looked at each other.

I heard our Three Old Ladies coming down the long corridor, back from their lunch-break and being teased by old Ron, who was saying he had mistaken them for a Poppy Day version of the Beverley Sisters. I saw that my Company's life was getting back into its usual routines and we ought to be somewhere else. I opened the door and beckoned.

"Just down the road," I said, "is a pub called The Eagle, round the back of the Corn Exchange. A few years ago it's where Crick and Watson burst in one day to announce they'd solved the sweet mystery of life – "

"Good beer too," said Robin.

"Can we adjourn there now, so that perhaps I can resolve some of my own mysteries?"

They both agreed it was a propitious venue for us to disentangle our own double helix. Matt became a zebra again, the better to walk back to his clothes at the University Arms, after causing four heart-attacks in the corridor; Robin set about gathering up his papers and lists, and tidying his office and organising his shaken Beverley Sisters for the afternoon; I went to my private and heavily-locked filing cabinet at the Pruhaus to retrieve that 'COSEC' letter for examination by Matt. We would rendezvous in an hour.

Came the time, came the beer and sandwiches. Having bought the drinks determinedly against Matt's resistance, and needing to feel in control, I deserved to ask the first question.

"Matt," I began, "it's great to see you again, of course, but tell me: if that Benson letter pretending to be you is a forgery, are you in fact working for COSEC? I visited them last year? "

He fidgeted. "COSEC is non-political – "

"Oh bollocks."

"Well, let's say it aims to help all Western students – "

"Against Communism, you mean?", I was asking the obvious.

"Well, aren't we all?"

I couldn't argue with that. He went on to explain that 'his organization' worked often in conjunction with student groups: "To sort of help them along. You've heard of 'The European Movement' I suppose."

I hadn't. I was too busy trying to run a business. I didn't get involved in politics. Where Europe 'moved' was beyond me, provided I didn't have to move with it. Out of the corner of my eye I saw one of Robin's bloody great Yorkshire eyebrows twitch.

"And you, anyway," I pointed my sandwich at him. "What the hell are you doing, getting into this mess?" Then something else. "And that charade with you lying on the floor back there – "

He squirmed. It was a delight to see.

Matt quickly put in: "I'll explain that in a minute, let's get our general facts straight first. Robin, you owe it to Tim. Go ahead."

Robin had been deeply into student politics, and his connections had still continued afterwards until I had rescued him from it. I suppose all the top student leaders are automatically considered and weighed up by MI6 as potentials for spy duties, and Matt (or whoever he really worked for) was put in touch with him when COSEC (or whoever they really worked for) noted that my business would be valuable to him or them or the European Movement (or whatever other phoney establishments the CIA was funding in The West).

"Matt," I asked, to clarify my position, "could that Benson letter have come from somebody else – 'on your side', so to speak? Could anyone at COSEC or one of your related contacts have sent it in good faith, and you not know about it?"

"Absolutely not. There's nobody there at all concerned in that sort of thing, within the UK anyway – they'd get all they needed straight from NUS in London. Anyway, the letterhead is a forgery" – I had just shown it to them – "I can see errors in some of the telephone numbers, that was to stop you from ringing I suppose."

"Besides," added Robin, sensibly, "Why would they give you their real address? It was just to get your confidence. Whoever has been doing this, must know you had been in touch with the real COSEC. Did you go with Olivia?"

I ignored that for the moment, and fixed Matt with what I hoped would look like the obligatory steely eye. I don't know if it worked, but at least he put his drink down and gave me his full attention. "I've no idea," I said, "whether you're in the CIA or MI6 or any such – "

"Tim –" Robin began.

"Shut up," I told him. He did, he did! Though his jaw kept moving.

"And," I went on, to Matt, "You're obviously not going to tell me because no doubt you're not allowed to, and if you do, they'll punish you with boiling oil or dripping water or stick your head down the loo (if they are public schoolboys) or torture all your family or what the fuck else… "

"You're on the right track somewhere in there," said Matt.

I had now both run out of steam and on top of everything else, was feeling sorry for him, which annoyed me. I let him have a word.

"This letter I didn't write," he said, waving it until I took it from him, "is really pretty good. Somebody knows about you and me and the ship, as well as knowing what your business is all about. It suggests a combination of people, in the background, who have been studying you for a long time."

175

"But they do," Robin put in. "They think long-term. Back in the Thirties," and he went on with the old Burgess and Maclean stuff we all knew about: how potential agents can be recruited, kept on the payroll, and not used at all for decades. "Not just those two or three – "

"Or four or five," said Matt. "Some have still to come out of the woodwork; and not just at Cambridge. In Oxford too, I'm being told. Where is Holywell Manor? Do you know a woman called Hart?"

I knew Holywell Street, it was where I used to visit hosts of New College students; but the Manor was at the far end, an outpost of Balliol and standing in front of a couple of roads with 'Manor' in their name; no contact I knew of. As a married student, we lived for a while in Manor Road in an upstairs flat and used to tether our one-year-old to a tree in the centre of the lawn so that he could get fresh air while being just unable to reach the flower-border and eat the earth: or so we had thought.

"Hart? No. Do you know a man called Oxdon?" I can't think why I hazardously threw that in, possibly I was more than a bit worried about some subversive background behind the Doctor. But, to my immediate relief, neither Matt nor Robin showed the least spark of interest in the name. I could continue to keep my various suspicions to myself. Matt was going on about the Communist threat at universities. Our much-laughed-at tame Communist leader Harry Pollitt had been advising our Leftie extremist university students quite openly to 'work from within'. And apparently there was a very active man at Nuffield. It was not just the big universities, though: there was a proselytising Communist lecturer at the Royal Academy of Music, of all places. I was at last beginning to wake up to the dangers simmering beneath the trivial student surface.

"Matt, Robin," I said, trying to concentrate myself upon our immediate problem, "it seems I've been feeding information about left-wing student leaders to somebody or other that you don't know about. Two things we have to know: one the one hand, is it Left or Right groups that want this information? On the other, are they an outside organisation, or is somebody spying on my company?"

Matt and Robin looked at each other, yet again. Which of them would answer, and what ought they to say? Did they even know?

"We in the free world – " Matt started. Oh Christ, not all that.

"Defence of the Realm," Robin started. That was more like it, I'd been in the Army, and I turned to him, Yorkshireman or not.

He went on: "If details were wanted by the Right, we'd get them from higher sources, governmentally. So, it is the Left are spying on you, taking advantage of the fact that you are politically naive – " As I protested at the adjective, he corrected himself, "or anyway, neutral, as you claim."

"And even if, until now, you have been milked for information by some outside agency calling itself Benson, that will now have been blown. You won't ever hear from them again. Whoever they might have been, they are sure to know, now, that you have met Matt and therefore found out that Mr Benson is phoney."

Matt had been listening to all this and he now brought our thinking to a nasty head; it was, he said, a festering boil that had to be pricked. I pushed away my second sandwich.

"Even if, until now, some outside Communist outfit has been working on you for all that college information, they must have been controlled by somebody close to you. I think you have a mole."

A spy, among the people I had recruited? Rubbish.

I protested: I knew my colleagues well enough.

"They're not all salaried employees – how about the Area Managers?"

I had no convincing answer to that: would any of them be using his position for Leftish politics? It seemed unlikely. I asked Robin what he thought: after all, he was always in among them.

He, intelligently, brought the whole problem down to practical levels which centred around my personal Directorial worries rather than the nation's. "If we do in fact have a mole," he pointed out, "that mole will now know that his or her existence is suspected by us, but not yet exposed. Therefore, he or she will be lying low for the moment."

"What do you mean, 'she' " I demanded. The inference was obvious. I had to justify my Olivia connection in Europe, or see her unfairly smeared, the way only distasteful politicians can.

Matt said he had to get everything in the clear. "I might be a spy. You might be a spy… An artistic knight of the realm, even… How well do you really know this Olivia? Or your PA, Rosemary?"

I told him that this was getting ridiculous, but had to admit to myself that anything was possible. I would ask Ron, as the senior person at the Cambridge office, to check quietly on Rosemary's background; and would equally quietly reassure myself about Olivia, which I knew was entirely unnecessary, but anything to satisfy Matt – and now, also, Robin.

Matt handed Robin a fiver and asked him to re-order drinks. While he was at the bar, Matt moved over a bit nearer to me and asked confidentially: "Robin tells me that all the student mailing lists come directly from you, is that right?"

"Yes, I have this private source. No, I can't tell you. They contain nothing but names and addresses. Before I give them to Robin I include one or two 'sleepers'."

"Sleepers!" Of course, with his usage of spy jargon, he misunderstood.

"No, Matt, fictitious names, we plant in every list, to the address of a friend, who will tell me if he ever receives a letter resulting from a list. It would only mean that the list had been stolen. The initials of the fictitious student will reveal which list the sleeper has come from."

"Anyone else know this, of your people?"

"Only Olivia – she keeps the check-list of initials."

"Any letters, ever?"

"Never. So nothing there."

As Robin came back with a tray, Matt lit a cigarette and asked me: "What happens to the lists after you've given them – "

"Ah!" I shouted suddenly: that was something else. "For God's sake, you still haven't told me, what was all that charade about, back at The Lion with the gun and you, Robin, playing schoolboys?"

They exchanged what were supposed to be conspiratorial glances but to my suppressed delight they both looked a bit stupid for a moment.

"We weren't expecting you," said Matt. "I told you on Castle Hill to stay away."

"We were setting a trap," Robin mumbled into his beer.

"A trap! Who for?"

"That's it," said Matt, shaking his head and his cigarette with it. "We don't know, but Robin thought if there was, in fact, a spy in your Company, we could try to catch him – "

"Or her", Robin put in. "I made a big noise back at the office as we were leaving, about a great pile of new lists you had given me, to work on, and we thought – " Over to Matt:

" – If anyone was stealing papers or copying lists or whatever, they would almost certainly sneak over there in the middle of the day, because everybody else would be out watching the rag goings-on during their lunch-break."

"So, you would shoot them."

"Two shots. The first, with Robin 'dead' on the floor, should convince the intruder I meant business."

"But then you would shoot him."

"Of course not," said Robin.

"Oh yes, if necessary." Matt looked at us both.

Robin spilt most of his beer. "It was a blank…?" (The question-mark should also denote the quaver in his voice.)

"When you get back, have a look in the corner above those cabinets." Matt sipped his gin sadly. "You people really don't know what you're getting into. On the other side of the Curtain, students are disappearing, being killed, eliminated is the buzz-word, together with their tutors, senior professors, even sometimes their families, at a rate of thousands every year." Leaning forward. "*Thousands.*"

We sat rather quiet. Robin uncharacteristically offered me a cigarette – but I remembered that I had told him, that morning, I'd given up.

Matt went on: "Lots of nasty things are happening in Europe which, here in the UK, you don't seem to bother about."

"I know. I'm afraid we never seem to take life seriously enough. We laugh at disaster too quickly." I recalled a recent light-hearted play put on by the local Rodney Players (who had also done a couple of mine), where the KGB man was named Nokemoff and the CIA man Dippimin, but I didn't mention it just now.

"Well, Tim, it's not a bad fault. Don't forget, I'm English too." I had very nearly forgotten. "Maybe I've been rubbing shoulders too much with our American friends. But do take this warning seriously. If Moscow did manage to infiltrate the UK's student leaders, and if they then got on to the NUS committees – "

"Harry Pollitt," said Robin. "Work from within."

" – because they would be ordered to be forceful but charming, they would be promoted to top positions. Nobody in other countries would ever have expected Communism to take hold. In the East, yes, certainly. Probably in Italy… And even in France after the war if the Sicilians in Marseilles hadn't broken that strike – "

"Ah!" I had read about this, somehow the Sicilian mafia had been made use of by the CIA. "Wait a bit," I said, "You wrote to me from Marseilles, back in – "

"Never mind that, it was a long time ago. Just bear in mind, Tim – and you Robin – that given the position you're in, sitting on a great heap of valuable names and addresses, which the KGB would probably give their eye-teeth for, and certainly kill for – " Robin and I tried to avoid each other's glance at this point – "because they're presumably the only lists available outside the Education Ministry, do you really think the Soviets would think twice about pulling the trigger?"

I said, to nobody in particular: "I should have stayed with the laundrettes."

★ ★ ★

I felt I'd had enough of Robin for one day. I wanted to send him back to his rhubarb, but all I could suggest was that he returned to his shot-up room at The Lion and picked up all those student lists the KGB and the whole covert world wanted so much, and stuff them – I said with a pause – back in their cabinets. I would check back with him soon, about the ominous coming Board Meeting in March. I walked him to the door, though, and asked him: "Today's meeting, and the share handout, how do you think it went?"

Robin pondered for a while. He was, after all, the one closest to me on the Board now, both on our side of the job, marketing the idea rather than selling the products; also in our invaluable sense of the now mortally ridiculous.

"Do you want comfort or the truth?"

"Oh Christ! If it's like that, neither."

He stood there on the pavement, scratching himself. He always said it helped. "I suspect they want you out. I feel, if they've got a majority, they'll use it. They are starting to work on us HQ people, too. I reckon they are banking on ejecting you with their share majority, and next, refusing to sign the Bank joint-and-several guarantee, which will then get rid of us at HQ; then either doing new deals with the creditors, or run the Company into collapse and set up a new one on their own. But don't let it get you down, old son. I've got my eye on the ball, my shoulder to the wheel and ear to the ground – "

"That sounds like a vulnerable position."

"Great for handling rhubarb," over his shoulder as he walked away.

Back in the bar, I found Matt thumbing through some postcards of the colleges. He bought a few, and I wondered who else he was 'keeping in touch with' these days, as he had with me after that voyage eighteen years ago.

"Walk me back to the University Arms," he suggested. I knew he had to leave for somewhere in France – I think he said somewhere in the Paris suburbs – to meet some poet or other; it appeared that this naive chap was editing what he thought was an entirely impartial literary magazine, "for the European cause", thinking his funding came from voluntary charitable foundations in the States.

"Western Europe is full of these innocents," Matt said as we walked round the corner into King's Parade. "It's the same in the Middle East. You get some 'League of Rich Widows' pumping money into the ideal of American Democracy, wanting to plant its flag in countries that don't want it in the least."

"Don't want democracy?"

"Of course not: they're tribal, have been for thousands of years, do what they're told by the local chief, who does what he's been told by the big chief. OK fellows, here's your handful of hashish, off you go, slit those throats. Who else is that little man in the family tent going to vote for?"

"But if that's so cut-and-dried, what happens to all the money being contributed?"

"Well, as ever, most genuine charity money evaporates in the hot air of admin. But getting back to Western Europe, the real money comes through covert, entirely secret official channels. Let's leave it at that."

"How did you come to get involved in all this? I thought you were in the Colonial Service?"

He pulled a face. "Look what happened to the Colonies!" That was a valid comment, I thought, thinking of my father's final years at various collapsing outposts of Empire. "When we met on the boat from Canada I had a cable transferring me to a secret group in Holland, after my last job in the Far East – "

"Yes, Fiji. But you sent the card from Marseilles."

"Oh well, as I said, that was a minor assignment. But a year later when I reported to the Dutch I was in a rather special position because I was British, but working for – or with – the Americans."

"Why was that so special?"

"The Dutch had kicked MI6 out of their country around that time, because they were furious with us due to a balls-up in London. A whole lot of files about their Underground and Nazi collaborators had been held in London for safe keeping, but they all went up in smoke. A fire in the Records Department. At The Hague they were livid. They expelled our people, so they came to lean far more on the US."

"On the CIA?"

He stopped and looked at me in mock amazement. "I've no idea what you're talking about."

We were outside a small café just past The Copper Kettle. "Coffee or tea?" he suggested.

"This place," I told him, "has been renowned ever since the nineteen-thirties for its waitresses… "

He moved towards the door.

"… The trouble is," I went on, "they're still the same girls."

He came back, and we walked on, turning into Silver Street and down towards the river. On our right, before Queens', there was at that time a small but well-known butcher's shop with a very attractive girl at the cash-desk. She smiled back as I went past, as she always did. Any wicked thoughts of mine had soon been dispelled when I saw her one night enmeshed with her Cypriot boyfriend, bigger and stronger and younger than me, and anyway a man I wouldn't want to offend in any way because his family ran a restaurant opposite Downing, and when I was at that slightly distressed end of Regent Street and exhausted by idiot students, I used to enjoy the most delicious mushrooms-on-toast which I even now drool over in memory.

"So anyway," Matt got back on track, "my job, as you now know thanks to our mysterious Mr Benson, is to help prevent the Soviets from spreading their propaganda among our Western students, and instead – "

"Spread your own?" I realised at once that it was unworthy of me, and I hurried on: "What I mean is, we have to resist them by promoting our own philosophies and beliefs?"

He demolished my airy-fairy thinking at once, shaking his head vigorously as we leaned over the railings of the bridge.

"Sod philosophies and beliefs, Tim," he said, quite angry. "Bugger all the talk about Lefties and Righties and their artificially stirred-up 'views'. Personally, I just don't like to see youngsters being taken for a ride by manipulators on either side. Fuck all politicians."

I said I had to agree with that, but rather him than me.

We weren't going to get any coffee at The Anchor today, I had overlooked the fact that this popular spot would be overwhelmed by onlookers on Poppy Day, waiting to watch the Battle of the River Cam.

"I would be happy," I told him, "to take you upstream to Grantchester, by punt." I told him of the student who came to me to insure his punt, which required the vessel to have a name, and the resultant marine policy with its essential wording from Lloyd's had recorded him as being 'Master, under God, of the good ship 34-24-34' and his cover included 'Piracy upon the High Seas'.

"However delightful to be kidnapped and pirated by you, Tim, I think if I am going on the water, I must choose a more comfortable barque on the Seine."

So we went back, up past Pembroke. We were in that area, surrounded by colleges, where a few years ago I had discovered that alphabetical list of Freshers, ending at 'L', that I've told you about, and still find a bit shocking. Thoughts about lists came back to me as I smiled past the butcher.

"You asked me earlier, back in the pub, about our student lists of names and addresses; and apparently – never mind the KGB – you yourself were ready to kill someone unknown who might steal them from Robin's files… " He stopped at the crossroads.

"We have no interest in those lists ourselves, we want to protect them from undesirables – "

"So you already get all the information you need about our students from Unions or the Universities?"

"Usually straight from the Ministries, and not just the UK". He was a bit irritable, as if I didn't understand – and he was right. He lit a cigarette, which I still slightly envied him – it takes a long time to give up at a moment's notice, I was finding – and I waited while he fiddled to make his lighter work. God knows where he bought it, a heavy, chunky thing, but I found it utterly untypical of the Matt I knew. He saw me squinting at it.

"Yes, I know," he said, "I got it from an Arab. It's a bit over the top but it takes pictures too. Just one for the scrapbook." Click.

We were close to the spot where I had recently visited a hearty Peterhouse student ending his Finals Year. In early May our chat had been enlightened by the romantic sound of a cuckoo in the Backs just outside his rooms, and we had sat and listened, entranced. Three weeks later, three whole interminable weeks of it, when I had re-visited and sat waiting for him as he did his final revisions for the exams, he came in with a shotgun and a look of deep satisfaction.

"We just don't need the names, you see," Matt was telling me, "But Moscow mustn't get them."

"So you don't even want to know about our UK students?"

"Look," Matt stopped and turned to me halfway up Pembroke Street. "For God's sake, Tim, nobody in Western Europe is the least bit interested in your lists, however well they have been typed and copied, or handwritten or scratched on walls. We only need information on them when they do something or go – " He cut short.

Ouch.

"Tim, I really must get moving now – "

"You said 'when they go'. Is this about Copenhagen?"

Matt dropped his cigarette and nearly fell after it into the gutter. I had no idea that snippet of information I'd had ages back, from Officer Cadet American Bill, could be so powerful.

As on the boat years ago when we had first chatted, he glanced quickly up and down the street. I almost expected him to produce a silver greyhound. As a complete innocent, I was enjoying this, but since it was obviously important to other people including Matt, I wasn't going to push it.

"What the hell do you know about Copenhagen?"

I knew absolutely nothing about Copenhagen except it had a Mermaid and was bloody cold in January without a coat. Oh, and there were women's clothes that made your luggage heavy when you flew away. I put on the most sinister conspiratorial look I could muster, and smirked at Matt knowingly. "You're secrets are safe with me," I said, as we parted near the top of the road; and he promised – a bit deflated – to be in touch.

I went down Corn Exchange Street. What secrets, I asked myself.

Behind me was the well-concealed Museum of Archaeology, open to the public though nobody ever came. It was run at that time by an old friend, Jack Trevor of Christ's, who knew some secrets himself: he had all the answers to the Piltdown skull hoax, and told me them, well before most. He also had a delightful au-pair girl to look after his bachelor needs off the Huntingdon Road and they used to come for supper, when we would play each other's records. He had introduced me to Mahler, and in return I had brought him Bruch.

Yes, Jack knew some secrets. I wished to God I did.

I wended my way back to the Pruhaus car park and just managed to squeeze myself into my car beside Maurice's hulking great tank (so, he was still out enjoying Poppy Day, was he, in a real University: you don't get much of that in Solihull, nor back in Essex, I guessed); and I drove non-stop to the only place and person I could truly trust.

★ ★ ★

Olivia had been doing some homework at the Public Library, round the corner, over Ebury Bridge, and turn right into Buckingham Palace Road.

"What is 'fellow-traveller'?" she asked as I came in.

I explained, adding that our Western starry-eyed camp-followers of Communism in the Twenties and Thirties had been called 'useful idiots' in writings by Lenin, and they still were, as Matt had just been pointing out.

Olivia said: "I think we know the woman who wrote that."

This lost me. She went on: "Remember last year, in the Lakes?"

She was, incredibly, right. We had spent a few days at a hotel on the edge of Windermere, where we actually met the old lady who had once been Trotsky's secretary and had now, for long years, been married to that intriguing ex-spy Arthur Ransome, of 'Swallows and Amazons' fame, and definitely one of ours… Strange world.

CHAPTER XII

I sat with Olivia on the old settee in the Pimlico flat. Something by the Beatles, or more likely that raucous new lot, was juddering down from Room Seven above us and our chandelier was trembling, as well it might, after being soaked last Autumn: if that woman's goldfish bowl broke again with all those heavy drumbeats, we'd be in more trouble. Outside on the landing, the chronically-underemployed Mr Hodges, the freelance drainpipe consultant or whatever it was he was telling the Social Services, emerged from the loo and plodded down to his streamingly-damp Room Three at the back, looking ever more like Groucho without that sense of humour: but what did he have to be humorous about, it occurred to me. Maybe I won't put his paltry rent up this year, after all... Our cleaning lady with the unlikely wooden leg had just stumped off to make her husband's supper.

"She hasn't!" None of our tenants could believe the limb was false.

"She has! I saw it when she was doing the stairs."

"Listen," I said to Olivia, "We need to talk."

She gave me a Roman "tut-tut" and placed a finger across my lips. "Tim, you've had a heavy day in Cambridge, you should relax with me and forget it all for an hour or two."

I appreciated the reasoning, but this couldn't wait.

"Listen though," I said again. "If there is trouble at the next Board Meeting in March, I'm going to be pretty preoccupied. I've no guarantee or even any real hope of security afterwards, let alone any income."

"*Pouf!*"

"Obviously our Europe venture has gone out the window, and anyway you're due at university this Autumn. Do you think it's time now for you to go back home to Rome?" It hurt like hell to say that, but she might be used against me if there was some sort of confrontation; I prayed secretly, though, that she would stay on and help me through.

She thought for a minute, turning down the black-and-white 'Steptoe and Son' we had been watching on the TV.

"There's more, isn't there? She looked at me searchingly. "When you came in I felt it at once – something new has happened."

So I painted the whole Matt-mystery-mayhem picture. It put a new topcoat – I could hardly say whitewash – over all my previous company worries. I explained how weak my position now was, and how all my colleagues were greedily aware of that. Robin I could probably trust, but –

"What you're saying," she lay back on the cushions and twisted a strand of that long black Mediterranean hair, "is, they'll all be ready to attack you any way they can, and me being here with you might be – *come si dice* – embracing?

That wrong word was nevertheless so appropriate that I didn't correct her.

She gave me her cockeyed smile. "Tim, we've had over two years, and we've both known I must go back soon; but just for now, let me stay and see if I can help. I've met nearly all your people, haven't I? So I can refigure – visibilise – " She petered out.

"Visualise?"

"Si. I can do that while we think about them all, but I am still apart from them, so perhaps I can be more unpartial." She pointed at the papers on my desk, which I had been shuffling from side to side. "You will have to do detective work about your men and this mole you say you have. I can help but nobody else can."

I had to trust *somebody*. She was right there.

"You are like the big detective with the room over the pub… "

I had taken her to the reconstructed Sherlock Holmes study at Charing Cross.

"… And I will be your Doctor Johnson."

The same day we had visited Gough Square, off the Strand.

"Watson."

"Watkinson, Johnkinson… both of them. So, we will hunt your mole. I know about moles, don't I?"

★ ★ ★

Olivia certainly did. Her studies of English had advanced so well, that she had undertaken a work of love: to translate parts of 'The Wind in the Willows' as well as the whole of the two 'Winnie-the-Pooh' books. In the former case we hit several difficulties: misreading her dictionary, she first found that the Italian for 'mole' was *'banchina'*, which is a dock, as in 'dockyard'; and when I got her out of that, she was sidetracked – as one is with reference books – into other meanings of 'dock', ending up with courtrooms and garden weeds. Ultimately it became clear that the word for the small myopic creature is simply *'molo'*, and we both felt foolish. (And yes, they do have them in Italy: my son and I were sitting with our sandwiches at Hadrian's Villa one Summer, when the little thing dug his way to the surface and sat blinking between us).

In the book, Mole's favourite cry is 'Oh my, oh my!', but although I thought it sounded great, Olivia declined my suggestion of *'O mio mio'* because it didn't make sense. We used it a lot, privately.

When she came to the battle-scene at Toad Hall she rather neatly improved a little on Grahame by introducing, as well as Stoats and Weasels (which are both apparently *'donnole'*) some ferrets, – *'furetti'* – but she called them *'furiosetti'*. Translator's Licence.

She and I both loved the Pooh books. I had read them both while I was in a hospital in Nairobi, aged eight, quite dangerously ill, I'm told, with blood-poisoning, but my hysterical laughter had kept so many other patients awake that the books were confiscated. To my immense annoyance I had to lie there listening to nurses in the distance, giggling.

I still read them again and again: as Olivia so rightly said:

189

"Underneath, they are not just for children, they are for upgrowns." This is so true: for instance, there is that bit where Owl wonders whether to push bossy Rabbit off the tree. Now that's an adult joke. Equally adult, does anyone agree with me, is the fact that I can never nowadays read the final chapter of 'Pooh Corner' without crying. I don't think a child would be moved to tears by that ending. (See also Note 10).

We had fun with the names. Olivia kept the originals for Pooh of course and also for Tigger, but Piglet came over nicely as '*Porcellino*'; and the problem of Owl, who so confidently misspelt himself 'Wol', she overcame magnificently by turning the Italian '*gufo*' into '*fugo*', which somehow brought in the idea of flight, and so even outdid Milne. Eeyore required a vowel-change to preserve the full sense of the name, and I can't help thinking that Olivia subtly improved the barely-suppressed anguish of that depressive animal in his Gloomy Place by making him '*Ai-orr*': the cry 'Ai' being a common expression of alarm or despair around the Mediterranean. Rabbit, though a good name in English as he 'rabbits on', was a problem we couldn't solve, as to 'rabbit on' in Italian is merely '*blaterare*', which we could do nothing with, so the irritating animal was just a straightforward '*coniglio*', and personally I was very happy with that in view of the 'gl'.

It was a huge relief that she was going to do some quiet research which I had no time to attempt, into the backgrounds of my suspects. I knew I could safely leave her to it. We turned off the TV and went round to Grumbles. It was strange to have cut off ' Steptoe and Son', and a few minutes later find ourselves chatting with Wilfrid Brambell at the next table, in full colour too as he was a smart dresser.

We said goodbye to Sylvia, that most memorable of all Grumbles' staff, whom I never failed to fancy like anything… That E-type was outside again, and the lovely little driver, whose face I was sure I had seen more than once on the news-kiosks.

As we walked home, Olivia said, apropos nothing but with a sideways look: "These London girls are so *simpatice*, with either of those two, I give my permission."

I said: "How about both?" and she hit me. But walking on in silence, I suspect we were both thinking about it…

★ ★ ★

Next morning I sat at my desk making a list – a mole-call.

"How many suspects do we have?" Olivia came in towelling her hair.

"I make it nine, if I'm to be really brutal – "

She giggled. "Brutal – you! Perhaps '*brutto*' – '*brutto muso*'." She kissed the back of my head. Perhaps the front was just too brutto at that time of the morning.

"Nine," I said very firmly after quite a long time. "There are the seven Directors, and then I suppose we ought to add Matt because after all, even he might be playing a double game and be an undercover Red, do you think?"

"I haven't met that one," she pointed out. "Nor your Professor in Oxford; but we'd better add them both just for a beginning."

"Yes, that is the nine."

"But it must be ten, Tim. You must add me."

"Oh, really!" I protested, but she insisted with a wave.

"I mean it. It is serious because your men will suspect me. I am close to you and all your important papers are lying around… " I caught a glint in her eye as she went on *accelerando*: "… on your desk and on the floor and on the TV and on my dressing-table and on my pasta packets – "

I grimly added her to the list, nearly breaking the pencil. I was still at the stage of reaching for cigarettes when under extreme stress.

"*Bene*," she said. She sat at my desk. "Now, I am going to do some work. You have among all these papers," waving both arms, "the names and birth-dates of your men? *Molto bene*. I am going to the Somerset House. Which is the station, is it Victoria or Waterloo?"

"Neither," I said, reaching for the A to Z. All you need is the Circle Line: Somerset House is not in Somerset."

She was putting her coat on. "I must go soon, to be sure."

This I knew. In order to 'be sure' she had to leave early. She had warned me more than once that every time she took the London Underground, she allowed an extra thirty minutes because she knew for certain that she would start by going in the wrong direction. As I keep saying, she was an intelligent girl. (This is the logical young lady who later, when left some money by a relative, had to decide between buying a car or an expensive fur coat; and chose the coat as being far more practical because it would always get her a lift. In Rome, no doubt the better decision).

"You," she told me as she went out the door, "go and find out the truth about your Signor Professore."

★ ★ ★

The Signor Professore was ageing before my eyes. No longer was Dorian in the attic: he had come downstairs with sombre tread, I thought to myself as I sat in the usual chair. He watched me with a gloomy countenance and a rather wheezing breath, while still stroking the cat. The animal had aged, too, and it blinked more slowly.

Dr Oxdon was alert, however, to what I had to say. Poised, I sensed. But I had come here to see if I could eliminate him from our suspect list. After all, I reasoned, it was he who had got us all the student data in the first place, so why use us when he already had that mysterious access? I took a deep breath: but –

"Have a Cape gooseberry."

He was pointing to some marble-sized orange fruits in a bowl on the beautiful oak joint-stool beside me, splendid with its fluted legs.

"Good heavens," I exclaimed, "I haven't seen those since – "

"Yes, since in your garden in Nairobi? You don't often find them here, I'm told. A friend flew in. They have that nickname, don't they, in Africa. Scientifically the name sounds like a nasty Schubertian disease: Physalis ."

192

"Perhaps," I said, taking one, "one should eat it with a pinch of mercury?"

That, he liked. Not for the first time I felt that he had become a lonely old man, aching for lightweight, even flippant conversation; for many years no tutorials with young students; little attendance any more at Top Tables even when he felt physically able; drink invitations from the SCR, so few now; most contemporaries gone, and all these new people with their loud voices so that you couldn't hear what that nice old Fellow next to you was saying. And you see, as soon as we started to chat inconsequentially, he was blossoming. I remembered how he had clearly relished the Scrutton 'Garden of Cucumbers'; and I wondered whether he would appreciate Olivia's Italian version of Pooh – I thought it was very likely, must send it to him… But now I had to be severe and talk business. It shouldn't be difficult…

"The CIA have been in contact with me," I began, in a suitably sensational tone, just to shake him.

"Oh dear" he responded blandly and in complete calm. "Has all this student stuff of yours been dragged into politics? That's the last thing you want."

As before with this whimsical old man, I found it difficult to get my message through.

I said: "You've been asking for our data on students' insurances for several years, and I've been happy to oblige because your initial introduction admittedly let us establish our – now excellent – relationships with the student unions; but now it will have to stop." There – I'd said it. "Stop absolutely," I ended.

Oxdon nodded, but I was sure that he wasn't in any way agreeing with me, he was just waiting for me to take a breath. It was that indulgent sort of 'finish-your-essay' nod. The cat stretched up rheumatically and rubbed against his chin. He smiled at me in a friendly and reassuring way. I didn't much like it.

"Tell me, Tim," he asked as he helped himself from the porcelain bowl, "We do a lot of research and I need you just to confirm a few – er – facts. Yes," he added thoughtfully, "Facts. Is it correct that your parents have just come home and retired?"

Well, yes they had, two years ago, down in Sussex. But what was this?

"And he was in the Overseas Civil Service? Stationed in Kenya in the Forties, down among the gooseberries?"

"Yes," I agreed again, puzzled. "We went out in 1934 and though I came home to school with them at Coronation time in thirty-seven, they went back and were there through most of the war. Why?"

Oxdon obviously knew all this already and was simply setting the scenery for something I couldn't possibly guess. He had leant asthmatically back in his chair, and waited for a short while, eyeing me over the top of those glasses, even now slightly askew.

Then it came: "What was your father's connection with Baden Powell?"

The incongruous question threw me into a sort of Wimp's Wonderland. What on earth had been cooked up, seemingly to cast doubts in some unspoken way upon my Dad's friendship with the founder of the Boy Scouts?

My reply in bewilderment: "Dad, and *his* father too, had been very early supporters of Scouting, following the family's return from South Africa – Potchefstroom I think – with the Ninth Lancers soon after the Boer War. They started a Troop in South London, at Wimbledon – "

"Southfields, actually." He nodded me on.

"Dad was only in his early 'teens, but enthusiastic from the start – he was that sort of chap. In fact, he even acted as a schoolboy air-raid warden in 1914-18, and also won a Scout medal for stopping a – "

"Runaway horse and cart, yes. We have that. He was awarded what they call 'The Scouts VC', wasn't he?"

"For goodness sake," I was getting rankled by all this, "what is there you don't know? And whyever is this relevant?"

Oxdon nodded again, presumably to appear understanding. But he waved me on.

"Well then, the bits I personally remember. Dad's daytime job was sales promotion for the UK Government, he used to call on masses of local firms, putting British exporters in touch. He sometimes took me with him," and I remembered with a chuckle, "Once we were at a vast pyrethrum farm and I floored him by asking, if it was such a powerful insecticide, however did it spread its pollen? But after-hours, he was soon appointed Chief Rover Scout for all of East Africa: that is," quoting from the postage stamps I knew so well: "Kenya, Uganda and Tanganyika – oh, and Zanzibar." Zanzibar had always seemed to me as a kid out there, a highly exotic add-on to Dad's territory. It was a slight disappointment when I finally got there on the way home, just cloves and white buildings and a lot of palm trees, except for that exciting wrecked German cruiser at the entrance to the harbour – or was that Dar-es-Salaam?

"And though all this Scouting activity was a sideline," I continued, "In all his spare time after his Governmental Trade Promotion work, he did it very well, really in depth, starting new troops for young Indians and Africans too, which BP greatly approved of, I've got his letters saying so. Just before the war he started a secret night-time Special Police team using his Rovers and their friends – "

"Forgive me, dear boy, but what about 'BP' himself? How close was your father to him? He had retired to live in the Kenya uplands at the end of his life, and we know that your father was listed as being one of the pall-bearers when he died; all that, we have. But why?"

"Why do you want to know?"

"We have a theory and a suspicion. All this will emerge as we continue. Now: how did BP get close to Dad?"

"After leaving me at school in 1937, they went back on, I think, the 'Llangibby Castle', one of the work-horses of the Union Castle Line which sailed to Africa 'every Friday at four o'clock'".

"Thursday."

"And Mum and Dad, being in the middle stratum of Governmental big-wigs, and as it was a small ship, found themselves at the same table as the BPs. Naturally, the Scouting connection came up; and they got quite close, sharing all the official visits the BPs had to make, showing-the-flag at Scouting stops along the way, acting as his ADC, I suppose you'd say."

"And when they all got to Kenya?"

"BP stayed pretty close to Dad. He didn't meet many people after that because he was ageing, and happily tucked away on his upcountry estate; but he and Dad received and sent lots of paperwork and information from time to time; and BP kept a keen eye on the Rover Scout development as it made such a good contribution to the war effort out there. The Rovers were really close to the Police; and Dad told me many Kenyans were very negative just then about our prospects against the Italians – who were massing on the northern border."

"Oh, very negative. We'll come on to that. Now, about Baden-Powell: did you know that in his earlier days, Army days during the Boer War, he had ordered executions?"

"I can't say I knew that, but I'm sure in wartime – "

"… and made a point of going to watch them?"

"A senior officer has to, Doctor, you must know that. And in those days of guerrilla warfare – "

"In other words, BP was no saint when the opportunity arose – "

I was incensed by this. Was Oxdon beginning to dement? I spluttered so vehemently that the cat jumped off him: "Doctor, your choice of words is disgraceful. How can you say 'the opportunity… '? Necessity, perhaps?" Where was this going?

He shrugged. "Ach, that is just semantics. I accept your criticism, largely because you are understandably in support of your father, and of course you only knew BP as a kindly old famous gentlemanly Peer of the Realm, not so?"

The accumulation of adjectives was an irritation, but I had to ignore it.

"Exactly what he was," I said, "Every word. My father was very proud to have known him, and greatly regretted he couldn't be a pall-bearer as intended, as he was away in the RAF."

"Ah!".

As usual, this old man was ahead of me. He looked at me thoughtfully, then picked up a sheet of paper on which I could see scribblings, not in green ink thankfully but in a sort of Quink purple which was bad enough. Green would have been a possible hint of incipient madness; purple couldn't be far off. Some newspaper-cuttings were pinned to it, even more alarming…

"Erroll." He looked at me over those glasses again. "What does that name mean to you?"

'Flynn', was my immediate response, as if we were playing psychological games… 'Robin Hood'… Sexy young girls naked in showers… Phoney swordfights… Bloody Australian… 'Too Much Too Soon', and you can say that again. I said with a laugh: "Were there Boy Scouts in Sherwood Forest then?"

He didn't smile: not even a bit. I realised that something tricky was coming up. He apologetically cleared his throat, and out it came.

"No," he said. "*Lord* Erroll. Working in Nairobi, ostensibly for the Government. Appointed, astonishingly, given his background, to be Kenya's Defence Secretary or some such official post just when Italy threatened to invade. Fascist. Very active at the Muthaiga Club your parents belonged to. Extremely popular with the ladies, especially the married ones with husbands safely away at the war."

I thought his neat phrase 'safely away at the war' was a good paradox, for use in some other context; but not this one.

"Shot dead," Oxdon went on. "In his car. Late night of 24 January, 1941." A pause as he looked across at me. "A few days after BP's funeral. Shot close-up behind the left ear, and of course it was a right-hand drive. Old fourteen-eighteen gun, the suspected weapon, but that means nothing; but black powder, which was strange… He was found by natives not far from his home on the Ngong road, it was presumed having had an assignation on the plains. Gun never found."

I did now recall the basic facts behind this murder, I must have read it about vaguely at school, I suppose, but at that time, aged fourteen, we were more concerned with the Blitz directly above us, and – only secondly – newspaper front pages with their sketch-maps along the North Africa coast, with names like Sidi Barrani and Tobruk (which fell that very week, I now see). So, with an effort, what could I remember?

A local high-living member of the Happy Valley crowd, Delves-Broughton, a baronet cuckolded by Erroll, had been charged but acquitted. It hadn't been Broughton's gun, forensic discovered at the trial. Nobody else had been nailed for this shooting, and frankly, nobody liked Erroll in any case, widely believed a Fascist. And it was wartime, which by common consent, not least among the local judiciary, forgave a lot. It had never really registered in my long-term memory, too remote, but these snippets came back to me.

"So," Oxdon pulled me back to the present, "what do you know about Erroll, from your parents?"

It wasn't difficult really, once prompted, and given that my Kenya memories were so pleasant, to wade back through years of childhood to those happy days in Thirties Nairobi, when at the age of eight my friend Brian and I would cycle completely safely and carefree down into the centre of town, update our stamp collections at the shop of the East African Standard newspaper, call on Dad at Memorial Hall across the road, pop into the powerful concrete Art Deco covered market to pick up something to chew, and then ride past Brian's father's pharmacy to the picture-house, there to watch in complete absorption the latest Astaire and Rogers that our parents had been raving about at breakfast.

But whatever was all this about Erroll? I had to say: "Dad never even mentioned him, he might have been a Top Brass, but we weren't in that circle at all. No connection whatever to the boring Happy Valley crowd, whom, if anything, one despised while envying their money. Dad was only a Muthaiga member ex-officio, he was just a middle-range Home UK Civil Servant out there on a thousand a year. They couldn't afford Muthaiga unless somebody invited them, could they?"

"They sent you to the private Muthaiga School nearby."

And I scored this time. "Indeed, at a considerable sacrifice to help my education, and that's why they couldn't afford to go to the

Club. And then when I was back home in England, with them paying for my schooling still, Dad was – ”

“Away at the war, yes. Adjutant at RAF Khartoum. Very hot and sweaty.” He looked up from the purple notes. “And back in Nairobi, where was your mother putting in her war work?”

I remembered a few chatty bits of scandal she had enjoyed passing on to me when we finally met up after the war, out in Canada, and suddenly, to my astonishment, I could see where this was going.

★ ★ ★

With excellent shorthand and general office skills remembered from her secretarial work in the Twenties, Mum's wartime job in Kenya had been in the typing-pool, first at a Government House annexe, close to the Arboretum and just down the road from our house on Chiromo Road, and later up near the Muthaiga district. The office, I now half-remembered, was run – largely in his absence – by the glamorous Lord Erroll; and on the rare occasions that he showed up in office hours, he was inclined to – as Mum put it – “come and sit on our desks and chat, ooh he was lovely.” Nothing more. But now, Oxdon had swiftly made it important.

Dad was away.

Oxdon said casually: “So Erroll was quite a lady killer – quite a catch – among the forlorn abandoned wives of the Muthaiga sorority?”

“Well, I don't suppose he was the only predator in those days in Happy Valley, in a wartime society that had already been decadent for half a century. But my family were among the run-of-the-mill governmental crowd, quite removed from the settlers in Happy – ”

“Of course, but people like Erroll hunted away from home, as well.” He sat up in his armchair and reached out to switch on a standard lamp – I hadn't even noticed that daylight had been fading. “He was thirty-nine when he died. Your Mum –?”

I had to think. “Forty-one.”

"Tim, you need to know this," he began gently, though surely it was a contrived gentleness? "The Erroll murder, after Delves-Broughton was cleared, has never been solved. It's still wide open – "

Me, searching my memory: "Surely, Broughton killed himself?"

"Yes, at the Adelphi in Liverpool, but that was later on and nothing to do with Kenya or Erroll, we believe. We know he had other reasons."

For the first time I noticed the 'we'. Who was behind all this?

He turned on a beatific smile. It horrified me. I had learnt to accept the tentative half-smile which appeared on occasions, but that had been his genuine response to anything at all 'smile-worthy'. What I had here was an entirely artificial display, and I felt it was pulled by a puppet-master behind the scenes. I know a politician like that, and it's not nice. I began to realise that I was being set up, even though all these events were from another, distasteful world and nothing whatever –

"Hear me out," he said. "Forget the decadent Happy Valley crowd; we don't think Erroll's was a personal jealousy killing at all. None of them had the courage and anyway none of them were sexually jealous, there's any amount of evidence in their overall behaviour, don't you know?"

"So why is my mother – "

"Hear me. Erroll was a high security risk in 1941. He wasn't just leaning towards Fascism, in fact he had already joined Mosley's lot in 1934, which probably wasn't very widely known just yet among the general populace in Kenya. But now, bear in mind, the Italians, at war with us, were only just across the northern border, with their colonies on the Horn, and they had now moved into Abyssinia too, and were massing their troops. And here was Erroll the Fascist in charge of Defence, or part of it. Picture that."

I was picturing it, vividly. Despite myself I was finding his expert presentation fascinating. Oxdon could see this, and he called to the kitchen: "Could we have some cocoa or something, dear?" Turning to me: "Sugar?"

A voice came back: "On its way."

"You can see, Tim, they had a problem. With all his liaisons, Erroll was very likely to give important things away. He never had been able to keep a secret, especially between the sheets. And now, invasion was a big threat. He had to be stopped, and shut up."

"Why not just that – sack him and lock him up?"

"He would just talk all the more, and all his hoity-toity friends would kick up such a song and dance: lots of them were unreliable too. No, he had to be got rid of. He was odious anyway: I met him once. Do have a gooseberry"

I was trying to piece all this together. "Are you about to suggest that Baden Powell was behind this 'elimination'?" It was unbelievable.

"Well," he replied thoughtfully, "Remember BP's whole life had been on the top floor of the Establishment, and he was no stranger to the highest people in Intelligence, was he? And he had long been both a successful warrior and steeped in covert work – perhaps the only one in Kenya, and we were at war." A sip of cocoa. "As it happened, BP had met Erroll a couple of times early in 1940. In fact, sent him a polite neighbourly note on his new marriage, to which I gather he had no acknowledgment whatever, and that would have registered badly with the old man. But no doubt he would have been receiving feedback on the fellow from Security locally and from Intelligence higher up". He looked at me thoughtfully over his glasses. "I mean, Tim, who better? He would know what had to be done."

He stopped for a cough and a drop of cocoa went on to the cat, who licked at it lazily.

"Of course, the old man was on his last legs... (look who's talking, I thought), but we think he may have been asked to recommend someone he could trust to do the job." He looked at me yet again over those slanting glasses.

My Dad? Kill anyone? He even stepped over grasshoppers. He must mean one of Dad's Rovers. I wouldn't know about that, I told Oxdon.

"Someone he could really, really trust. This was an essential act of patriotism, with all our East African territory in mortal danger, let alone all the lives at risk. Kenya was almost undefended: most of the KAR were up in the desert."

"So was Dad."

"I'll come on to that." Ominous.

"We think that your father may have refused at first, but then agreed when the risks were explained to him; but he asked for the job to be postponed until BP died, to ensure that if the truth came out, any scandal would not in any way tarnish the Scout movement. Of course everybody knew that BP was fast fading. He died earlier that January and the shooting was on the 24th., remember?"

"Is there any evidence to support your silly story?" I was justified in being rude, the way this was going, and without any cigarettes.

He referred again to the purple ink. "Not a thing – "

"Well, then – "

"Except, you see, all the background circumstances. Let us count them: One: the timing, as we've just discussed. No sooner is BP dead – "

"But Dad was away in the RAF – "

"Precisely, and therefore – two – he was subject to military orders, which would not have been the case before he went. And so: under orders, having a good alibi on the surface, while a fast little RAF plane could get him in from Khartoum to their private airport out on the plains outside Nairobi, and back again, very comfortably… There would have been a car waiting." He laid down the cocoa cup. "You should drink some more of this, it's very calming."

"You were about to list the background circumstances."

"Of course. Three: the means. I've just covered that, he could get there very easily, and very privately with RAF back-up. Four: The motive. Clearly, national interest. But you see, Tim, that if your father had been caught, he would be on his own – this is commonplace and both he and BP would have accepted that. Operatives are always 'on their own', aren't they? Read any novel. If things had gone wrong and Dad had been caught, perhaps by some late-night passer-by, he would simply have been arrested and presented to the Courts as a jealous husband, the perfect line to take by the authorities, no matter how much your Dad or Mum might have argued their innocence." Another break for a cough. "Five: the lack of anything else having emerged since – there haven't been any convincing deathbed confessions – "

"I thought – "

He shook his head. "Only a couple of silly Happy Valley freaks, like you always get, sozzled neurotic sensation-seekers looking for a headline, and they can all be dismissed; and not even in that crowd has anyone come forward to say anything really helpful. But more to the point, the official investigations petered out very quickly; reading transcripts of the trial, one would suspect the lawyers had been told to play the whole affair down. Nobody liked the man, only his title I suppose. All the obvious suspects had domestic alibis – "

"Supplied by their terrified wives?"

"Husbands, just as likely."

I tried common-sense. "You know you have nothing whatever against my father, let alone my mother. She did make occasional jokey references to Erroll, I remember now, when reminiscing about her wartime job, but Dad" I stupidly emphasised, "has never mentioned him at all, in all these years." But I knew at once that I had blown my case for the defence…

"Six," said Oxdon, and waited while it sank in.

Then he went on: "One has to ask: why not?" Short pause. "Isn't it the sort of event that any normal Kenya veteran from 1941 might occasionally reminisce about?"

"Oh, and number seven: why did your so-close-to-BP Dad not fly down for the funeral? As you said, he was listed, actually reported in the papers, as being one of the pall-bearers, and in such emotive circumstances he would have had no trouble whatever getting time off to fly down, given his Scouting position in the Colony. So why didn't he? We think he was ordered to stay away, to make it look as if that trip down and back would be impossible for him – and so his non-attendance would cement his alibi for the coming Erroll job."

He sat back. All seven points were dangerously sharp.

"Well," he smiled, "all I've been saying is simply supposition. Have another gooseberry. But it makes a great story for the Sundays, doesn't it? "

★ ★ ★

I was horrified. Were there truly plans to print all this nonsense? It would destroy my innocent parents, who were well into their long-awaited quiet retirement, none too healthy after too many years in the tropics, and who prized their privacy far more than the CMG that Dad never got. Oxdon was watching for my reaction.

"Oh yes," he said. "It will all be published. Unless – "

"This is blackmail." I bit hard into my gooseberry as he gave me that brittle smile.

"I suppose so," he agreed coolly, "But you see, we must continue to have those Life assurance proposal-forms, just the copies, you understand."

"Wait, please," I pleaded. "I may well be kicked out of my company by next Easter."

He brightened. "Ah, that's absolutely fine. Our work will be complete by then, so this whole arrangement can end at that time. Splendid."

This, I supposed, was good news for me in a negative way; but I still had to know who I was dealing with, and had been, for all those years. Was this the mysterious and well-informed Benson connection, for instance, or was Oxdon – by his own admission "the all-knowing" – from some entirely different group?

"Professor," I tried to make it sound fierce and demanding, "When I first came in today, I told you that I had been visited by the CIA, or maybe it was MI6. Either way, they warned me that Moscow wants our lists. They have explained why, and I now understand this. But you said a while ago that being dragged into politics was the last thing you wanted – "

"I think not. I was talking about you. We, as it happens, are deeply into politics – "

"But I have to know, don't you see, who is behind you and your use of the data. It's getting out of hand," I ended, feebly perhaps but inwardly beginning to seethe.

The old man sat thinking, and then surprisingly crumpled up the sheet of Quink and threw it across the room, missing the waste-paper basket but momentarily stirring the interest of the cat, who gazed across but decided it wasn't worth the bother. What was the significance of Oxdon's action, could I have gained an advantage at last? Seize the moment.

"Tell me then." I stood up defiantly and drummed up an angry shout. "Are you working with MI6 or with the CIA?" I banged a fist painfully on the joint-stool. "Is it the Kremlin or – or the East Germans? Israel?" I grabbed two more Cape gooseberries, and chewed at them viciously while he gaped at me. "What do you know about Dutch? Deutsch? How about – " I fumbled furiously for the notes I'd brought with me, "how about Holywell and the Harts? Driberg? The rest of the Oxford ring? What about… er… Abbiss? Barter?? Binns??? Bonnett????"

He was still blinking at me with his mouth open. And well he might: the first few names were well-known Communist suspects, but the rest were straight off the top of my troubled head, drawn from my memory of my old Fourth Form register. But I could see that he suspected something of the sort. No fool, then, old Oxdon.

"How about the rest of the alphabet? Xerxes? Yashimoto?" Suddenly he erupted into laughter, shaking all over. The cat had sensibly vanished, and his daughter came to the door to make sure he wasn't having a seizure. Maybe he was. I nearly was as well, and sat down breathless, while his shoulders still heaved.

Still twitching slightly, and wiping his eyes with a grey-looking handkerchief, he spluttered: "This has nothing to do with spying, dear boy. We aren't remotely interested in students."

* * *

"What!" I nearly got up again.

"No, no." Shaking his head, still wiping. "It's the parents we're after."

I echoed this in amazement. "But when all this started, eight or nine years back, all we were getting for you were those lists – "

"Ah," he pointed at me, "Yes, the home addresses."

"But what good were they to you?"

"Marginal, really." If it hadn't been Oxdon, I would almost have thought he was giggling. "We used them a little for statistical purposes to get some feel about student presence in various towns; but to be frank, Tim, it was just basically a tactic. Just like your covert friends, Left and Right, we can take the long-term view." He spread his hands. "We, too, can plant and wait. Many good seeds will germinate slowly." He gave one of his real spectacle-shifting smiles, as he relished his metaphor. "You were desperately needing the student data to run and build up your business. It worked, didn't it? We were in no hurry and decided we should, if you'll forgive me dear boy, get you – how does one describe it – firmly on the hook, don't you know?"

On the hook, indeed. But why?

"But how do you intend to do anything with the proposal-forms?"

"Health," he said, simply. "It's all about health."

Then he chuckled. I suddenly knew he was going to confide in me. "The tables are turned," he said. "Since we are now near the end of our relationship, I owe it to you to open up and make some confessions. We've known one another for a long time and we're probably much in line politically; and anyway we already share secrets, on top of which I have you – what does one say in the KGB – over a barrel with all my facts about Erroll, and that." Another cough, another gooseberry, and one for me.

"We are looking for bad health."

I was perplexed. "But almost all the health questions on the form are irrelevant: they've had a few broken limbs on the sports field, yes, but apart from childhood illnesses, it's usually a blank page. TB

206

was a big worry when we started, but by the mid-fifties it was suddenly no big risk because it became curable. My own doctor used to run a clinic but he woke up one morning and found himself out of work; so now he's a GP… " He cut me off at last.

"To use the vernacular: bugger the students." I liked this: he was rejuvenating before my eyes. "On every Life Insurance form there are supplementary questions, about the good health, or otherwise, of the rest of the family, not so?"

"Well, yes, but – "

"My associates are extremely, monumentally interested in the bad health of sub-standard parents, especially the men of course, but – "

"Why especially the men? And why can't you get all such information from official sources like the National Health Service?"

He sighed, he was dealing with an idiot. He spelt it out slowly: Because… we… are… not… official. I thought that was obvious."

"You'll have to tell me a bit more," I told him, "and in plain English. Think of me as transfixed by your fish-hook and pinioned over that barrel."

To this day I don't know in what way the metaphor enthused him and I'd rather not dwell on it; but he was clearly encouraged to tell me more of his secrets.

"Your students have to declare if a parent is ill, and specify the reason. As you are sending us four or five thousand forms annually, we already have two or three hundred declared very sick fathers, and we will meet our final target by your suggested closing date next Easter. From that three or four hundred total, we expect to find at least fifty who are not only terminal but whose address suggests they are Right-wing inclined. We would therefore expect, at a rough guess, at least half of them to be willing to serve in a good cause."

Great Scott, we were entering Wonderland again.

I asked: "What on earth can you and – er – your group whoever they are, do with fifty dying old men?"

"Think about it," he smiled; it was definitely back to the old genuine smile which had always sent those glasses sideways, and despite myself I warmed to it. But not for long, because he still threatened me. "And think long and hard," he added, "about those plains outside Nairobi, that dark night in 1941 and the missing pall-bearer, don't you know?" He reached out to ring a little bell on his side-table. The daughter came in.

"Tim, we've covered a lot of ground today. It's agreed that we carry on as before? Come and see me again before Easter, won't you, and I will then enlighten you a bit more. You see, I am a scallywag."

He was quite clearly going off his rocker. But as I left, and much as he must have done to generations of undergraduates over the years: "Glad we've had this little chat." Then however, he added: "Oh, and remember the hook and the barrel."

I slammed the door, and not much ashamed to admit it. He had dried up on me after all. I wasn't in his confidence in the least. I was being blackmailed, dictated to, and used. I reached for my non-existent Stuyvesants…

★ ★ ★

I was also being rather silly: I went back, ringing the bell sheepishly.

His daughter was smiling as she opened the door. "People often come back after a couple of minutes. Usually it's when they've thought of an answer. You know: 'esprit de l'escalier'."

I told her I hadn't much esprit left, and I'd fallen off my escalier.

She sympathised, but added: "He's getting old, but he still has some interesting things to say if only people would listen."

"For goodness sake," came the voice from the study, "I wish you two would stop drafting my obituary. Bring him back in and sit him down with the syphilis-fruit."

She pretended to look shocked but was obviously well-briefed. She must have been over fifty but dressed younger – wild hair swept back above a casual loose, ill-coloured, very North Oxford scarf. I thought of that super-eccentric presumably-female Don who so often strode down from Somerville… Or even, if transmuted, the equally disturbed music professor one would see wandering Broad

Street at that time, his hair like an infested beehive... but nevertheless I love his symphonies.

It struck me yet again that Oxdon must surely be remote now, from all those people. Marooned in a comfortable but stagnant backwater as he was. I was once more starting to feel sorry for him; and I saw his really-rather-feeble attempt to blackmail me via my clearly-innocent father as perhaps the last throw of dice that he knew to be loaded against him: he was evidently himself under pressure from 'somebody above', somewhere. At least I could now cross him off Olivia's list. This was not our mole. And that, I suppose, was why I had felt I should go back.

"Professor, my own position is not what it was: I am not a free agent now, I have a Board of Directors and I have to be answerable to them. As you know, I have made sure nobody knows of our connection, nor will they, so long as I remain in charge. But our relationship will most certainly come out into the open if I stop being in charge. That would expose you, in a way I suspect you would not like."

"No, that is something we would not like, Tim. You are correct."

"Therefore, it is in your group's interest that I do remain in charge, and to help me to achieve that, I must know what you are up to. Are you with me, so far?"

"I can hear what you are saying."

"So, please: what use do you intend to make of the family health data you are getting from me?"

He sat thinking, and then – with some relief it seemed – he decided to come clean.

"All right." He scooped up the cat as he often did. I think it was his comfort blanket: it certainly looked like one. "Our country is in grave danger. Look back just a few years," he said quietly, as though there were spies all around us, behind the heavy curtains and inside the sinister photocopier... (God knows, I found myself thinking, there might well be: has he had the place checked for bugs?).

"Grave," he repeated. "Eden, then Macmillan and finally Hume all fell victim to 'events', as dear old Mac put it. But you see, he was quite right: those events really were 'outside', nothing to do with our running of the country. Then, you see, came Gaitskill. He was a moderate, Left but only just Left, shall we say a Socialist who nevertheless loved his country, and for his country, worked within the rules: an Englishman – one could have trusted him." Long pause: of course, Oxdon used to be a lecturer.

"And he died. Suddenly. Why?" He looked at me but I shrugged feebly. I had read Politics but not Forensics. Was he suggesting that, here in England, of all places, they were becoming both the same?

"So we get this Harold Wilson, glib North Country wonder-boy, pipe-smoking upstart who always uses cigars when nobody's looking. So: a cheat. If a man will cheat in little ways, how much more in big ways when under pressure and given the chance? Do you truly see anything genuine there? We don't. They tell me, MI5 don't, either. They say he's being looked into, and a lot of his buddies with their precarious knighthoods. And he reinstates Philby, for Heaven's sake! There are signs and indications," he concluded, out of breath.

"Well anyway –" I started, but it would be counter-productive to interrupt just yet, he was becoming confidential.

"The Scallywags," he said.

I was quite lost by this, though I sensed it was some sort of code.

"In the early part of the war," Oxdon continued confidentially, "a lot of us got together – mainly High Table people but there were lots of others, graduate researchers and so on. We pledged to work together, behind the scenes, a sort of intellectual *maquis*, against the threat of invasion."

"You probably know," he went on, shifting for more comfort in his chair, and of course I didn't know at all, "the Auxiliary Units set up after Dunkirk to form a top-secret military defence force?" His voice went up at the end, as though to confirm that I was accustomed to Top Secrets, and I found myself nodding like a conspiratorial idiot.

"Churchill set it up with a chap called… ", he tailed off and thought for a minute. "Name like a boy in a storybook, can't remember. But one of their top people, when they were disbanded, went into teaching – you may meet him, you go to Loughborough don't you?"

"So he was a Scally –?"

"No, no, he was in the military lot, all blood-and-guts. But our lot, we were the Scallywags. You might say, the harmless brains.

"We were no good, any of us, with guns or bayonets, or even the farmyard pikes and scythes they tied together, and all that; but we had brain-power, and sometimes that counts. We called ourselves The Scallywags just because," he tailed off rather feebly, "well, it was a good anonymous name, don't you know, didn't give the game away. After all, they nicknamed the Home Guard 'Dad's Army'."

"If you were all University people, why not 'Grads' Army'?"

"Yes, of course we thought of that". This shut me up effectively and I let the Professorial scallywag continue.

"Your proposal-forms, Tim, can tell us which men to approach. They are patriots, they are terminally-ill. Any personal sacrifice they may make, would only bring forward and – er – abbreviate their physical end."

I was incredulous. "You are recruiting a death-squad of respectable Conservative suicide-bombers!"

"To be quite frank with you Tim, yes", he said, absolutely calm. "But give that long word a small 'c'."

"The country must be protected" he thumped the arm of his chair. "If Wilson's gang, pretending patriotism, in fact invites the Soviets to come in and take over, at first via a powerful Fifth Column already being cultivated and nurtured – largely at the colleges through the Student Unions, by the way – can you deny it? – then we will be swamped before most people in their innocence and naivete and apathy even realise it. We must be ready. For the fight-back. There will have to be voluntary sacrifices… The Scallywags would return and see to it, and see it through. On a wartime basis".

There would also have to be a quick withdrawal by me from this, which he jovially accepted: he seemed much younger, his enthusiasm was a rejuvenation. I took a couple of gooseberries, sexually-transmitted though they might be; clearly, my head was in need of some respite and a drop of Laphroaig…

★ ★ ★

At the Swan, Marian had good news: the church bells were under repair. I wondered which of the locals had heroically sabotaged them, but gladly booked myself in. I decided to defer the Laphroaig until I had eaten, and went into the cosy dining-room armed with – no, not a dry sherry but for old times' sake a rather special white port: I had been introduced to this as a young soldier, at a tiny riverside pub in Leintwardine near the Welsh Border, and though a bit on the un-dry side, it went down very well, paradoxically at the *start* of a meal.

The Swan's temporary chef, I deduced from his menu, was still living in the Fifties, so I romantically joined him there and ordered, equally nostalgically, a prawn cocktail followed by Chicken Maryland. At once, I was back on Kings Road with Sarah… Wells and the four-poster with Sarah… Sheffield, even, with – Oh, stop it!

Wine, sir? There wasn't a Pouilly Fume, nor a run-of-the-mill Fuisse, so a carafe of the House Stuff which was not too bad at all. But no point trying to show off: I was no James Bond, after all. (Nor was he, I sometimes thought in more recent years).

I reckoned I might drag myself back into happier days with an Armagnac Arbellot to go with the coffee, also as an overdue nod to Olivia; but they had never heard of it. I thought 'Sod it' and went to the other extreme, with the cheapest possible Spanish Fundador, and had three of them. I forget what they tasted like, but the coffee was good – for Newport Pagnell.

As you will have gathered, it had been a tough day; but it wasn't finished yet. I found my way erratically to the public telephone. After a couple of inexplicable wrong numbers, I found I had successfully rung Olivia and drank her health down the line.

She had nothing much to report, just digging in the Records

with more still to do. She had gone the wrong way on the Circle Line, of course, right round in fact, and eventually came to Somerset House from the East, but as she proudly pointed out, had not had to change trains, so she felt she had won, and at no extra expense I had to work that out but she was right Then I told her we could eliminate Oxdon from our list of moles, which was a relief even though it had raised all sorts of other hares – and fearing her inevitable reaction to the phrase, I almost hung up…

But then she had a sensible suggestion. As I had to be in Cambridge tomorrow, would it not be a good idea to bring back to Pimlico all the current student lists? Every last one. They could be put into a safe deposit in London, just in case of any further trouble. Yes, I agreed. She had a second suggestion, that by the sound of me I should have an early night; but it was already too late for such indulgence.

I would see her tomorrow evening, loaded to the roof with all the lists and running the gauntlet, whatever that was, of the dreaded KGB who would kill. Never mind that, my glass was empty, it was at last time for my treasured Laph-however you spelt it…

Oh, what a long day…

Marian brought the drink across to my usual chimney-corner, and also a few sheets of paper for note-making, which I had normally had to request. Great girl, Marian…

My job for the evening, I started explaining to myself up the chimney, was to puzzle out precisely who I was dealing with covertly, and who I was coping with on the sidelines, and who I was being studied by at Oxdon's crowd, and could I do anything about it all… And who I was…

We had these lists, you see, I pointed out confidentially, after an hour or so. And what was worse, my glass had got empty yet again.

Matt, who was either CIA or MI6, or perhaps both, didn't want them. What? These lists. Everything they needed on students they were getting, through COSEC and the NUS and the Education Ministry. Somebody called Bollocks had started it, somebody had told me long, long ago in an American accent I thought, and I pondered that for a while. Was Matt with the Russians? I felt I couldn't quite work it out, but that meal had been nice. Good old Maryland.

That nice girl came over every now and then with refreshments. Nice girl, that… Begins with 'M'…

Mr Benson was from 'the other side'. That must mean the Kremlin. They didn't want the lists either, just a few top student names of those most involved in politics, like Wilson, smoking a cigar in his pipe, which seemed somehow erotic; but now Russia would soon know that we'd found out about Mr Branson all right, and his bottle of sauce, ha-ha. So what would they do?

Nobody wants the fucking lists. And much more importantly, there was a mole, o mio, mio, because everywhere I was planning to go, it chimed – oh God, chimes – chimed in with his requests; so the mole has to be somebody in the office, and there are dozens… No, well, several…

And if, if, we found the mole, what would it matter because if, if the NUS start their own insurance business I will be closed down and then with all those debts, if – Oh God, all those debts. It was getting jolly – jolly-well near to – "

Suddenly nothing happened.

"Bedtime?" suggested Melinda, or Marina, or Maryland or whatever her bloody name was, nice girl though, and I didn't argue. It was getting bedtime, so I just left them all. I hadn't written anything on those bits of paper but I tore them up anyway – you can't be too careful, can you?

CHAPTER XIII

I was perfectly all right in the morning, and set off on the bunny-run, waving a friendly hand to the church tower. (My salesman years of experience insist that at this point I must refer you to Note 5 at the back!).

I was diverted before Bedford by roadworks, and sent down to Ampthill, to cut across to the A1. More memories. Professor A E Richardson, the artist and architect, President of the Royal Academy in his day, was marched through Ampthill as a young soldier during the First World War and saw a beautiful Georgian house, vowing to buy it one day. The day came, and he did buy it, but all the splendid eighteenth century furniture had gone to auction.

He made it his life's hobby to trace it and so far as possible buy everything back. From school, when I was the pretentious Secretary of our pseudo-Aesthetic Society, we used to visit him in small parties and be shown over. It was a treasure-house and he took us round personally. He bubbled with enthusiasm. But here is the best part: he had a Sedan chair; and to celebrate the end of the Second World War he found two friends and had himself carried round town in it, to attend a street party. On the way home, it being dark, they were stopped by an officious policeman for having no lights. "But, officer, I'm not a vehicle," he said. "Look, I'm a parcel."

I'm sure I've told you that before but what the hell?

Once back in Cambridge, I went round to the Lion to see Robin, and collected all the current lists which he had finished with; he would in future always let me have them as soon as he had sent out all the letters. He agreed this was sensible under the present circumstances. He wanted a quick word, so he came down from the ladder, at the top of which he had been swaying while filling in what looked like a mousehole except it was in the ceiling. Neither of us mentioned it.

He said he was sure the Area Managers were planning something to happen at the March meeting. They had given the HQ Directors to understand they would like a private meeting, one at a time. They didn't want me to know about it. Robin said he would have to go along with the others, obviously, but would keep me informed.

I drove back to Pimlico with all my lists. The next day, Olivia and I took them, together with my original 'Victor Lazlo' Letter of Introduction from Oxdon, and a few more sensitive papers which had been getting in the way of her pasta and face powder, to a safe deposit place in a drive-through basement just off the Strand. Olivia was not very impressed with the security, even though she – or I – had to show identification like fingerprints… She said a friend of their family, a distant cousin I think it was, could break into it in ten minutes. When I say 'distant', I understand he lives in Palermo.

She was equally critical of the keys they gave us to my box. "*Mamma mia*! What an unimportant key! It is just like that bunch you have for the tenants' electric meters." I invented a plausible explanation – true for all I knew – that this was a clever disguise to conceal how important it really was; but it didn't cut much ice.

"This key will guard important papers but I think it will break in the lock. We in Italy have better lock people"

"You probably need them," I feebly retorted. "When you have finished your notes on all our mole suspects," I said, "put them into the box as well," and I gave her one of the two keys.

Robin rang me that evening. "I've been talking to Ollie," he said. "He says that because he is your personal adviser as well as the company's accountant, he can see himself perhaps being in a difficult position; so he thinks he'd better stick with the company, stop advising you, and would I let you know."

"This sounds like trouble brewing?"

"Could well be; but believe me, I'll keep you posted."

And then just as I was about to hang up: "Oh, by the way, we think it is terribly important that you make yourself scarce, really, really scarce until March. We think you'll be OK but meanwhile keep your head down. Just bugger off somewhere. If you show them any anxiety at all, it could activate things. Above all, make sure you don't have any contact, any, at all Tim, with the Area Managers – whatever – before the March meeting.

" Scarce, OK? Just piss off. 'Bye." And that was that.

★ ★ ★

So I followed the advice. But it is so difficult to 'make yourself scarce' suddenly, to order. A three-month-long empty diary was out of the question, so I had to invent a whole range of ways to look busy, whilst not being available at home or at the offices, and it was an eye-opening experience, hiding from the phone. For the first time I came to understand how those hundreds of precariously-employed middle-range Whitehall Warriors contrive to justify their existence.

You have to pretend to be busy, ever so busy, but just out of reach. You think up all sorts of minor amendments and petty potential rulings that will promote the impression that you are deep into abstruse problems that make you essential and irreplaceable. Don't you know?

I went on a tour of all the universities in parts of the country not covered by the four Area Managers, taking Olivia with me. What? Well why not, everybody else does if they can find a way to justify it. We talked business, didn't we?

In Scotland, we ranged from the smoke of Sauchiehall Street to the grim granite of Aberdeen, and met in Edinburgh some student union leaders who later became politicians and Lords, a pain in the arse even then; but we also visited and loved St Andrews and tickled the chins of the flatfish in the aquarium. In Wales we drove right round the coast since nearly all the students are at the seaside; but also ventured inland to visit Plynlimon, the mountain where both the Severn and the Wye have their source, and which I had cycled to with two pals from school, twenty years before – an exercise in nostalgia which much appealed to Olivia: "You English schoolboys, ten days on bicycles and sleeping in haystacks, *Mamma mia*." Actually, that was only one night, we chose B & B the other nine nights; and anyway it wasn't hay, it was unfortunately straw and we got up and left, scratching ourselves, at five in the morning.

Next Olivia and I flew over to Ireland. Belfast at that time was riven by this or that political agitation, so I had left it to Robin to issue whatever marketing stuff he could; and we went down to Dublin in the Republic, mainly because they had got in touch with me some time ago and asked if they could be included in our SLAS scheme with its evident student benefits. I had gone to the Insurers and got their agreement, so this was a serious business meeting... It got hilariously out of hand almost at once:

The President of USI (Union of Students in Ireland) was delighted to "meet with" us, and we agreed lunch at Jury's. Where else? This was the venue of choice at that time.

Lunch was fine: we discussed the insurance needs of his students, we looked at our statistics from sales results over in the UK... Lunch and its afterthoughts being ended, we became a little more relaxed and called for occasional refills of the Gaelic Coffees to which he had subjected us... We talked on, drank on: this was, after all, Jury's. We found, to our surprise, that we were still sitting at the table when dinner started... The menu was brought to us. We sat and tried to focus.

Suddenly, the President of the USI began to sing. Loudly. Good voice. Some very Irish song. Fifty other diners began to look at us, haughty and disapproving; after all, this was Jury's. I shrank behind the flower-vase, as I saw the Head Waiter steaming across to our table. He aligned himself menacingly alongside the Student President who was in full flow. He fixed him with a stare. Oh God, I thought... Then – he joined in, loudly too, through to the end of the song.

We went back to England. We were safer there; and I had a bit of time to give some thought to Oxdon's unpleasant blackmail threat, and some completely unexpected connections, nothing to do with this story. (But do see Note 8, when you've finished the book).

★ ★ ★

March came: Olivia was still doing her researches. I was getting from the library, books on bankruptcy. I had made a list of people I would have to tell, if things went against me. Yes indeed, it was March, and still no hint who might be our mole. If we had one, he was still anonymous.

The Board Meeting which I dreaded was at the Oxford office, where the ever-happy and unassuming Tony now ran our somewhat sumptuous ex-Jerry offices, rather like a small green pea in a large golden pod... or have I said that?

I drove there, on what was apparently a glorious Spring-like morning, which seemed to have enthused Robin, who was with me, but the weather didn't do very much for me personally, as I morosely contemplated my likely demise.

Robin was unusually lyrical: "What a glorious Spring-like morning," he told me as we went down into Henley. I had been thinking it was rather cold.

"Yes," I said.

"My word," he enthused, opening his window no matter that it caught me in a draught around the neck, "Doesn't it make a difference, don't you think, when the sun catches the fresh glint in the young leaves and the fields glow gold and shimmering with a sort of liquid magic like this...?"

"Yes," I said. The sun had not yet reached my side of the car and I thought the clouds were a bit threatening.

"Just listen to the birds," he told me. "The happiness as they greet the new bright days of Spring, and the promise of their mating season is infectious, isn't it?"

"Yes," I said as I nearly ran over a scavenging crow.

"Don't you really get the feeling," he went on remorselessly, as we drove up the hill out of Henley, " this must truly be God's own country – "

"Yes," I said, and at last I had got him.

"For Christ's sake," he said, "Stop saying Yes."

"Well, shut up for the sake of God and his own bloody country."

We drove on, happily, to my impending doom.

★ ★ ★

I checked into the Randolph as of old, saying Hello to that old lady who lived there permanently, thanks to the pension from her prematurely-defunct husband. One pondered, looking at her comfort, what had ground the poor man into his early grave?

I walked round the corner past Ellistons, up to our offices. I smiled slantingly at Elsa, a delectable recent teenage addition to the clerical staff whom I would later take for surreptitious lunchtime picnics to Godstow; I have to tell you, I saw her again recently in The High, and she still has the best legs in Oxfordshire. (Note 15)

I went into Tony's (ex-Jerry and thus still very impressive) office. Everyone was already seated, which itself was suspicious. But more sinister was the rotund stranger, sweating in a serious suit, sitting alongside Max and Sid.

As one might expect, Max started. "Tim, this is Somebody-or-other" (I have made no attempt to remember his name) "who represents us, and we would like you to agree for him to attend this meeting as our advisor. He is a solicitor."

I looked at him: too bloody sure, a smooth lawyer from Leeds, what else could he have been. But I could scarcely refuse: all my fellow Directors were nodding agreement to this request, though none of them would meet my eye. Robin was as bad as the rest, and I had to wonder whether he had been misleading me. Or, as he had told me, just keeping in with them, the better to protect me…

I had never before fully experienced that awful sensation known as a 'sinking feeling'. Partly, yes, that is common, as when you are caught out at school by a very strict disciplinarian; or shrinking under the baleful eyes of a policeman on a hilltop outside Witney. But real deep-down collapse and terminal disaster, if you've suffered it, you will know what I mean, and agree that this is a good description: you feel that your lower body, the bowels and the bladder, have opened and out-poured. It sometimes, in some people, physically means just that; but for most of us it is a sort of mental evacuation – and here's an interesting phrase – a 'gut feeling'. I had it.

Ollie, who at least was looking at me, then announced that as he was my personal accountant and adviser, he felt he should at this point step down as a Director of the Company. At first I thought: 'wait a minute, he has just said the opposite, according to Robin'; but he left the room anyway. I kept quiet. Was he up to something?

Max – who else? – then set in motion all the nasty business by proposing: One, that the previously-arranged agenda for this meeting be set aside and we should proceed at once to Any Other Business. Put to the vote: all the rest were in favour, with me abstaining.

Two: that the Chairman for this and future meetings should be Edward. Aha, I thought, the other Area Managers are keen to butter him up, this unexpected flattery is aimed to get him on their side; but I voted in favour. I thought, as he is a sensible man and a trainee lawyer, this would do no harm.

After that, they all called for me to resign as Managing Director. It was pointed out to me smoothly by the fat man in the suit, that the bulk of the shareholding was against me and if I refused to resign, all they had to do was call a shareholders' meeting which, given the new distributions, would inevitably kick me out.

I won't take you through all the bureaucratic rigmarole which wastes so much of our lives… It seemed that my HQ Directors had been subjected to what in my opinion were a load of dubious facts and corrupt statistics, which had persuaded them to vote for my removal. (I accept that the Area Managers might have had some valid points against me and even my other colleagues, so the sensible approach would have been a discussion, but it was clear that Max and Sid and their Man From Leeds preferred a quick attack with a steamroller…).

I ended up that midday as a Director still, but only just, pending removal altogether from the business as soon as they called a shareholders' meeting, and till then with no duties and therefore no salary. With their powerful shareholding, Max, Sid and (trailing along) Maurice – plus strangely Edward – now held sway. Within a few minutes, Max and Sid became joint Managing Directors with a very comfortable basic salary plus commission on everybody's production (hitherto they had been no salary, commission only, and only on their own production); Maurice and Edward got a lesser but still useful salary but – significantly – it was dependent only upon their own production; Edward was offered an extra fee for being Chairman but he declined it as he felt the position should 'float' in a small business like ours. All three of my HQ Directors were in one way or another subtly diminished.

They all went off together for lunch at a well-known place down St Aldates; so close to Pembroke Street, yet even Jerry had never taken me there – too pretentious, he'd said – and since he evidently preferred the Dorchester, or first-class on the Queen Elizabeth or something, if our local restaurant was that overblown they were welcome to it. I only hoped the sweaty man paid the bill.

Me? I slunk out on my own, smiling my sad smile to the very desirable and wonderfully-designed Elsa, and – longing for a smoke – went ploddingly along The Broad to Blackwells. On the way I got part of my equilibrium and sense of humour back by considering how lucky I had been and would always be, whatever might happen to my business, when I was linked to my College, this marvellous city and its unmatchable army of eccentrics; people like the wonderful Dr. Spooner and the salt. He knew, somewhere in that tangled brain, that if you spill red wine on a tablecloth, it's a good idea to put salt on it quickly; so – yes, you're ahead of me – somebody at dinnertime spilt the salt, so without hesitation he poured red wine on it. Lovely.

Only in Oxford (or maybe in Windermere?).

I bought a helpful book on bankruptcy, and sat reading it in the little White Hart pub, where I had a pie and mushy peas. The pie was OK but the peas weren't mushy enough to suit my mood.

I knew that my rebellious colleagues all had a long-scheduled Management Meeting in the afternoon, at which, as a Director without portfolio, I was evidently not involved; so to preserve my diminishing sanity I walked up to Jericho and went to 'The Scala', that little off-beat cinema where I had for many years discovered remarkable films, many of them lost to the general public. In those days it was all 'continental noir', and that day they were showing the sad-but-charming *Jeux Interdits*'. Rene Clement was the director, and what a pity he later produced that 1965 unhappiness 'Is Paris Burning?' Good title. Great idea. Flop.

But about *Jeux*: this has one of the most wonderful background music themes, on guitar. Every time it is played on the radio, the announcer says 'by an anonymous composer'. What is the matter with these stuffy self-appointed 'authorities'?

Surely at the BBC they can't be all that gormless? What's wrong with their archives? Even the announcers would only have to exert themselves a little, to check the cinema reference books where the film's music is credited. I said so to the Radio Times but they didn't print it. My old friend Halliwell would have made them pull up their languid complacent socks.

I then, disconsolately humming the tune, went back to The Randolph with a bottle in my pocket – why pay silly prices? – and went to bed with it, still fuming about the BBC's Radio Three...

Why do their incoming Managers automatically assume that they know better than the older people they replace? So many ideas and productions from years ago, are quite simply *better* than the stuff we now seek to supplant it. I know this. Most of you know this, too. But who's going to stop the down-slide? I went to sleep dreaming about Scallywags... Storming with machine-guns into Broadcasting House...

★ ★ ★

It was about four in the morning that I awoke. Christ! I thought, what a bloody fool I am. Early today the gang would be at the Cambridge office, ravaging the files… And my remaining secrets, instructions for sending copies to Oxdon, arrangements with our creditors, all sorts of private papers, advertising deals with top Insurers that were strictly off-the-record… I got up and drove like mad.

At the Pruhaus in Cambridge, at six-thirty I arrived alongside the milkman and found the elderly Glaswegian caretaker (I must here correct that: I had always thought he must be Glaswegian simply because, at first hearing, I could never understand a word he said, and had to ask him not only to repeat but sometimes even to spell it: it turned out he came from somewhere else, downstream) and he let me in, thank goodness.

I went straight to my personal metal set of drawers that served as a filing cabinet. I emptied it, bunging everything into a cardboard box, and then locked it again, nothing inside at all, as an act of spontaneous defiance which I rejoiced in later.

Then I drove to Bedford, where alongside the watery mid-river prison of an earlier renegade, holier than I, I knew that our friendly Bank Manager was always available by nine with his bacon sandwich. Breathless, I told him what was happening, and got his promise of goodwill.

I then steamed down to Kent, to our main Insurance Company creditor, where I was sure I would get support from Hugh. I did.

By mid-afternoon I was in Guildford with the tricky job of not just facing, but convincing Jerry that on his small but comfortable lakeside fish-stocked estate he would have to cut back on the Black Label until I'd sorted things out: I didn't want to hurt him, as he was ageing and showing early signs of ill-health, but luckily he accepted the situation – he was at last becoming a realist.

By supper-time I was back again at Grumbles with Olivia, at a table for four, and we were shortly approached by a good friend, Adrian, an actor successful in various TV roles, with his black girlfriend Billie, who was a very attractive jazz singer. Adrian was well-known for being 'outrageous': that PR adjective most likely to get a mention for him in the gossip pages; but, as with most struggling thespians, it was – appropriately – an act. As he came up to our table, he said loudly: "Tim, you don't mind sharing your table with a spade, do you?"

I took a quick look at the lovely Billie but she was smiling.

"Good Lord no," I replied, "Some of our best friends… I just can't stand the white trash they associate with."

I waved towards Olivia. "Are you OK with Eyties?"

Which set the tone for an enjoyable evening. (Note 16).

★ ★ ★

But now I reckoned I needed to talk about my plight to some professionals. I started, next afternoon, by ringing my personal accountant (for matters outside the company), whom I'd known for years: Bernard up in Finchley, but he had left the office.

"He's gone home already," said his secretary.

"Has he alr-," I replied, but felt I had to bite back the word in the nick of time, suddenly realising that it would sound rude and be judged anti-semitic by the tight-arsed fools who are seeping into our lives, our Courts and our innocence.

Bernard did, next day, recommend to me a very charming young lawyer, just north of Oxford Street, who gave me a great deal of useful advice. The only trouble, when I look back, was that this very simple advice was wrapped up in him ascertaining from me at once one very self-evident fact in my favour, and he spun it out over several weeks, and God-knows-what fee per hour. He could well afford to be so charming, it occurred to me later. Nice chap, though; aren't they all?

This simple fact actually emerged by itself, free of charge, in the midst of all the intended litigation, when I had lunch with Robin and Ollie. I know my whole story seems to centre around lunches and dinners, but that's the way it was. The whole era of 'long business lunches' has been derided, but when the morning and afternoon hours are fully taken up by routine sales activity, those meetings at food-time were a vital opportunity to talk serious stuff with serious people. It did get out of hand in some quarters, mainly in the big national companies: I remember once, at a lunch with Directors of a vast Scottish Insurer, launching into business matters as the soup arrived, and being chided: "Oh come now, Tim, wait until the cheese." This never happened when I was lunching with any Directors of small businesses like ours: our time-tables seldom allowed such luxury.

I met Ollie and Robin at the same little Italian restaurant, just off Kings Road, where I had once taken that girl I rescued from the window of Peter Jones. It was called 'Au Pere de Nico' but so far as I remember, Nico had been from Naples. As always, Robin started talking, as the antipasti arrived.

"It was bloody lucky you took my advice and kept away from the Area Managers," he told me, licking his knife thoughtfully. "We were petrified that you might have talked to them about share prices."

"You didn't, did you?" Ollie put in anxiously. He was hidden behind the menu, possibly a bit unused to all that Mediterranean food and seeking something recognisable. "Although you had agreed quite early on, how much the HQ men were to pay, I hope you are still debating prices with the AMs, am I right?"

I was sensing good news, and ordered a bottle further down the list. "Neither Max nor Sid have paid me anything at all, I suspect they hope to get the shares for nothing," I told him, "and Maurice is still arguing,' I imagine. And on your instructions I've kept away from Edward too."

"No contact whatever?"

"Absolutely none. We've been away, incommunicado."

"Thank God," said Robin. "You're back in business."

Ollie spelt it out. As Company Secretary it had been his job to get the share transfers registered, but to do that it is imperative to declare the purchase price, and then pay the appropriate Stamp Duty. He had heard nothing. In short, the gang had jumped the gun (I had a terrible job in Pimlico that night translating the phrase). Nobody could legally have voted me out after all.

I refilled the glasses and called the waiter. I noted that, for once, I didn't feel the need for a smoke.

"So," I said, steadying my glass and deep into my *penne arabbiatta*, "How soon can I get back?"

It was a depressing answer. Company protocol and all the legal Articles of Limited Companies would give the new Managing Directors a good few months of complete power before, as a protesting majority shareholder, I could get back in and be rid of them.

The eventual outcome would be clear-cut from the start; but while they were sitting in the Company chair, they could take all sorts of nasty steps designed to wreck the business from within, so that when they eventually left, they could benefit enormously in their own, newly-formed competing businesses, by having crippled mine. They could also default deliberately on all our debts. They would leave me in the ultimate shit.

"That's about it," said Ollie. "Nevertheless," he went on, "we do have a different approach. Let's set aside the fact that, at the end of the day, you have a shareholding majority. Much quicker, being still a Director, if you can command a majority at Board level, you can put everything right at the next Board Meeting, by a simple show of hands, up in Finchley at Max's office. But you will have to plan it very carefully. Remember there are four Area Directors, against three HQ, and then you. But one of the Area ones has a casting vote.

"So they have a majority, on the face of it."

"And I can't help," he ended, "because I've resigned."

...

And, I reminded myself when he had gone: we have a mole.

★ ★ ★

On the crucial day, Robin, Ron and Tony met me early in the morning in Pimlico. I now knew I was OK with Robin of course, given his Matt connection. As for Tony, he had soon felt that he had been misled, and anyway he was resentful at Max and Sid cutting him down both personally and financially. Ron, submissive as ever and absorbed in his Life Assurance dusty routines, and his family troubles, had been carried along initially, I supposed, with the tide of the Area Managers' assault on me, and had also been chiefly concerned in securing his long-term income, for which I couldn't blame him, as he had given up a lot to come to us.

Ultimately though, it was Robin who had cleverly clinched things by warning them both about the hidden Agenda of Max and Sid, and thus persuading them to vote along with the AMs for the time being, and so exposing, to us all, their real intentions.

So there we all were, mobilised for the attack, "like Badger, Ratty and Mole", Olivia said. But the vital victory had been won, very quietly, the previous day.

★ ★ ★

I took a bit of a risk by asking young Edward, our Chairman no less, to meet me for lunch, in Henley, in that nice square hotel by the bridge. I knew that he regarded me favourably since I had appointed him in the teeth of opposition and had defended him against the antagonism of the other three AMs. And he had read Law.

"You do know," I began, "that the transfers haven't been done, and why?"

He nodded. "I imagine you'll be calling a shareholders' meeting as soon as you can, to outvote them all?"

"Until I can achieve that," I went on, "you Area Managers hold the reins and can be as destructive of me as you like, for months." I sketched for him some of the possible destructions. "The AMs can grind us into the ground by deliberate extravagance, running up huge bills we can't pay?"

"Not me," said Edward. "It's all been a bit too much for me; and to be honest, the in-fighting and the dubious ethics have rather turned me against the insurance business, or at least your side of it.

I'm inclining back to the law as a career," he ended. "I'm sorry Tim, because I owe you a lot."

"If that is so," I said after a deep breath, "If you do owe me something, you can cancel out that debt, if there is one, at a single stroke."

"I can guess what's coming."

"Of course you can, with your training. At present they've made you our Chairman, and if necessary you have a casting vote. Tomorrow in Finchley –."

He reached across the table to pat my arm. "Tim, I won't be anywhere near Finchley tomorrow. You can appoint your own Chairman and secure the vote."

He drew from his pocket a letter with his resignation as a Director, and in front of me he dated it that day, and also declined the offer of shares. We then had a happy lunch, a drink or two, and strolled up to the bridge to watch the Eights. Problem solved.

★ ★ ★

The four of us, driving in my car up to Finchley on the morning of my planned comeback, discussed first of all whether we were attacking Toad Hall or acting out something by Baroness Orczy, or Dumas. I only hoped that our mental swordsmanship would see us through; but we had everything pretty well lined-up.

At Max's office there was a noticeable lack of the old bonhomie which had always, in the past, pervaded our meetings, even at the most anguished or pivotal times. Nobody made any jokes. The Area Managers seemed to have no idea what was coming, and for the first ten minutes they were looking at their watches and obviously wondering where Edward was. Just before ten-fifteen I said: "Oh, by the way, I have this letter; we have to elect a new Chairman."

The four of us elected Robin as Chairman, with Tony as Secretary; it was then explained that, due to their dilatoriness, the three Area Managers had not agreed terms for their shares and therefore no transfers had been registered. Ollie had written: "I have been advised that I should not register them in view of the conflicting instructions I have received, and in some cases I have not been given the consideration to enable me to assess the stamp duty payable… " and Tony read this out.

Then the legal clincher: "Nor have I received that stamp duty. As a result the transfers have not been presented for stamping."

After that, the rest was easy. But very rewarding.

We moved, four-to-three, that Max and Sid should at once resign as joint Managing Directors, to be Directors without salaries or duties, and we set up a review into the possible refunding of their swollen salaries over the past few months; we cut down Maurice a bit because his ostentation was damaging us at student unions in the Midlands and perhaps at NUS; and it was proposed and agreed four-to-three that the bill, so far still unpaid, from the sweaty man in the sober suit at George Street in March should be paid personally, by those Directors who had retained him, not by the company.

I relish one exchange I had, in the course of all this, with an apoplectic Maurice, who demanded: "If you are cutting us all out, how do you expect to keep the company going?"

I was suddenly inspired. I said *"Il faut reculer, pour mieux sauter."* And it kept me happy for weeks.

Anyway, I was back.

★ ★ ★

The meeting unwound pretty fast, without any of the usual friendly after-chat. Both the gallant Tony and Ron had left early, about their various productive business activities, no doubt; the three displaced Area Managers disappeared, I supposed to start planning their new competitive insurance businesses (but where would they get their names and addresses?).

After a while, Robin and I walked back down Ballards Lane towards that big pub on the corner. We were going for a drink, but fortunately I reached into the pocket of my mac (yes, I know it was Summer but it was raining, OK?) and my car keys had gone.

I looked down the road. My car had gone, too.

★ ★ ★

I found a phone-box, in the street down by the pub, I think it was. I rang Olivia.

Before I could say anything, she shouted into the phone: "Tim, I have news. It was not Japan, it was Korea."

"What the hell?" I shouted back. "Listen, my car will be – "

"Your car is here, it's just come, I cannot see who – "

"Shit! Don't open – "

"Someone is on the stairs… Tim, I'll leave a note – "

Silence.

"Darling – " But I heard a crash as a door was forced. She said nothing more but there were four little taps on the handset at her end, as with a spoon, and then the line had gone dead.

We called a taxi and sped, at the usual black cab speed of ten miles an hour, if all clear, down to Pimlico. I never knew before that day, that it was seven hundred miles from Finchley to Westminster. Our driver bimbled happily along… Ambulances doppled past…

We arrived. My car was not there. We rushed up to the flat: Olivia was not there. There were break-in marks on the door.

I skimmed through the scattered papers to catch up on the notes she had been making, from her researches into our staff, which I had asked for; and there was something about Ron, of all people. This was so concise, it only took me a couple of minutes. Ron had been a Far East prisoner, yes, we all knew that, but not in Japan 1939-45, he was too young to have been in the earlier conflict, Olivia had discovered, but in the Korean War. And, I suddenly realised, in Korea there had been much brainwashing of Western prisoners… Very much. Sophisticated Communist stuff, deep into the brain…

I then saw a large sheet of paper, prominent on my desk, with just a scribbled note in big, bright red felt-pen: "Horace 1600" and alongside it, curiously, our bunch of fiddly little gas-meter keys.

Robin was bemused. I asked him, what was the time? Just past three-thirty.

"For God's sake," I said, "We've got to get to Trafalgar Square by four o'clock."

Robin went running out into the road to find a taxi but I knew they were scarce mid-afternoon on Warwick Way – school collecting time in Belgravia; instead, in an inspired moment, I rang Jeremy at Grumbles and he sent hurtling around to us the girl in the E-type. Somehow, we crammed in, and she wove her lovely way dextrously along Victoria Street, past Lincoln staring from his chair in amazement, and slid neatly up Whitehall.

Amid all this, which I was enjoying as much as my sexy young driver, I saw that Robin had got his breath back and needed to know what the hell this was all about.

"Ron is our mole," I had to shout against the traffic. "Yes, really. He always knew where I was going to see our respondees, so he could send the Mr Benson instructions – nobody else could have known that."

"Yes, but – "

"He wants all my private files, about student lists. All my deals and agreements, like with Oxdon – "

"Who the hell is Oxdon?"

Oh, shit. "Anyway," I said, "Ron has kidnapped Olivia and is taking her to our safe-deposit for the lists and all my secrets. I think she will be driving, because she plans something to happen at four o'clock in Trafalgar Square… "

"Why there?" he shouted back as we went up past Downing Street.

"Horace is Horatio Nelson. It's like a clock, with the sun on the National Gallery at midday, so four o'clock must be over on the right, past St Martin's. That's right on the path to our safe-deposit in the Strand. I'm sure of it."

"How do you know she'll be driving?"

"Why else would my car be missing? It's registered for security clearance at the deposit entrance. And he has to be threatening her, don't you see?"

We tumbled out of the E-type and thanked that lovely vision, who throatily sped off, both exhausts spitting. We stood on the pavement at three-fifty-five, just past the church, I think it was outside some big Commonwealth office or something like that.

"He'll probably have a gun, threatening Olivia."

"Good God, do you think so?"

"We've got to be prepared. We must grab him."

"Have you got a gun," asked Robin.

"Are you joking? I haven't fired a shot since I was seven."

"Seven! Whatever were you doing with a gun at age seven?"

"In Kenya in the thirties, we were all taught to shoot, with a 2.2"

"To protect the Empire?" Robin suggested.

It had been far more complicated than that, but nowadays nobody will listen. However, I remembered that both my parents had routinely slept with a pistol under their pillow; also my aunt who worked for a charity Missionary School up-country and carried her pistol everywhere... It had never been aggressive, merely self-protection because policing outside the town centre was a bit thin on the ground.

"At home, all I had was a Daisy airgun," I told Robin. "Just enough perhaps to kill a pigeon at close quarters. Although," I recalled, "I did shoot our shamba-boy twice. He chased me round the garden."

"Twice?"

"Well, the first time was an accident."

As we spoke, between all the buses and taxis, at last we both saw my Jaguar coming round the corner. As I had guessed, Olivia was at the wheel, Ron beside her, surely with a gun. As they came up to us, she suddenly swung the wheel so the car lurched and came clumping up on to the pavement. She switched off.

We both ran up, opened the passenger door, and dragged Ron out, gun and all. He went limp and didn't resist.

The traffic at once began building up behind us, and hooting;

this is the most efficient way in the whole world, to expedite business.

I quickly said to Ron: "Don't let's be silly, we have to get clear of here, before the police come doppling along to sort out the traffic, and start asking questions."

"All right, Tim," said Ron, "but I need to explain."

I shut him up. "Not now. Give me the pistol before the police – "

He did. He sat down shrunken on the steps of the building, while I asked Robin to go back to Pimlico with Olivia, calm her down as necessary (it wasn't) and at the very least make her a nice cup of tea. They reversed into the road and drove off.

I looked at Ron. He was sitting despondently on the stone steps. This was our mole – I couldn't find an adjective: at one extreme, 'dangerous' was wildly overdoing it; at the other, 'pathetic' was too unkind. I remembered he was a staunch churchgoer with a sick wife and some pretty horrid memories – I supposed – of wartime: one had read of solitary imprisonment, bullying, and degradation, followed by the inevitable brainwashing and cynical indoctrination to produce an artificial but committed servant of the Communist ideal. He had been returned to the UK as a 'sleeper' sworn to loyalty to 'them'. A gentle, charming man with a time-bomb within his head.

I had nothing in my own background, I thought, there at Trafalgar Square, to compare with all Ron's tangled pressures. Who was I, to make judgments?

"Let's go into St Martin's and sit for a while," I said. He nodded.

In fact we talked quietly at the back of the church, for over an hour, while for the first time he unburdened his mind of so many poisons. He was confused a little, he wept a little. I found this difficult, because he was older than me and so much more experienced. Yes, he had been tortured; yes, he had been in some way 'indoctrinated' and fed mind-changing facts and figures which seemed to convince him, when combined with various 'medicines', that he owed some sort of long-term 'loyalty' to 'them'. After he came back to Cambridge, 'they' had occasionally been in touch, with non-specific threats to his family… Nothing definite.

But I remember this: "If you were subjected to near-starvation," Ron said in that pew in St Martin's, " combined with mind-blowing noises, and lights, and vicious orders being shouted throughout the night; if this went on for months so that you could no longer count days; and if, then, suddenly, there were three days of glorious silence with good food and Bach and Mozart and, yes, lovely Oriental girls: would you not welcome whatever was said to you in a friendly fashion, with nostalgic tinges of English humour too? And next," he went on while I sat there mute: "I was being told that the Americans were working on ways to spread plague, and yellow fever, and – and – so many bad things… "

All I could do was nod.

"It gets to you," he lamely ended.

"So," I had to summarise this, as far as possible in a way satisfactory to everybody. Sod them all, I thought. Like Matt.

We had our mole. We had defused him. He wouldn't default again, after that confession. He was a very useful man in the office, and would always be.

I told him to stop doing it. I told him the company needed him. I told him his job was safe. I went home.

I've still got the gun. It wasn't loaded.

CHAPTER XIV

"The messages you left were brilliant," I told a somewhat ruffled Olivia back at the flat. She and Robin had skipped making tea and gone for something red in a glass, a little more deeply comforting for a young Italian girl just rescued from kidnap. I don't think it was Blackcurrant cordial, either.

The Horace time-clock message, the four taps on the phone, and the bunch of keys had all helped to put me in the picture; but one thing remained a worry:

"How was it that he let you drive?"

"Of course, he was holding the gun," she explained, "and also I told him the people at the safe deposit would only let drivers they knew, into their car park – "

"Great Scott! It's a pokey basement, there isn't any car park."

"He didn't know that. It was lucky, no? And I had to waste time so I could be in Horace Square at four o'clock, you see?"

"Lucky also, you had a teaspoon," I added, and Robin's confusion was lovely to see; but another thing was concerning me, too.

"I didn't even know you had a driving licence." And of course, she hadn't, just a few tentative lessons back in Rome, God help her. Had she been worried by having to drive on the left? I was way ahead of her with the answer to that.

"In Italy, like in Paris, we just drive in the middle." I was starting to feel even more sorry for Ron. He must have been praying fervently, gun in hand, to whichever of his Gods would listen, for no inquisitive policemen.

We discussed Ron at length, and my decision to keep him on

236

the staff. I was faced, to begin with, by eyebrows that appropriately reached Pennine and Appenine heights; but eventually they both agreed with me: Ron would do no further damage, if only because we would be watching; but also, with the AMs gone, he was going to be indispensable while we tried to rebuild. My guess was that his relief would bind him to us, risk-free, in the future. And so it was…

Talking about the future, Robin said, our biggest problem might be getting access to students' addresses all over again. The NUS may well prevent it: they were well ahead, as we spoke, with plans to set up their own in-house Insurance Brokers and they would feast upon students countrywide through their eight hundred local Unions. If they give those local students a cutback of commission on all business sold – for instance – at the annual Freshers' conferences, it would almost at once kill us, stone-dead. And they would probably find a legitimate way of banning us from all our Handbook inserts.

"So," he pointed his cheroot at me, "the lists you give us will be our only life-blood."

Oh, hell, I thought to myself. But: "Plus," I reminded him, "the Life enquiry spin-off from our great little Belongings policy." This was always selling excellently everywhere, it had no rival, and our Life team would deliver the policies personally and then talk about SLAS.

Robin looked at me sadly – I was getting used to it. "NUS have just brought out their own Belongings Policy, not just *based* on ours but almost word-for-word from start to finish; and a bit cheaper."

He delved into an inner pocket and passed me an extravagantly expensive-looking leaflet. I looked at it. So much for pleasantry at the Pheasantry. Not just the terms and conditions, but even the sales and marketing… Alas, you can't copyright ideas.

Olivia had been sitting quietly. Then she said: "If the NUS are going to pay commission to the Unions, you may lose your connection with the Professor."

"What Professor?" asked Robin, understandably.

"*O merde!*" She stumped out, calling herself stupid, in at least three languages.

"It doesn't have to be secret any more," I called. And I decided I might as well at last bring Robin into the full Oxdon picture, my frayed and fast decaying source of student information. I ended up by explaining that even that prime source was drying up anyway, in a few months.

He listened carefully, then: "So we're fucked, aren't we?", unusually considerate when Olivia was out of the room. "All of a sudden we have the NUS commanding the market, plus three ex-Director rivals from within who know all the tricks, and by the sound of it, no leads."

I told him – Olivia had just come back in with a new bottle – I would not give in just yet, despite all he had spelt out –

"And all the debts?"

Yes, and despite the hideous debts too. Something might turn up. More to the point, we had – I had, mainly, over the past fourteen years for God's sake – built up a very substantial clientele of still youngish people who had graduated and were now earning good money on the lower rungs of lucrative career ladders.

But Robin Coldwater had still more bad news for me. "During their three months running the company up until this week, I think you'll find the AMs will have siphoned off all those names and addresses."

Shit.

"Well, in their place, wouldn't you?"

I fell back on the last comfort we had. That was the renewal income we had built up. Every annual premium paid on a Life policy, then carried a tiny element of commission to the introducing Broker. This could run on for thirty or forty years; only two-and-a-half percent, but it was an insurance man's basic lifeblood, designed to help the Broker to maintain contact with his client – and it added up.

But not enough: maybe by now just sufficient for one person to retire on if he had modest inclinations, no ex-Partners with guaranteed pensions, and preferably without personal debts to insurance companies that ran into six figures. I was getting gloomy.

238

And yet, strangely, I didn't want the cigarette that Robin offered. I was over it, I'd beaten that if nothing else.

It dawned on me that I would have to go back to Oxdon and warn him that the NUS was moving in with Insurance on the local Unions, and our pleasant little local arrangement was due to be not only killed off, but exposed. This might prompt some other sort of help from him and his Scallywags. It would certainly shake him.

★ ★ ★

I knew I had to go back to leafy North Oxford although the old Professor was clearly going off his trolley. My worst worry came early, even before setting off, when I had to explain the expression to Olivia, this being just before the days of supermarket mobility.

"What is trolley? My book says electric autobus."

I responded by giving up, but taking her with me, dropping her off at a riverside table at 'The Trout' in Godstow, where she could enjoy the rush of water and peer down at the contented families of fat chub, while reading an early Bond (Would it have been that paperback with bullet-holes in the cover?) and no doubt working her way also through a Campari or two: I'd pick her up later.

I said to Oxdon's daughter: "I'm afraid I may have some bad news about the data we've been supplying." She replied with a sad smile: "Bless you, but I honestly don't think it matters any more. They have more or less abandoned him, though very nicely." By now I was sharing the sad smile. "But do come in, he will be terribly happy to see you and talk again."

Oxdon was sitting hunched in his chair, his back to the light from that ill-kept garden. The grass needed cutting. There was no cat, and looking back, I'm sure that was the missing factor that worried me most – the old man really did need his comfort-blanket.

"Tim, dear boy, do sit you down."

"Professor," I began, "I simply cannot any longer – "

"Of course, old chap, remember that everyone still tells me everything, don't you know? You've been removed from your

Board, but now you're back again. But, I suppose, in reduced circumstances, yes?"

"But I can't, any longer – "

He waved a hand dismissively.

"Dear boy, it really doesn't matter any more. My colleagues have all the recruits they need, but I think the threat has disappeared: of course the Left killed Gaitskill, but Wilson has been scared stiff by the rumours of surveillance, so we have stood down the Scallywags – they will wait in the wings in case they are ever needed."

It was nothing to do with me, but I was intrigued by these terminal old vigilantes: who wouldn't have been? I had to point out the obvious: "Surely they'll all die off in no time?"

He had an answer for that. "Ah, we have a built-in solution, we call it 'successive recruitment' and it can give the Scallywags perpetuity. We have a Membership Secretary, who is a well-known surgeon on Harley Street by the way, and he will appoint his own successor in good time. His job is to arrange for each of our members also to appoint his own successor, from among other but younger sufferers of a terminal illness. It will be a permanent Task Force to defend the country against – how shall I say? – that little bit too much Socialism."

I was admiring his precision and clarity, the engrained tutorial way of presenting these facts, when he had one of his coughing fits, but a bad one. As it ended and, with his head lowered, he seemed to recover, he looked across oddly at me and there had been a sudden change – an unusual, puzzled look in his eyes. A look, in fact, of hostility. A hand wavered up to his brow.

"What are you doing here?" he snapped and I went cold as I realised that the old man was evidently developing some sort of mental problem. I felt it best to smile encouragingly but say nothing.

There was a silence, as he pulled himself together. He shook his head as if to get rid of something. "*Ungluck*," he muttered, then "*Unlogisch*."

I just sat there, hoping his daughter would come. He was holding me with his eye, for all the world like the Ancient Mariner.

Then he gathered his thoughts. "There was something about America," he pondered…

"Students?" I suggested, and his face brightened. "Yes!" he said happily; but then, a cough and: "No. No, Tim, you must never believe what they tell you." He leant forward with a glint which warned me he was on to yet another level. "Suppose, just suppose, that you are a very attractive woman, very beautiful, who is being endlessly cheated on by her extremely rich sex-obsessed husband, quite openly so that she is constantly humiliated by all his colleagues. Yes? Now then, Tim: they go out one day and he is shot dead. The person who shoots him is then also killed. Within a few months the lovely woman goes off with an even richer man, whom she has known for some time. So: this new rich man was not even in the country at the time so he has an alibi. Who is your chief suspect for arranging the murders?"

"Well," I supposed, "the wife – she clearly has most to gain."

He leaned back and the glasses shifted like anything. "What if the lady's name was Jackie?"

I was stupefied by this; there were plenty of theories about the JFK assassination, but this was a new one, to me anyway. However, Oxdon was gradually regaining his composure.

"Ah, yes," he said thoughtfully. "America… Yes, students. Forgive," he added, "a nuisance of old age. Let me think for a minute… "

We sat quietly and I listened to the traffic on Banbury Road. All of a sudden two black kittens raced into the room, skidding sideways on the old oak floorboards and both ending up in a leap on to the Professor's lap.

We both smiled then, but ignored them for the moment because something rather deeper seemed to be going on, if only he could concentrate.

"Tim," he started, "some time ago, I forget when, you talked about America. I think you said you were interfered with by the CIA and MI6. I don't think MI6 will do you harm, but in the States there is big trouble brewing about the CIA interfering in – what can I say

– intellectual matters, here in Europe, and especially students. Do you know COSEC?"

Yes, I said, we'd been in touch; but I let it go at that.

"Well, they were set up by the CIA, right from the start, after the end of the Forties, and I have young friends at an American university who are planning to expose many connections probably through their newspaper, and that is one of them. Everywhere," he went on, "students in the West are being dragged in, used as cannon-fodder against the Moscow-organised 'professional' students who pack the Russian youth rallies, most of them phoney middle-aged muscle-men who wouldn't pass their School Cert. if they had all the answers on the desk alongside."

I was relishing that vivid example when he had another coughing attack, and I had to wait a full five minutes. He had been repeating very clearly the warnings I'd had years ago from American Bill, and most recently from Matt. And the old man seemed so young again.

But then, once more, and again differently, as soon as the coughing was over his eyes had the look of a stranger as he focussed on me. I got that creepy feeling…

"Jericho!" he cried without the least warning, "What do you know about Jericho?"

My bewilderment took me just half a mile down the road to that fashionably-decadent part of inner North Oxford around The Jericho Tavern, which included the equally decadent Scala Cinema which, you will remember, I was wont to visit in times of need for recuperation, with its double seats in the back row, and its partiality for continental *films noirs*. Were 'they' even having me watched when I took someone to the pictures? I began to run through the last few weeks…

"No, no," he went on, his hand twitching, "The real Jericho – the ancient city, perhaps the first city ever in our world – they say 8000 BC for the city, but I have just been told by an excavator, most confidential, young woman in a big dig out there, up in Summertown, we must not tell… They have dated the earliest to perhaps twelve thousand; and very close, by Galilee, a fishing village found when the waters went down, perhaps eighteen thousand… " He stopped for breath, then: "Think, Tim, my friend – that long ago."

Well yes, I knew a bit about this. (And have since done a few courses at Rewley House, the wonderfully off-beat Centre for Extra-Mural Studies down in Wellington Square where you could buy, sorry, earn an eccentric diploma on almost anything. I remember the start of a twelve week course on astronomy, where we had to get our group comfortably settled in, and the tutor was looking for us to help with the facilities, and tiring of our dithering: "We will be visiting and analysing the remotest corners and secrets of the universe, and we can't even organise tea-bags?").

I knew about 'The Fertile Crescent', the start of our civilisation, (if perhaps you left out China), centred on Palestine and Mesopotamia, and its two rivers of antiquity. So? If that was where human beings first came together in a stable society, so what?" He was going to tell me.

"Think!" said Oxdon, his eyes now sparkling with an almost teenage enthusiasm that was completely clear and rational. "When many people first came together, not just for protection but for social reasons, and they had fire you see, and so much light. You see, no? A whole accumulation of lights, at night. Never before."

I couldn't argue with that. But where was he heading?

"Somebody out there would see those lights. Somebody would come and investigate, don't you – "

"But we are told – "

"Ach! 'We are told'! There are a billion galaxies, a billion. And in every galaxy, a million stars. And for most of those stars, some moons. So many planets, don't you know? Tim, don't waste any time doing the sums – the probabilities themselves are a waste of time. It is certainty."

"So you are saying, it's inevitable there are people out there?"

"Well," he laughed, understandably, "hardly 'people'; but there is life. We can't imagine what it looks like. It could be just a cloud

243

of intelligent dust; it could be a venomous creature the size of Greenland, full of deadly poison... But wait."

It was such a treat to see him so full of life and excitement, even if it would not last more than a few minutes, that I was perfectly willing to wait; what did it matter that his brain-cell connections had gone, so long as he was happy, involved, harmless, and – for all I knew – talking complete sense.

"If beings from another planet, a close planet, were watching and saw bright light, they would want to come and investigate, yes? It would take perhaps eight thousand years, yes? Of our years."

"Our –?"

"Don't you see, Tim? For them it might be only a fortnight, or an afternoon. They would have a quite different timescale."

It seemed reasonable. I began to concentrate, despite myself.

"So, aiming at the new lights – our Earth's first man-made signs – they would arrive where? Jericho? Palestine! On a vehicle we would see as a shining star. It would hover. Where? Bethlehem, Tim." I still let him go on. "And then, later for us but very soon by their timescale, taken up again... Ascension!" And he ended, almost triumphantly: "And you see, there is The Shroud!"

Oh God, I thought, not that. But after a second or two, I started listening again.

"An old fool at High Table years ago told me, the image on that relic in Turin was genuine, and caused by radiation from an earthquake! Is that not very silly, Tim?"

Quite stupid, I agreed. Laughable. Radiation? Ho-ho, I said.

"Nein," shaking his head vigorously. "No, no. Radiation, yes, yes, but you see, it was radiation from the space-craft. It is evident."

There was nothing I could do about this, just nod. I am always suspicious of phoney preachers and God-botherers, but this not only seemed curiously feasible but even straightforward; I couldn't see anyone making money out of it, but he still ought to send it to a film company, or at least alert the Daily Mail. "What is even more, Tim, we have other reports from early times, other religions, don't you know? And even in the Bible there was an earlier – "

"Yes," I remembered, "one of the prophets." For the first time in twenty years I wished I had paid more attention to the old divinity teacher at school we all knew, not too well I hope, as Homo Henry. "He was gathered up, in a cloud or something. Was it Elijah?"

"Chariot of fire. One Kings seventeen. Yes, Tim, a chariot of fire. But don't you see, it is more important: if they came then, they may have come from the beginning. Coming back out of curiosity to see how we were developing."

I began to see that he was not talking about religion. I thought it best to let him expound: if I was to be the catalyst for all his ideas, so be it. It was pretty thought-provoking.

His mind had now wandered on.

"They are here," he said. "It's germs... Bacilli... Bacteria... Look how they have the ability to mutate so quickly, *nicht war*? They can surely think! And given they can think, Tim, given that, could they not also calculate, invent? Plan, design their own mutations? What else could the answer be? "

I was now getting a little worried about him, he was breathing fast and audibly and had gone rather red. Also he was completely ignoring the two kittens, which was very unlike him. I tried to interrupt the flow, but –

"Another thing, Tim." He pointed out of the window. "Our galaxy, the Milky Way, yes – all the galaxies – every one is designed exactly like an atom... We, Tim, sitting here inside our little atom of a galaxy, may be just a tiny part of... of... of somebody's underpants in some other huge galaxy we will never know. And then the other extreme: here, in this room, we may both be sitting in *our* underpants on countless millions of tiny galaxies full of – of what – of *people*?" He ended with another coughing fit.

Each time this had happened, Oxdon seemed to me to have switched to a different subject, to some extent to a different personality; and I waited anxiously to see what would emerge next; but he calmly cleared his throat and went on along much the same line of thought. Also, I was pleased to see that he had started stroking the kittens: it would help.

"This must change Darwin, you see, change it all completely." He waved towards the city and the colleges. "I've been telling them for years. Nobody listens. We are all just an experiment, you see."

He paused and looked at me as though I was a roomful of his students, in a lecture-theatre of the past. I tried to give him, by my expression, the reaction he was seeking.

"An experiment?"

"We don't know what they are, what they look like, perhaps invisible to us, as though we are being watched through a microscope, yes? But if they invented us... in a laboratory... Probably students in the Universe buying insurance when they go home?" He laughed, the glasses slid, he managed not to cough. "And in general, Tim, they made, they constructed us very well: look at the intricacies of an animal's body. The mechanics, the wiring, the systems, blood, nerves, digestion, the magic of a beating heart, even an ant... All things bright and beautiful, all creatures... You see it, Tim, don't you?" He broke off sadly. "Nobody would listen... "

I made the right sort of noises, and tried to understand. So, I stupidly thought, the camel really was designed by a committee... A student committee, out there...?

"But then," he went on, "over the years, the millennia, some parts may need attention. And they come back and do it, correct it, put it right. They are experimenting with us. Perhaps they thought – a student thought one day – one of their huge days – that a zebra would survive better if it was striped black, a chameleon if some other student wanted to try out his – or her – or, or its ability to change one's colour – and that would be tested on moths too. There is a little moth, Tim, just a very little moth, it likes to hide inside three kinds of flower, and they are all different colours, so what does it do? It just changes to the right colour every time. Who taught it, Tim? It isn't as Darwin said at all. Not God either, or anyway not that sort of God. When a change is needed, or additional gifts are required, like the moth, they come and do it. And we can't see them."

I opened my mouth, but he anticipated me.

"Why?" he cried. "Because, Tim, we are being farmed... Like

bees in some great hive… Cultivated. But what for, eh?" He sank back.

Feebly, I said the only thing I could. "Time will tell," I told him. I thought to myself that the old man would know soon enough.

He had got it all off his chest and I think neither of us felt we need follow the argument through. Very likely, I had to concede, we *are* being farmed; and if so, some external veterinary surgeon may sneak in from time to time to adjust or correct our development and evolution. After all, down here on Earth we now do it domestically, in our primitive laboratories, don't we?

He visibly relaxed, and we got round to the kittens.

"Ah, a gift from a friend in Rawlinson Road. We lost my old furry companion recently – he's at rest down the end there." After our talk, a new thought occurred to him "He's been harvested, Tim, don't you know?" He blinked.

"But now, after all, we are looking to find names for these two twins. My daughter's friends say Gilbert and Sullivan, but that to me seems just a *bischen* too popular, too obvious really – "

An inspiration hit me. "How about Rodgers and Hammerstein?"

He loved it. "Oh yes," he cried. "Yes yes. It will really annoy the neighbours!"

He let them into the garden as I left; and outside in the road I could hear him calling: "Hammerstein… Hammerstein… "

At least, I told myself, walking down the sleepy road towards the normality of Summertown, it could have been worse – surely you can't call a cat Garfunkel.

How wrong can one be?

★ ★ ★

Robin and Olivia were laughing and joking cosily as I arrived back in Pimlico. "Go and find an Italian of your own," I told him.

"There is good news," said Olivia, handing me a letter. "I opened the envelope because there was a lump in it."

Discourteously overlooking the fact that it might have exploded,

247

and that she had thus been prepared to sacrifice herself for me, I took the folded letter. As I opened it, a small pile of cigarette butts fell out, and with them a cheque for £1,000. There was a short note: "Lunch and revelations? Get in touch. David."

One way and another, a small celebration was called for. We had the decency to invite the E-type girl to join us at Grumbles, but she was already there. Unattached though, so that was all right.

EPILOGUE

I said to Olivia: "We must find out all about David's mailing methods, what his student lists are and how comprehensive they are. At last I can get it straight from the horse's mouth," and at once I knew this was going to cause trouble.

"What is this horse?" You see – trouble.

"Er – just meaning information from the primary source."

"Eh, I like this," she said happily. "You have these phrases: the horse's mouth... The cat's whisker... You English who so love animals... The fly in the woodshed... The dog's bollocks... "

"Wait a minute," I said quickly. "Where did you get that one?"

"At my school in Rome, they knew much English, those nuns."

A bit too much, I reckoned. Must have been the war.

"They were Spanish," she told me.

Ought to have been the bull's bollocks, I thought, judging by all those enormous macho hoardings along the roads; but let's get back to talking about business and David.

"Tell me," she said, "does he do travel insurance for students?" I didn't know, but why was she asking?

"Well," she curled up on our settee, proud of the research she had been doing, "the NUS already has a Travel Service, and so, of course, do all other national Unions. So, *evidente*, they must sell insurance together with the travel tickets." She shook her head at me, frowning to tell me off. "We did not talk about that, when we went to those countries. "They sell it straight from the cat's – "

"Horse's." I knew about this Travel cover. It had been arranged long ago, by mutual agreement soon after the end of the war, and allowed all insurance claims by a travelling student in any Western country to be settled in the local currency where the loss or medical expense occurred. It was so well established, it had never crossed my mind to query it, let alone compete. The market was all sewn up, and placed with a firm in Holland…

Holland – wait a minute.

"Si. Where there is COSEC. And where also is the CIA, your friend Matt told you?"

That's true. I had to concede Olivia might have stumbled upon something. All that research…

"About all such student travel," she went on, twisting that strand of hair, "I think it has been set up so that **every time a student travels anywhere, the details may be passed to the CIA.** Even before COSEC began, all the Unions had a meeting about this travel scheme, how to work together, and it was – "

"How do you know all this?"

"It was in some newspapers of the time. It was in Copenhagen – "

So this was the great secret I wasn't supposed to know, according even to Matt. It was the CIA who set up the Copenhagen Travel Conference, and thus their Travel Insurance Policy; of course it was the CIA who, at that time of limited foreign currency allowances, had made the funds available to pay every claim on the spot, anywhere, and in the local currency too, which in turn enabled the whole spy operation to work. And ever since, through the information on their proposal forms, the CIA had been milking *every* student's travel plans. They knew exactly where a Leftie was going, and for how long, and how much money he took with him, so therefore how little money he had to take if he was being supported by somebody at the other end. Very neat.

I told her what a clever girl she was. A wave of the hand. "While you have been running around with dementing old professors and demented young insurance people, I have visited many libraries and newspaper files up in Edgware; '*eccetera eccetera*' as the bald man says in that film. So, after all these little facts, *doppotutto* – is that not a nice word? – it all seems likely, no?"

Likely, yes, I thought.

★ ★ ★

David and I met for lunch on that floating gourmanderie under the railway bridge at Charing Cross, the 'Hispaniola'. Framed by the bustle of the Embankment on one side, the busy river on the other, and overhead the trains clattering in and out of the station, it was surprisingly quiet in the dining-room. As the swirling tide came in with its clutter of debris from the downstream docks, he gave me his secrets.

"Tim, I'm only telling you this because I think we can work together. I've no need of all the data you've had to rely on, squeezing lists out of all the universities or whatever it is you get up to – "

It had certainly got a bit tricky, I told him. That was something of an under-statement, since my Oxdon connection was no more; and a passing tug crossly told me so. I almost hooted it back. But a revelation was coming:

"The government gives me all the information I need."

"You *what?*"

"The regular annual voting lists, the electoral rolls, all over the UK, give us all we need. They are available, free for the asking – "

"But surely –?"

"And all the first-time voters, because those aged 18 or so are marked with an asterisk. We simply obtain all the rolls, and address our letters to the first-time voters in all the areas that are likely to be a bit upmarket; and if we run short, we move a little bit downmarket too. There's no end to it, and it's all free and available every year."

"Good God! That means you also catch a whole lot of youngsters who don't actually go to a university, but somewhere else?"

David gazed dreamily out at the driftwood and floating plastic. "Officer cadets... Young farmers... "

"Engineers? Accountants..?" I helped him.

"Curates... "

Curates??

He nodded. "Very small pensions, in the Church. Maybe large

251

families, that's sort of traditional, isn't it? Then, most of all, when they retire as vicars or something, they have to get out of the vicarage promptly and they'll need to find a place to retire to, so it's a good market for mortgage cover. But then, you know, so many others, like the self-employed; like, say, actors – "

"Oh God," I moaned, "not actors – "

"Well then, actresses," he suggested, much more positively, and innocently offering me a cigarette which, thinking quickly, I carefully declined. As I shook my head, he said: "Now that you know, do you think we can work together? If we can offer all our enquirers a choice, your people and mine would go in separately and compare one scheme against the other, there's a good chance most of them will start thinking 'This or that' instead of 'Yes or no'. Well then, Tim, how about it?"

I had stopped shaking my head a whole paragraph ago, and was now nodding it instead. Another tug was chugging past, towing a long line of barges full of unspeakable detritus to be dumped at sea; and I felt all my personal shipload of anguish going with it.

I told him: Yes. Yes, indeed. We shook hands on it. *Uberrima fides*. No question.

"However," I cautioned, "You do know that the NUS is starting its own Brokerage?"

"Yes. But what the hell – they'll be bureaucrats. And don't forget, we can get at the eighteen year-olds before they do."

That may have been good to hear at the time, and for several years it was true; but as things eventually turned out, the NUS in-house firm has ended up as an important brokerage (Jerry would have given them Capital Letters), with something like a hundred offices and a thousand staff, while I am now working from home, watching them selling my ideas from the Fifties. Even so, I'm still my own boss and answerable only to the Bank and the taxman; while they have recently been taken over by a huge International – so who won, I often wonder.

Back then in 1965, however, I sang all the way home; I also tore up that cheque. Well you would, wouldn't you?

★ ★ ★

Back at the flat, Olivia could scarcely believe my good luck. "O mio mio. It happens," she said, "only once in a blue lobster – "

"No, no," I said, "Moon."

"No, no," she replied. "It is lobster. I read it in one of the old newspapers: one lobster in a million is blue."

One good thing, I thought to myself, has come out of all this turmoil: she won't be traipsing around town, reading any more bloody newspapers. Are we OK for some *penne arabbiata*?

With the David deal in place, my business recovered and modestly rebuilt itself. Ron stayed with me, faithfully, until retirement, and we never, ever, mentioned Trafalgar Square. Tony went on to build up his own very successful business which quite soon outshone anything I had done: we meet occasionally, socially. He sleeps less, though.

I never saw Matt again. He did once ring to say he'd like to meet, "to check on progress", and mentioned staying in (I think he said 'on') Old Church Street in Chelsea, though he'd prefer to see me at the Six Bells round the corner. I waited a couple of hours but he didn't show up. He had sounded rather agitated on the phone; and I supposed he was having some sort of problem that didn't concern me. Nothing at all since then; and given the later news about CIA activities, I stopped wondering why.

I also soon lost touch with Robin, much to my regret, and I looked for him up in the Rhubarb Triangle without success. Given his Student President background, I suspect that he, too, was tempted into the glamorous but sinister world of the CIA, or at best MI6, who are always on the lookout for promising graduates who can play – subtly – both sides against the middle. I hope he has prospered and now has someone else to twirl his knife for him. He and Tony were closest to me, throughout my 'troubles', with the invaluable knack of both boosting me and when necessary bringing me down to earth.

The three Area Managers, having nursed their wounds, went on to form their own businesses, ploughing their lonely furrows in the bizarre and claustrophobic world of student insurance – and did it very well, from what I hear. We met every now and then in the course of business and – you know what? – we got on very well, all things considered. As I have already commented, it is amazing how humour, and especially the witty ridiculous, can break through. I'm sure many small business-people will confirm this: outside pressures seem to squeeze out a deeply-hidden hilarity: a nervous reaction, I suppose it must be, but a rewarding one. I always remember, at that devastating Board Meeting near Easter where they all voted me out, I made a comment that they were "trying to nail me". Sid said, I have to admit rather cleverly: "Well, it's a good time for crucifixions." Very neat.

Olivia had to go home, taking Molo and Porcellino and Fugo and the rest with her, for the enlightenment of the bambini. We had loved each other but always in the knowledge that there was a time-limit. We keep in touch; and one Christmas recently when I didn't get a letter from her, I sent a postcard of the Albert Memorial. It said: "Take *that*!!" and within a week I had three pages.

COSEC was utterly confounded in 1967 when there was a colossal showdown and scandal in the States about the covert activities in Western Europe by the all-pervasive CIA. A student magazine called 'Ramparts', previously unknown but suddenly famous, exposed all (or most) of what had been going on ever since the late Forties. God knows how many millions of dollars had been pumped into West-leaning organisations, via a whole pack of 'charities' fronted apparently by all sorts of 'little old ladies' and well-meaning innocents. The publication 'Encounter', was based in Paris and run, with the best will in the world, by that fey poet whom Matt had to visit after leaving me: it turned out to be Stephen Spender, who never knew what was behind him. Much of this is summarised in the final section that follows (see Note 9). It ends by hinting quite strongly, I see, that despite all the self-righteousness after the US Senate Enquiry, the status of CIA covert activity may be largely quo. I can't think who added those comments. It certainly wasn't me, Your Honour.

Grumbles flourishes, as I write, where Jeremy still puts in an appearance when not travelling the tropics. It is one of the few genuine survivals of the Sixties bistros, almost – not quite – unchanged, and mentioned in several novels of the time. One has nostalgic memories of other such places, now nearly all gone. Michael Eddowes ran his chain of intimate and smoky 'Bistro Vino' places, carefully sited close to a good pub so that you could bring in your own bottle, and have a great plate of sausage-and-mash for under three shillings. So many friendly places have been stupidly overtaken by the poncey pretensions of the 'nouvelle cuisine'. I always thought the adjective came after the noun – I must ask Maurice – but perhaps giving it this prominence simply betrays that pretension? But then, as we old folk say, and yes, we are right, nothing is as good as it used to be. And Wilfrid Brambell is dead. So is nearly everybody.

★ ★ ★

I married, eventually, the girl in the E-type; but I was only ever allowed in the passenger seat. Jeremy was our best man, at Caxton Hall, but I always like to think he was inwardly seething. We visit Olivia in Rome quite often, and we still like the Argentina cats far more than the humans who litter the place. Oh, Olivia was reading this and wanted to know about 'litter', in relation to cats and people (and, I fear, rubbish and rickshaws…) It will take some time…

★ ★ ★

I very recently, and completely by coincidence, came into contact with my wonderful dream girl, whom I have called Sarah. We have spoken by phone. She is not married now. She would be agreeable to meeting. I am scared because I still have my dream from sixty-odd years ago and old age is no time to destroy it. I cannot forget the poems we romanticised over: Yeats – you know the ones I mean. 'Pilgrim soul' – 'glad grace' – 'embroidered cloths' – 'only my dreams' – 'tread softly'… Oh, indeed; and 'nodding by the fire', too. I am scared to meet, even if my understanding E-type wife comes along. (They were, at different times, at the same school, amazingly, which I only discovered last year).

What is it about schools in Hampshire? The schools seem to be as rewardingly fishable as the trout-streams, but I mustn't say that sort of thing nowadays, must I? My first-ever girlfriend boarded there too, but down on the coast, though strangely I first met her in King Alfred's other home-town – but that, as they say, is… in another storybook (my 'The Bunny Run', out now and waiting for you).

But about my lovely Sarah: what do you think? Must we stay nodding by our radiators?

★ ★ ★

Finally, here's a funny thing:

In the Public Records Office out at Kew, browsing the other day, I stumbled upon their section on shipping passenger-lists. I found the hand-written draft of a list for the 'Illyria', that crossing of mine in the Autumn of 1946. It had never been printed and distributed because of the post-war pressures of the time, so we had never seen it on board.

I was in it, so was Matt. But – no mention whatever of those two boring young Canadians on their innocent way to – where? Could it have been Prague, where Europe's Communists were holding their monumental student mass rallies? Who were they really? And whatever did I say to encourage them about my ideas for selling nationwide to a captive student market?

But, you know, I've been too long in the business to worry my old head about that sort of thing. Too long. Are you sure you don't need my help with your pension arrangements?

ΠΟΤΕ$

1. My 18-month service as a 2nd Lt. is altogether another story which you might find entertaining. See my spy-catching novel "The Paper Caper" (Troubador, e-book if you can scrape up £3.99); it's quite largely based on fact, when I had to edit an Army newspaper. In the story I use it to trap a Cold War super-Agent with the help of my lovely ATS nurse, and greatly assisted by the wise counsel of my old Colonel who reminds me that "the bigger the shit, the smaller the splash".

2. A famous Victorian (but who?) when travelling in Italy, had an argument with some bumptious official – you know how these Continentals are? – and stormed away saying over his shoulder: "I shall write about you to the station-master at Windermere!" His bemused companion queried this, and was told: "Years ago, I told that wretched station-master that if I ever met a more stupid man, I'd write and tell him."

I recently wrote about this anecdote to a couple of dozen newsworthy but intelligent people, asking if they knew who that Victorian was. Nearly all of them kindly replied – a first for me – but they all simply wanted me to tell them when I found out. Eventually, thanks to that splendid radio critic Gillian Reynolds, I was referred to the equally splendid Nigel Rees ("he knows everything," another of my correspondents confirmed; there is a name for such brilliant people but I can't remember it – if isn't 'polyologist', it ought to be). The crusty Victorian wasn't Belloc, nor Chesterton, though I still think it, too, ought to have been; nor any other of the usual suspects. It was a Master of Balliol, Rees told me,

257

whose name I have already mislaid… So much for epigrammic fame – had they been his 'last words' they would be immortal.

But don't go away, here's another one:

An equally crusty Victorian came down to breakfast on a day of torrential rain. He tapped the barometer in the hall, and it said: "Set Fair". So he hurled the thing through the window, shouting: "See for yourself, you fool!" But who was he? Postcards only, please.

3. Inventing, putting together, marketing, selling and following-up a 'Special Scheme' of any product, let alone Insurance, can be boring to the uninvolved, (even if they aren't in a hurry to find out about the CIA's spying on British students), and I have therefore relegated such details to this section, a separate Note for each enthralling activity as it comes up: for the moment they are all hiding at the end.

4. I have only recently discovered that my young Classics teacher of 1946 is now the eminent philosopher Mary Midgley, still very lively in her nineties. The "Garden of Cucumbers" poem which I believe Mary wrote as a teenager, is included in her fascinating autobiography "Owl of Minerva" published 2005. But I'm pretty sure it first appeared in the "Mosaic", the school magazine I edited back in 1946. As Oxdon realised, I remembered it word for word. You would, wouldn't you?

5. Not only Newport Pagnell, with its quarterly chimes and its nice whisky, but the whole of the upper River Ouse gets a fuller treatment in my interlinked-short-story effort "The Bunny Run" which is a stretch of the river, of the Oxford-Cambridge road that criss-crosses it, and of the imagination. (Troubador, e-book, a mere £2.99)

6. Rupert Brooke's 'Heaven' takes St. John the Divine deliciously to task, from a fish's point of view, for his assumption, (Revelation. ch. xxi. verse 1) that in the Glorious New World "there shall be no more sea". (Come to think of it, though, we should remember that

in those year-dot days, the oceans must have been utterly terrifying to all but the murderous, who had learnt to ride them. "Eternal Father… " makes the point pretty well even for more recent days, and that's another splendid poem: the word 'peril' needs cutting short for maximum effect, doesn't it?). Brookes's very short poem is splendid to learn, to recite as a party-piece: the final line has only eight words, and the first six of them need to be declaimed. Then a pause, and a quiet last two. You'll see what I mean.

7. This beautiful little poem forms, at the start of Mervyn Peake's weird novel 'Gormenghast', his dedication "To Maeve", his wife. I wrote and asked if I might print it here, but got no reply. Go at once and read it now – it won't take you a minute, online or somewhere – and if you are anything like me you'll have somebody in mind whom, with this exquisite wording, you'll never forget.

8. After I had written about that meeting with Oxdon, I had cause to think back. (This a factual note, nothing to do with my main story, so skip it until you've read the book, unless Lord Erroll's death is of importance.) To my astonishment, and considerable initial alarm, everything I had recorded him as saying about my parents at the time of the Erroll removal, was in real life perfectly true. Thinking of course that I had been making it all up, it slowly dawned on me that I had given the Professor a whole lot of valid facts; I realised that it must have come out of my subconscious. So I bought the four main books about the Erroll murder, and amazingly a totally unexpected but very likely fact dawned. I deal with it on the pages following these Notes, under "Matters Arising – 1", and I sincerely hope the Boy Scout Movement will forgive me. Dad, too, as I say at the end.

9. My second Matter Arising, after these Notes, is a more factual glance at what the CIA was getting up to over this side of The Pond, from the late 1940s to the mid-60s (as they had to admit in 1967 due to "Ramparts") and, I am inclined to believe, long after. I'm pretty

sure this has never been made public so, as I don't want to fall from some high window, we must remember that you have been – still are – reading a work of fiction, as true as I'm riding this camel. Therefore read on after you've finished my story, but keep your head down.

10. After I had put Olivia straight about 'grown-ups' she usually got it right, but once came out with aged adults as 'grand-ups' which I think worth recording. Strangely, we were again chatting about Milne, and the mature appeal of some of his fun. In the two books of verse: 'When We Were Very Young' and 'Now We Are Six', for instance, a young child is unlikely to appreciate the sadness behind the Dormouse's banishment by the know-all Doctor (whose attitude to the profession is reminiscent of Belloc's: "They answered, as they took their fees, there is no cure for this disease"); nor the subtlety behind Milne's character of the nurse in Changing The Guard (Alice is marrying one of the Guard, A soldier's life is terribly hard). Also, the hilarious punishments suffered by Bad Sir Brian Botany go completely over the top: "They pulled him out and dried him and they blipped him on the head" – why dry him?? And: "They pushed him under waterfalls… " – why go and find another waterfall?? It's all brilliant, but it's upgrown, and grandup too.

11. The Life Scheme.

It must be remembered that, right up to the mid-sixties, at least half our enquirers (sending back the reply-card) were ex-National Service, and a good many of them already married, or certainly soon to be.

Jerry had sensibly chosen a useful type of Life policy called 'Five Year Option,' or 'Whole-Life Convertible'. This started out at the lowest possible rate of premium (as one would pay throughout one's life for payment only on death – a well-known precaution under certain circumstances such as protecting the family against Death Duties, but meanwhile useful only for security or for borrowing against), but it carried the guarantee of convertibility after (usually) five years into any other sort of fixed term policy such as an Endowment to mature and pay out a lump sum, perhaps on retirement or to clear a house-purchase loan at a specified future date, usually twenty years. SLAS allowed such conversion at any other time, not just five years. It also permitted, at any time when the client was able to start finding some spare cash, conversion to a With-Profits scheme, where one received annual increments to the sum assured, based on the profits of the Company.

A great advantage to this type of scheme (though under-appreciated by less intelligent critics), was its delay of higher premiums until the students had qualified and were earning, because those later years would carry the bulk of the premiums at the time when they could benefit from the Income Tax Relief allowed in those happier days (a sensible concession wiped out in the 1980s by the heartless Chancellor, who seems to have had little time for Insurance Companies: on an official visit to the Chairman of Lloyds he was heard to say in the lift, looking at his watch, "We'll give these people twenty minutes").

I never knew how many of our clients did, after five years or later, convert to With-Profits. I hope many did because I noticed a couple of years ago that the Company in question was paying the best profits of any UK Insurer. If any of my Life clients are (still alive and) reading this, I told you so!

12. The Belongings Scheme.

As you will have gathered, the insurance of what one might describe as "bed-sitter belongings" in the early 1950s demanded the listing, with full descriptions and identification-numbers where appropriate, of individual items, which could then – subject to security precautions – be covered against "All Risks" – that is breakage and damage and loss as well as the basics – at a price. The only policy I knew of which would give blanket Fire & Theft cover to the whole unspecified heap of one's room contents, was the "Officers' Kit" scheme they tried to sell me at Aldershot: your kit was covered worldwide so far as I remember, including in transit;

and I suppose the policy included All-Risks on specified items, that would seem likely, not just to help the Officer but to boost the premium substantially. It must anyway have been a loss-leader paving the way to later Home Insurance and no doubt Life, much as I saw its potential with our students.

They were not just in a similar situation as young Army Officers, masses of them had actually been young Army Officers until a few months ago; to introduce our Scheme was pretty obvious, once it had occurred to me. The chief difference was bicycles.

Both Oxford and Cambridge are renowned – have been, probably, ever since the penny-farthing but certainly since World War Two – for their profusion of bikes. My own, secondhand even when I acquired it at a 1949 jumble-sale, lasted me for over ten years and gradually passed away in a rack outside my late College, where I had left it on going down, still to be used when I was in town, but otherwise a bequest to any student needing a quick getaway.

Our Insurers were aware of this bad risk, because the theft of bikes was notorious and often in the Press. A gang from Cambridge would drive over to Oxford in a big lorry, pick up a couple of dozen decent specimens, and on the way back would re-assemble them all, so that they could be sold a few days later, unidentifiable. This enterprise didn't work in the opposite direction because all Cambridge college bikes had to be identified with a number painted on them. The Insurer's willingness to give cover against theft (but not damage) was seen by me as courageous, until I realised that all resultant claims were being paid from the advertising account.

Of course we still wrote more specific policies such as for items of individual value, and quite a lot of PA (Personal Accident), mainly for idiots on the sports field; but the one I remember is the man who said he had cut himself badly on the lid while opening a tin of macaroni cheese. It must have been a very tasty brand.

I reached for a claim form. "Which hand?" "Er… " Rather a long pause. "Actually it was my tongue."

I put the form away and reached for my grocery list.

13. Timing the mailshots.

Freshers were, even in those days, subjected to a great barrage of advertising when they arrived, and in view of the coffee coupons, political society leaflets, contraceptive temptations and a hundred other approaches of lesser or greater importance at a time when nobody wanted to waste a single minute on reading stuff, given the animated social activity all around them, we soon gave Freshers' Week a wide berth. Nor was there any sense in having posters put on Hall noticeboards for the first three weeks (of any Term, in fact) because it would be robbed almost at once for its drawing-pins.

The answer was to hit these First Years before they arrived; and we did well by placing a loose insert (incorporating the reply-card) in all the Student Handbooks posted by most Unions to home addresses, where the availability of our Belongings Scheme would meet with enthusiastic parental approval and be bought by post. (Hence, as you will see, Robin's Dagenham visit and the "insert in the local Pipers"). With any luck, many of the respondees would also tick the box for SLAS details: they would have it all by post in the same envelope, and we would hunt them down in mid-Term – but no earlier.

Any direct letter about the Life Scheme into their College or Hall pigeonholes, similarly, would wait – until the second Term of the year, except in the very important case of Final Year students, whom we would always remind urgently in November that the SLAS concession, which was in most cases well over 15% off their premiums for those first five years, needed to be secured before they left in the Summer: with Finals coming up, how about making an appointment now, for that happy fortnight when it will all be behind you?

Incidentally, having designed a small logo for the SLAS, to appear on all our letterheads and leaflets, I went some way to overcome the noticeboard problem by having special drawing-pins made by a splendid firm in Essex, sporting the logo and boxed into 100s. I would enclose a box with every poster we mailed to the permanent Hall Secretaries. It amused those kind young ladies as a gimmick, but it was also useful, since it would appear on everybody else's posters as a constant advert, perhaps in all four corners, for us as well.

14. Following up the enquiries.

As a routine, every reply-card we received about the Life Scheme was at once sent a three-page 'Long Letter' including a set of quotations based upon the client's age. When a sufficiently promising quantity of cards from one of the provincial Universities had accumulated, I would phone the relevant Union Secretary and reserve an interview room; then write to all the students suggesting (i) a time when they might care to drop in to see me, and (ii) if they weren't able to do that, I would look them up at their Hall or digs during the next few days, so would they please leave me a message on their door (I always enclosed a small card for their use) with a choice of suitable times. My suggested times were spaced geographically and every fifteen minutes because I knew there were always many non-showers due to lecture and tutorial commitments; but the system worked fairly well and Day One was pretty rewarding.

I would book myself into a nearby hotel so that I could make the maximum use of the evenings (I have very fond memories of, for instance, the old Plough & Harrow on Hagley Road when I went to Birmingham, or the little Nelson right opposite the University at Leeds).

My 'home calls' would continue on Days Two and Three, but though they started at eight-thirty each morning and sometimes carried on until after ten at night, I usually spent much of the afternoon at a local crummy cinema, as I explain back in the main story… Those post-prandial hedonistics were something I looked back on nostalgically, once I had Area Managers doing the running around for us.

15. When I first started dictating letters to Elsa, I remember giving her a single sentence to illustrate what I wanted as a general rule.

I think it went like this: "There are four main punctuation marks, colon: the colon which leads forward to a list of items or phrases, semi-colon; the semi-colon which separates those items, semi-colon; the comma which is just a short pause for breath, comma, and the full stop, full stop." It seemed to work, full stop.

16. I think it must have been Adrian, on another occasion as we shared our 'salade pimlicoise' (I can't find a cedilla on this machine, indeed I've spent half-an-hour figuring out how even to spell the bloody word: si-, sy-, ci-, cy-...); anyway, recalling I suppose the hymns in his old School chapel, he announced that he was going to rename his girlfriend 'Chaos' because she was "dark and rude."

(Apropos names from hymns, are you one of the few people who still haven't heard of the Victorian children who used to giggle in their pews about 'Gladly'? My cross-eyed bear.)

MATTERS ARISING
= 1

THE 'REMOVAL' OF LORD ERROLL IN 1941

Happy Valley "Personal Revenge" or a regrettable wartime necessity? And could the required finger on the trigger really have been my peace-loving, God-fearing but patriot father? (Please run through my, albeit fictional so far as I knew, account of the interrogation I had from "Professor Oxdon" in Chapter 12, before wading into the pretty convincing stuff that follows).

a) PERSONAL REVENGE?

Of the four available books on the subject, three concentrate on the Happy Valley crowd and their sleazy social antics, which of course makes a good salacious read and can bring tidy royalties. The assumption is that somebody in that group wanted Lord Erroll dead for reasons of his or her own; and there are plenty of interesting candidates. But in every case one has to ask: were any of these sad people truly murderous by nature? Or even subject to such terrible jealousy when they had all been happily sleeping with each other for years?

And if so (and there was one such lady, trigger-happy, suicidal, self-harming, and American as well), why go to the discomfort of doing it in the small hours, in the rain, in the pitch darkness of the Plains in the wartime blackout, even if you *are* barmy, when it could be done just as easily in the daytime, in comfort, back in town where her bottles were?

These three books do touch – remotely it seems, in passing almost – on the political possibilities and Erroll's known links with Fascism; but they hurry on (almost as if under orders) to dismiss the idea as hopelessly irrelevant. That is precisely what happened, astonishingly in my view, at the start of the trial, with that inexplicable direction, from the prosecuting Attorney-General no less, to ignore any conceivable suggestion of a political motive for the killing. Why, why, why, one asks? .

It almost seems as though all three writers have somehow been persuaded (I hesitate to suggest "briefed") to emphasise the guilt of somebody in the Valley and the Muthaiga Club in order to stir up the murram dust and shield a secret security trail that would embarrassingly lead in a different direction… And the trial itself was surely a cover-up.

Nevertheless between the lines one can glean no end of information, in bits and pieces, which can be assembled to present a highly likely picture.

"In a way you could say that I did," Broughton told the 15-year-old Juanita, shortly after being found innocent. He was telling the truth, I think, and hope to demonstrate.

b) WARTIME NECESSITY?

Of the four books, the three referred to above: "The Murder of Lord Erroll" by Rupert Furneaux (Stevens, 1961); the better-known "White Mischief" by James Fox (originally Jonathan Cape, 1982, plus of course the imaginative film with its wrong ending); and much more recently "The Temptress" by Paul Spicer (Simon & Schuster, 2010), sidestep the security risk of a proselytising Fascist holding the post of Military Secretary in charge of Kenya's defences, when the Northern border was lined by thousands of jubilant Fascist Italian troops who had just triumphed over Abyssinia and other parts of North Africa! Not to mention the urgent need of Mussolini to achieve a Battle Honour against Britain so that he could keep up with his superior and currently victorious ally, Hitler.

But: Oh no, Erroll is British, a Lord, long ancestry, nothing to worry about, just Happy in his Valley…

However, happy indeed to relate, the fourth of these thoughtful studies, "The Life and Death of Lord Erroll", by Ms. E. Trzebinski (Fourth Estate, 2000) assumes throughout that his 'removal' was definitely achieved by our security services. I am absolutely sure she is right: the man would have been seen as a huge risk at that precarious time, by those 'in the know', even had he been a solid well-controlled family man – as a wild card, notorious for boasting both between the sheets and afterwards, he simply "had to go".

(The Governor of the colony is reported to have used those very words, a year or so earlier). And right at the very top, of course, was Churchill, fearful of a major calamity that would bring nationwide despondency (as did indeed happen a little later with our loss of Singapore).

But strangely, Ms. Trzebinski seems to miss her own target. Yes, her book is enormously researched: at the back are no fewer than 918 references from her 12 chapters, and then a bibliography listing over 200 books and articles etc., so if they are all relevant to what I'm writing here, I may be uttering complete rubbish. But I must press on because of my father…

Trzebinski gets herself deeply into the clandestine bureaucracy which she detects in the plot leading up to the assassination. Rightly, I'm sure, she dumps overboard the great shoal of red herrings from the Happy Gang, with some of them seeking notoriety in oblivion by hurling themselves on the hooks of the Press ever since 1941. (Why is it, silly nobodies do this?) But instead, she weaves a gigantic network of plotters and supporters and back-up people, all involved in the complicated tangle she seems to think necessary for Erroll's elimination, and all of them knowing that "something was up" at least, if not who, when or where.

Whyever does she envisage such a big unwieldy operation with all those minor characters entangled in it, all for the sake of a couple of bullets on a dark night, on the Plains with nobody about? Surely nothing could be much simpler, the sort of thing that happens all the time?

Moreover, had the affair been so bureaucratic – involving dozens of people according to her 'revelatory' Sallyport Papers – by now, over 70 years later, somebody would obviously have spilled the beans, on the internet if not openly to a thirsty newspaper. Would such an army all have gone to their graves tight-lipped when the Erroll Mystery seems to be an everlasting money-spinner?

I suggest we revert to the main characters, but read them from a different angle: their earlier 1930s background, and how it inter-relates.

c) WHAT WAS REALLY GOING ON?

Let us assume for the purpose of the exercise that Erroll's was indeed a necessary political elimination. In May 1940, with the discovery at the home of the American spy Tyler Kent of the 'Red Book' that listed all members of the Fascist "Right Club", Churchill – newly become Prime Minister – ordered the rounding-up of all British Fascists. Erroll, known sympathiser, was the only one in a position of military power, but he was out of reach.

Now, consider the track-records of our three main characters (and incidentally, their Intelligence connections):

JOCK DELVES BROUGHTON (b. 1883) was by no means a dithery old man, as sometimes presented; but still in his fifties. A Guards officer from 1902 to 1919, (which is not to be sneezed at), and invalided as a Captain, he was then for several years kept on in the regiment, note, though deskbound; and as an active officer in that position he was very likely to have had Intelligence duties: what else? Far too senior to go on payday duties, and useless on the parade-ground with that bad leg, how better to make use of him? On retirement he then ran his family estate but he was also for many years a magistrate, which is seldom mentioned but puts a somewhat different slant on his capabilities. He owned land in Kenya in the early Thirties or before. And by then, we are told, he knew Hugh Dickinson.

DIANA CALDWELL (b. 1913) was one of the free, adventurous, liberated girls of the 1930s. (We should not forget the many feisty young women we were dropping into occupied Europe soon after). She flew her own plane all over the place, and, note this, we are told she was already well-known to MI5 and MI6. She is said to be socially chatting-up the Vice-Chancellor of Austria, no less, shortly before Hitler's invasion: whatever for? To whom was she reporting back, working under this exciting glamorous cover? More to the point, she knew Hugh Dickinson in 1935, around the time she met Broughton.

HUGH DICKINSON (b. 1906) was a Regular officer in the 9th Lancers (which, *as only I am likely to realise*, may be highly significant). He crops up everywhere in the Broughton/Diana saga, and it is easy to deduce from most of the books, not just Trzebinski, that it is he who knits the whole plot together. Consider:

1. If he knew them both separately in 1935, he probably introduced them socially, or was ordered to do so.

2. When they set off for South Africa in mid-1940 (and by the way, how did they get permits and book passages at that time unless they were on a mission? A few months later, no lawyer was able to go out from the UK to act for Broughton, even for £5,000!), Dickinson was close at hand. He told people he had requested a transfer to Kenya to be near Diana because he loved her so much! What eyewash! This was hardly justification for a 'compassionate posting' even in peacetime, and quite ridiculous with a major war on. He probably thought he was making a joke until he found that people believed his amateur cover story.

3. Dickinson's transfer has confused our authors a little: he was moved across to the Royal Signals? Royal Engineers? RASC? Three books, three versions; but all agree that he was only on attachment, and remained basically a 9th Lancer. Bear that in mind.

4. In Durban, finding that Kenya was barring entry to single women, Dickinson arranged the marriage (if it was genuine) and the new passports; to have made an application for Diana to be allowed to enter, exceptionally, unmarried, would no doubt have attracted unwanted newspaper attention to all three of them. And yet, belatedly, without knowledge of the marriage, and inexplicably, unless he knew what was planned, the Governor of Kenya sent a message: "Let them all come." Why?

5. Our Lancer Subaltern then turns up in Nairobi but keeps in the background, hovering on the Valley periphery "because of his great love". However, on the fatal night he is well out of the way, either laid-up down in Mombasa with an alibi and a poisoned leg, according to one report, or equally laid-up in a rest-home suspiciously close to the scene of the crime with a nervous twitch and an alternative alibi. (Was the truth ever established?) But in the latter case, why is he said to have had thick mud on his boots next morning? He doesn't half get around, does Dickinson, lancing about everywhere.

And a couple of weeks after the killing, all three of them go off for an eight-day safari: the abandoned husband, his separating wife distraught at the loss of "the only man she ever loved"; Oh, and Dickinson.

It seems howlingly obvious, doesn't it, that Diana and Jock, recruited by the ubiquitous Dickinson, never really married. (Later in life she told a friend she never intended to). They never shared a room, even for appearances' sake; they never seem to have shown any sign of real affection, despite being very recent 'newly-weds'. This was simply presented as the most likely set-up to attract Erroll; and the moment they got to Nairobi, Diana laid it on thick, homing in on Erroll at once: almost indecently fast. Of course she didn't for a moment love Erroll, she had come to help kill him. (Apparently she had affairs with other men on the boat going out). Looking back at it all, one almost feels sorry for the man.

The Governor, we have seen, was clearly involved, *ex officio*. I reckon the Lady Mayor of Nairobi was also in the picture: the

271

Broughtons went straight to her the moment they arrived and were with her for both lunch and dinner that first day. And then, on the crucial morning, and as soon as Erroll's death was announced, the Mayor rushed to the mortuary to look at the body, and asked to have his identity tag: whatever for, was she checking to make sure the right Happy Womaniser had been nailed? In court, she appeared hostile to Broughton for no apparent reason, but presumably this was an act to cover her tracks, knowing he would be acquitted and with an eye on her political future. (Which went very well, incidentally!)

By the time of the trial, it seems certain that the judiciary knew all about the truth, and the shocking instruction from the Attorney General to rule out any suggestion of a political motive, takes the breath away. Here we have a blatant attempt to drag the Happy Valley into the dock, alone.

And the police were in on it, too. Arthur Poppy, the CID chief, had been brought to Kenya specifically to set up a fingerprinting service a few years earlier (I met him at his office, with my Dad, in 1935 or maybe 36 and he took my prints as a joke – I think they laughed that I was the first person to have his prints on file in Nairobi – I wonder if they're still there?); but he didn't ask for any prints on Erroll's car until hours later, after the car had been towed away and thoroughly cleaned. Nor was the area around the scene roped off, so that any telltale car-tracks were soon useless. Also, note this, Poppy stopped Juanita from giving evidence.

What else? How about the Defence Counsel? We are asked to believe that no barrister could come from the UK "because there was a war on". But it had been OK for the Broughton Trio to sail out a few months earlier. I suspect that the excellent Henry Morris KC in South Africa had already been lined up for the job, no doubt by Dickinson, so that Diana's rush down to him was a bluff. How otherwise could such a successful lawyer be so swiftly available, even for £5,000? And was it normal to agree a fixed fee in advance of such a trial, unless one already knew the outcome was almost certain and the case wasn't going to run on too long?

When the main prosecution case turned on identification of the gun, wherever it was, an enormous amount of time and energy was clearly going to be quite pointless. Reading the transcript, one can vividly sense that the matter was going nowhere; and that Morris knew it, right from the start. You can't help feeling that the Prosecution knew it too, and this simply adds to the impression that the entire trial was an extended sham – which would account for Broughton's relaxed air throughout.

So, when he 'confessed' a few days later to young Juanita that he was guilty, after all, "in a way", he was – in a way – unburdening himself. Agreed, he never left the house, but he set up the shooting. He knew Erroll's exact movements, and when he called at June Carberry's bedroom door, possibly twice either side of 3 a.m., wasn't he almost certainly making a phone-call with last-minute instructions, as well as establishing his own alibi.

But phoning to whom?

Dickinson, the man of the double alibis (and muddy boots!), would be one's first choice, except that as 'an Officer and a Gentleman' he was regarded, or regarded himself, as too valuable an operative. Further, as is so often the case, the Service – whichever Service was at the root of the scheme – would want to use somebody as their liquidator who, if things went wrong, could have been cast to the wolves, with an incriminating alternative motive, in order to let the Government off the hook. Oxdon makes this clear to me at our Chapter 12 meeting, in his slur about my war-deserted mother being chatted-up in Erroll's office.

And that brings in my Dad.

d) WAS MY FATHER THE RELUCTANT HITMAN? (This must be read in conjunction with my fictional meeting with Dr. Oxdon; and with particular reference to his 'seven points', all of them valid – as has slowly dawned on me).

1. We went out to Kenya in 1934, when I was six. Dad had always been deeply involved in the Scouting world (as Oxdon says) and

pursued this as his main off-duty interest alongside his day job as HM Assistant Trade Commissioner for KUT and Zanzibar. He formed his Rover group at once, I think, because in 1936 when Baden Powell visited Nairobi, they lined up at the station to greet him, I remember. (BP was very chatty to me afterwards, and I recall being fascinated by his telling me that his father had been born even before Napoleon came to power! I also remember that shortly afterwards, I had a weird vision of a baby in a wooden pram – tumbril? – in a crowd of old women knitting, and heads messily rolling towards me: it was all happening on my bedroom wall, and I was malarial. There were a few Henry Moore things in there too, which was worse). What my Chapter 12 left unsaid is that Dad soon built up a powerful strike-group drawn from his Rovers (he was soon made Rover Commissioner for East Africa by BP) in their late teens or early twenties, to act as a covert support for the Kenya Special Police, in many of their night-time raid operations, rounding-up suspects and known ne'er-do-wells in the settlements around Nairobi. I think this group was largely disbanded in 1939 or soon after, as so many of these youngsters went into the Forces. But I'm sure the Police files will bear me out.

2. Dad himself, however, continued to work alongside the police – and at a high level, apparently, because when I was back at school in England, some time in the early 1940s (I have the letter somewhere), he wrote describing an occasion out on the Athi Plains at night when he was "on a job" in a car with the Chief of Police and they had been rammed by another car and overturned, rolling down a slope and covered in battery-acid. His letter ended: "This won't be in the papers!"

3. Above all else, my father was a patriot. Born in Agra as a son of the Regiment, and then educated at the Regimental School in Potchefstroom soon after the end of the Boer War, he continued moving with his SQMS father wherever the Ninth Lancers (Hugh Dickinson's regiment, note) were posted, ending in Dublin during

the Irish 'troubles'. Both he and his father treasured their regimental link (Grandad's endless reminiscences about the "red-and-yellow Ninth" during the school holidays used to entertain me, then drive me mad). Dad's approach from Dickinson, suddenly in Africa and in perilous wartime with a secret proposition, would have been almost irresistible.

4. Unlike me, my father was very much an Action Man: muscular, stocky, ginger and hairy. He was also a good shot. I remember one day when Mum and Dad were out, I was prowling around their bedroom in our house on Chiromo Road (now Riverside Drive, they tell me, or something else in Swahili) and finding a gun under his pillow. It was a .32, I forget the make, though I pinched a couple of cartridges to show the boys at school, but they weren't very interested as all their parents also had guns under their pillows, which surprised me because in those pleasant pre-war days it hardly seemed at all necessary, at any rate to an eight-year-old. When I returned the bullets, he cuffed me on the head, but only gently. He had bought the gun secondhand when we docked at Port Said on the way out in 1934, while I was getting my topee at Simon Artz, as one did in those days. Because it was an old gun, it doubtless had the black powder which the Court would be so excited about.

5. He also had his .38 Service revolver, a Webley I expect, handed down from his own father and dating back to – at least – 1914, when Grandad had been commissioned and put in charge of a big assembly of Indians because he knew their lingo. (When their end-of-the-week parade was delayed they used to chant – and I can't spell it – "Jildi jildi all the week, but peechi peechi payday"). Dad kept the Webley until he retired back in the UK in 1960, and handed it in to the police. I remember that I remonstrated with him, because I wanted to keep it as a family heirloom, but he was, as ever, scrupulously law-abiding. But I also asked him about that little under-the-pillow .32. He told me: "Oh, I dropped that in the Nile when I was at Khartoum and we went shooting crocodiles."

6. Quite recently I happened upon an old tattered notebook, filled in pencil with Dad's highly-prohibited diary notes of his and Mum's journey home to England in 1944, down the Nile by train, bus and riverboat, prior to waiting around the delta for a convoy ("a bit tricky passing Malta"). Most of it is just general frustration about the food, the delays, the missed connections; but a couple of the entries might have some significance in this attempt to understand Dad's possible role in the Erroll affair, so long overdue.

(a) He has meetings in Cairo with "Stirling". Now, by this date the famous Stirling was in Colditz, but his position had been taken over by his brother, who was based in Cairo.

(b) He notes that an RAF officer named Jewell, who had been his colleague in Khartoum when he was Adjutant there, is "just back from Turkey". But Turkey was neutral in early 1944, swaying between support of the Allies or the Nazis, and secretly meeting Churchill in 1943, so does this suggest covert activities and that Dad was linked to under-cover people?

(c) He writes of shooting crocodiles with his .38 Webley, so it does seem that he no longer had the .32, as he told me.

7. The aftermath is probably the most revealing aspect of this possible involvement of my Dad in the Erroll affair, together with Oxdon's "seven points" in chapter 12. Facts unknown to previous writers include:

(a) The pall-bearer mystery. Since Dad was actually listed in the newspaper the day after the funeral, it must prove that it had been a last minute cancellation. Doesn't this suggest that the Erroll action was being deliberately delayed until BP's imminent death, but then required immediately, as Dad would have wanted to insist upon?

(b) Mum often used to say that Dad had "changed somehow" in the early 1940s, and she put it down to that crash when the car rolled over (I wish I could find Dad's letter, to check on the date). He wasn't ever morose, in fact wherever they were posted over the next twenty years – Canada, Rhodesia, New Zealand, Nigeria and finally Trinidad – he continued to be much in demand as a brilliant after-dinner speaker full of wit; and much-liked by all, the various Government Houses included. But at home, away from all that, there was a quietly pensive withdrawal. And not once, ever, did he mention Erroll, throughout a twenty-year retirement; when Mum chattered away from time to time, he just 'turned off' rather than join in.

(c) Stranger still, despite his enthusiasm since early teenage in the Scout Movement and his really close connections, once they left Kenya he never again had any contact with Scouting, none at all I believe.

8. There is a final note, just emerged, which may well be significant: Jack Bingham (the real-life inspiration for 'George Smiley') as a young man joined MI5 in 1940 with the specific brief to keep a close eye on UK's high society Fascists. In a recent article, his daughter remembers her shock at some of the well-known names she heard (while sitting on the stairs, I imagine). Bingham, too, was a "son of the regiment", his father the sixth Baron having been a Lancer.

9. Summing up, this whole crowd of pointers, many known only to me it seems, has led me to think that my father must be pretty high on the list of candidates for the actual shooting. I never had a chance to ask him, of course, and anyway I don't think I would have done. After two strokes in the 1970s had put him into a bizarre but comfortable Home in Oxfordshire for those with mental deterioration (the delightful old Doctor who owned the place, making silly mistakes at his desk, said: "You know, I'm only two steps behind them all"), Dad didn't know me on my last visit in 1980. With a big smile of happy non-recognition, he said: "Hello, are you going up-country?" He was back in Kenya at last and perhaps I was one of his Rovers.

If it was Dad's finger on that trigger, he was a staunch patriot acting under orders, and he could be relied on to keep a secret. And if now, after nearly seventy-five years, it turns out that I am divulging it, I remind myself that he always told me to tell the truth – when the time was ripe.

MATTERS ARISING - 2

THE CIA ADMITTED SPYING ON UK STUDENTS (1950-67) – BUT BEYOND? AND STILL??

My third chapter briefly outlined the origins of the CIA and their increasing involvement in Western European academia and the wider world of aesthetics, from mid-1946 through to the early Fifties when their juggling with student purse-strings, and the setting-up of COSEC in Holland, put them in a position of considerable power. (It would help if you skimmed through Chapter 3, I'm sure you've forgotten most of it – I have).

But it remains, you must understand, for me to take a look at what happened shortly after the *end* of my story, when the CIA's student involvement was still in full flow. To their consternation, in February 1967 an obscure US student magazine 'Ramparts' published a sensational exposure of all this undercover CIA activity; the news was seized upon avidly and in depth, mainly by the New York Times, every day for several weeks. It makes terrific reading and you can find the micro. copies of the NYT in most big libraries, or presumably it all still lurks on the internet unless their spooks have scrubbed it.

The truth gradually emerged that there had been – still was – deep CIA involvement since the war, in European student, intellectual and trade union affairs. In subsequent years many books have dealt with this, and I can best refer you to the following, some by ex-CIA men, which in turn will refer you on to scores of others as they have long lists at the back:

Agee, Philip : Dirty Work (1978). pp.188-210.

Aldrich, R.J. : The Hidden Hand (2001). pp 122-8, 342-370, 633-6.

Campbell, Duncan: The Unsinkable Aircraft-carrier (1983) p 120.

Marchetti, V : The CIA & the Cult of Intelligence. (1974)

Saunders, F S : Who Paid the Piper? (1999)

US official reaction was predictable: the 'Ramparts' exposure led to much huffing and puffing in Washington, and in no time at all President Lyndon Johnson was said by the NYT to have "ordered the CIA to halt all secret aid to students". Ah, but read on…

A few days later, a list is given on February 19 of about fifty "Units linked with CIA" most of them apparently bogus charities, and among them COSEC. Then on the 24th. curiously, "CIA aid to students is backed by White House as Legal Policy"; however, this appears to rebound two days later when Vice President Humphrey seems to have been more in tune with the public's wavelength: "I'm not at all happy about what the CIA is doing"; and this Governmental disapproval was encapsulated by a Minister who happened to have been appointed to "look into the question of CIA subsidies to private organisations", John W Gardner. He said, specifically: "It was a mistake for the CIA ever to entangle itself in covert activities close to the field of education… ". But was this just a bluff? I think so.

Certainly there was a full-scale Senate enquiry and another earnest declaration by Johnson that all such covert behaviour must stop. But, look at the wording. It is subtly slanted in such a way that it allows a lot of things to continue: *always, with politicians, study the small print.*

The President declared as national policy that "no federal agency shall provide any covert financial assistance or support, direct or indirect, to any of the nation's educational or private voluntary organisations: (*"the nation's"* – geddit?). So there would be no problem with covert activity with students across the Pond, among *other* nations – it's evident though not made clear.

A year later, CIA man Richard Bissell blandly told the Council on Foreign Relations: "If the Agency is to be effective, it will have to make use of private institutions on an expanding scale, though those that have been 'blown' cannot be resurrected. We need to operate under deeper cover." (from Marchetti, op. cit.). And further: "Essentially the CIA's activities with and at the universities continued as they had before the NSA scandal broke. *They do so today.*" (Marchetti, p.235 writing in the mid-70s.).

Barely a month after the 'Ramparts' news-break, both the French and the Polish students chose to withdraw from COSEC. I believe that many others followed, but I have been denied access to the NUS archive (held at the library of Warwick University). It is not clear to me, what NUS has to hide; it may be just that they don't like me. Should you be interested in finding out more about the COSEC involvement with CIA (and perhaps even the NUS's too?), the files you need to ask for are indexed as: "Box 40, Travel".

That's right – Travel.

I lost touch with COSEC's Director, Gwyn Morgan, after my Olivia-assisted meetings, very enjoyable, at various venues; and a recent attempt to meet up with him at his London club was first warmly welcomed over the phone, but then rather abruptly cancelled, presumably after he'd made another phone-call or two? I couldn't immediately pursue it, and when I did a couple of months later, Gwyn was dead. So: is the CIA and NUS connection still active, and if so, for what reason?

★ ★ ★

Before we go any further, what follows is mere supposition. After all, my book is fiction…

Student Data Collection. Presumably nowadays, more than ever, the security services want to know what our wayward young students are up to. If a mild, innocent but perhaps low-achieving member of some West Midlands ex-polytechnic with his 'home' in the local sink estate and his origins somewhere off the map, (and there are plenty of them), suddenly buys a one-way ticket to Kandahar, we have come to accept these days that there is a shaven-headed operative chewing gum at a computer in Virginia who will very quickly know all about it. But I suspect that this covert monitoring of student travel has been going on, much more simply, ever since the late Forties, long before sinister electronics took over our innocent world…

And I have come to believe that Student Travel Insurance was set up by the CIA themselves. After all, a hard-up student travelling to a somewhat unfriendly country and planning to stay there for some time – as shown on the insurance form – is presumably being hosted by somebody "on the other side". This would have been helpful information in the 50s and 60s.

The one word which everybody wanted to keep quiet, even Matt in my story, is 'Copenhagen'. I suspect that this Danish conference, in the late Forties, of the Travel representatives of so many Western student unions, and their surprisingly efficient scheme that emerged, including an extraordinary surmounting of all the rigid exchange controls current at the time (one could take only a meagre £50 out of the country, so how pay an insurance claim?) could not have even been considered, let alone set up successfully, unless it was engineered, behind the scenes, by the CIA. Claims paid in full in the local currency of the country concerned: quite miraculous. (Probably something similar already existed behind the Iron Curtain, within all the Moscow-controlled student unions of East Europe, perhaps arranged at Prague?)

But whyever would the CIA do this?

I guess that they contrived to obtain the details of all students' travel movements through their declarations, entered innocently on the proposal form, of the suspiciously cheap Travel Insurance available from their Student Union's Travel Office. The scheme, adopted by most Western SUs at the Copenhagen meeting, was placed through a small firm, based conveniently very close to COSEC's in Holland; and that firm would then have been enabled by the CIA to meet claims in any local currency wherever they occurred. Otherwise it was surely quite impossible, at that time, for such a tiny Company to offer such a facility? (They only had one recognised branch outside Holland at the time, yet could carry all those risks internationally and pay claims worldwide?).

If I am proved wrong, I'll be apologetic, deeply, but surprised; because snooping on any outsiders, so very shocking according to Lyndon Johnson's poker-faced White House in 1967 (and again in 1975, as the NYT records), was in truth always seen as perfectly acceptable. After all, in the latter year the CIA admitted that for over 20 years they had been opening or otherwise examining incoming mail from Russia (ever since 1952 – over two million items) – and this was considered by the local politicians 'ungentlemanly' only because it was happening on US soil.

So: One – God knows what the CIA and MI6 and that crowd still get up to over here, in Europe and not least the UK, spying on students and the rest of us. But Two – what the hell? These days, it's all for our own good, don't you know? As old Oxdon would have said.

Don't you just!

★ ★ ★